1,000,000 Books

are available to read at

www.ForgottenBooks.com

Read online
Download PDF
Purchase in print

ISBN 978-1-330-19990-9
PIBN 10050997

This book is a reproduction of an important historical work. Forgotten Books uses state-of-the-art technology to digitally reconstruct the work, preserving the original format whilst repairing imperfections present in the aged copy. In rare cases, an imperfection in the original, such as a blemish or missing page, may be replicated in our edition. We do, however, repair the vast majority of imperfections successfully; any imperfections that remain are intentionally left to preserve the state of such historical works.

Forgotten Books is a registered trademark of FB &c Ltd.
Copyright © 2018 FB &c Ltd.
FB &c Ltd, Dalton House, 60 Windsor Avenue, London, SW19 2RR.
Company number 08720141. Registered in England and Wales.

For support please visit www.forgottenbooks.com

1 MONTH OF FREE READING

at

www.ForgottenBooks.com

By purchasing this book you are eligible for one month membership to ForgottenBooks.com, giving you unlimited access to our entire collection of over 1,000,000 titles via our web site and mobile apps.

To claim your free month visit: www.forgottenbooks.com/free50997

* Offer is valid for 45 days from date of purchase. Terms and conditions apply.

English
Français
Deutsche
Italiano
Español
Português

www.forgottenbooks.com

Mythology Photography **Fiction**
Fishing Christianity **Art** Cooking
Essays Buddhism Freemasonry
Medicine **Biology** Music **Ancient Egypt** Evolution Carpentry Physics
Dance Geology **Mathematics** Fitness
Shakespeare **Folklore** Yoga Marketing
Confidence Immortality Biographies
Poetry **Psychology** Witchcraft
Electronics Chemistry History **Law**
Accounting **Philosophy** Anthropology
Alchemy Drama Quantum Mechanics
Atheism Sexual Health **Ancient History**
Entrepreneurship Languages Sport
Paleontology Needlework Islam
Metaphysics Investment Archaeology
Parenting Statistics Criminology
Motivational

Phillips Brooks's Sermons

In Ten Volumes

1st Series — **The Purpose and Use of Comfort**
And Other Sermons

2d Series — **The Candle of the Lord**
And Other Sermons

3d Series — **Sermons Preached in English Churches**
And Other Sermons

4th Series — **Visions and Tasks** And Other Sermons

5th Series — **The Light of the World**
And Other Sermons

6th Series — **The Battle of Life** And Other Sermons

7th Series — **Sermons for the Principal Festivals and Fasts of the Church Year**
Edited by the Rev. John Cotton Brooks

8th Series — **New Starts in Life** And Other Sermons

9th Series — **The Law of Growth**
And Other Sermons

10th Series — **Seeking Life** And Other Sermons

E. P. Dutton and Company
31 West 23d Street   New York

The Law of Growth

And Other Sermons

By the
Rt. Rev. Phillips Brooks, D.D.

Ninth Series

NEW YORK
E·P·DUTTON & COMPANY
31 West Twenty-Third Street
1910

COPYRIGHT, 1902
BY
E. P. DUTTON AND COMPANY
Published March, 1902

The Knickerbocker Press, New York

CONTENTS.

Sermon		Page
I.	THE LAW OF GROWTH	1

"For whosoever hath, to him shall be given; and whosoever hath not, from him shall be taken even that which he seemeth to have."—LUKE viii. 18. (March 11, 1877.)

| II. | HALF-LIFE | 20 |

"Truth shall spring out of the earth, and righteousness shall look down from heaven."—PSALM lxxxv. 11. (Sept. 27, 1885.)

| III. | THE POWER OF AN UNCERTAIN FUTURE | 39 |

"Watch, therefore, for ye know neither the day nor the hour wherein the Son of man cometh."—MATTHEW xxv. 13. (Nov. 22, 1874.)

| IV. | THE SPIRITUAL STRUGGLE | 61 |

"For we wrestle not against flesh and blood, but against principalities, against powers, against the rulers of the darkness of this world, against spiritual wickedness in high places."—EPHESIANS vi. 12. (Sept. 14, 1878.)

| V. | THE BATTLEMENTS OF THE LORD | 80 |

"Take away her battlements, for they are not the Lord's."—JEREMIAH v. 10. (Feb. 20, 1881.)

| VI. | CHRIST OUR LIFE | 99 |

"In the name of Jesus Christ of Nazareth, rise up and walk."—ACTS iii. 6. (May 1, 1887).

CONTENTS.

Sermon		Page
VII.	My Brother's Keeper	115

"Am I my brother's keeper?"—Genesis iv. 9. (Nov. 15, 1885.)

| VIII. | Rest | 133 |

"Come unto me, all ye that labour and are heavy-laden, and I will give you rest."—Matthew xi. 28. (Oct. 12, 1890.)

| IX. | The Material and the Spiritual. | 150 |

"And as he went out of the temple, one of his disciples saith unto him: Master, see what manner of stones and what buildings are here!"—Mark xiii. 1. (June 10, 1877.)

| X. | The Double Cause | 167 |

"And his name through faith in his name hath made this man strong, whom ye see and know."—Acts iii. 16. (May 4, 1889.)

| XI. | Go Into the City | 184 |

"Arise, and go into the city, and it shall be told thee what thou must do."—Acts ix. 6. (Dec. 27, 1874.)

| XII. | The Holiness of Duty | 199 |

"Wherefore the law is holy."—Romans vii. 12. (Nov. 12, 1876.)

| XIII. | Peace which Passeth Understanding | 219 |

"The peace of God, which passeth all understanding."—Philippians iv. 7. (April 23, 1876.)

| XIV. | The Relative and the Absolute | 236 |

"And there was also a strife among them, which of them should be accounted the greatest."—Luke xxii. 24. (Jan. 10, 1886.)

CONTENTS.

SERMON		PAGE
XV.	THE STRENGTH OF CONSECRATION	253

"And Samson said, Let me die with the Philistines. And he bowed himself with all his might; and the house fell upon the lords, and upon all the people that were therein. So the dead which he slew at his death were more than they which he slew in his life."—JUDGES xvi. 30. (May 14, 1876.)

XVI.	THE DANGER OF SUCCESS	273

"Verily I say unto you, They have their reward."—MATTHEW vi. 2. (April 12, 1874.)

XVII.	THE SPIRITUAL MAN	294

"But he that is spiritual judgeth all things, yet he himself is judged of no man."—1 CORINTHIANS ii. 15. (No date.)

XVIII.	DELIGHT IN THE LAW OF GOD	311

"I delight in the law of God."—ROMANS vii. 23. (May 3, 1874.)

XIX.	THE ARK OF THE COVENANT	328

"And the ark of the covenant of the Lord went before them."—NUMBERS x. 33. (Dec. 19, 1875.)

XX.	SONS OF GOD	346

"Beloved, now are we the sons of God, and it doth not yet appear what we shall be."—1 JOHN iii. 2. (Oct. 10, 1875.)

XXI.	THE FEAST OF TABERNACLES	365

"And I that am the Lord thy God from the land of Egypt will yet make thee to dwell in tabernacles, as in the days of the solemn feast."—HOSEA xii. 9. (Jan. 1, 1888.)

THE LAW OF GROWTH.

I.

LAW OF GROWTH.

"For whosoever hath, to him shall be given; and whosoever hath not, from him shall be taken even that which he seemeth to have."—Luke viii. 18.

It is interesting to know, of any one whose character and ways of thought we are studying, what words are oftenest upon his tongue. And it would seem as if this proverb, which I have just quoted from Him, were a favorite utterance of Jesus. Three of the Evangelists record it, and the circumstances with which they connect it are different. St. Matthew mentions two occasions on which Christ used the words.

It would seem, then, as if the truth which these words record seemed to Christ very impressive and important. He found in it the occasion for the most earnest exhortation to faithfulness. Such a fact must deserve our best study and come very close to our life. Let us try to see what it is.

"To him that hath shall be given, and from him that hath not shall be taken even that which he seemeth to have." In one case when Jesus used the proverb the parable of the talents had come just before. The immortal picture was just fresh in the Disciples' minds,—the careful, prudent, faithful merchant, whose five talents had attracted five others, and turned themselves to ten; the poor, timid, helpless creature who brought his one talent, all caked and useless with the earth in which it had been lying. And while the people were listening with that suspicion of injustice, that uneasy sense of something wrong, which almost always comes when prosperity and misery, success and unsuccess, stand side by side, Jesus went on frankly to declare that the truth of the parable was a truth everywhere; that everywhere there was a law of growth, a law of accumulation and of loss, which drew more blessing where blessing was already, and condemned to decay that which had no real vitality. It was a sort of "survival of the fittest" declared to be existing throughout the world.

And, just as soon as such a truth is announced, there are a multitude of voices which proclaim how true it is. Many of them speak in bitterness and anger. Indeed, it is the taunt of every disappointed soul. "Look," he who has failed says, "look and see how everywhere the prosperous prosper and the unhappy attract unhappiness by a terrible affinity. Behold how, when a man is rich, riches fly to his overloaded coffers of their own accord, while the poor man by his side grows poorer every day. Yes, it is true enough; let a man be going up and all the world hurries to help him; let him begin to go down, and where is the friend that will not push him lower?" So men speak with all the exaggeration of bitterness. Now, we want to leave out all the bitterness, for that is an element that never helps men to the truth. We shall see by and by whether the truth is one that ought to make us bitter. We want to stand now calmly and look over all the broad world, and see how true it is,— this centralization of blessing, this tendency of all privilege to attract other privilege.

It appears in the distributions of business. He who is fullest of work, he to whom the multitude are resorting to buy their goods, or to secure the building of their houses, is the man whom each new customer seeks out, while his neighbor sits with his tools around him, waiting for work which flows in a full stream past his doors, and lets no drop free to trickle in. It is true in learning. The more a man knows, the more the sources of learning open to him on every side. All the mouths of the world seem to be opened to tell him everything they know. The same is true of wealth. When a man reaches a certain point of wealth, his money reduplicates itself almost without his efforts, even drawing into itself the hard-earned profits of the toil of poorer men. And it is true of public favor. The man whom all are praising is the man whom all men praise. Popularity draws the eyes and voices of the crowd, and gathers with most unneeded profusion about some one or two people in the town. And of that far more sacred thing, Friendship, see how true it is. To him who has friends, friends are given. They come crowding up to claim some little fragment of the kindness of the much-loved man, leaving the other man, who has a whole heart to give away, with no one to ask him for it.

Or think of usefulness. One man cannot walk anywhere but at his feet there start innumerable opportunities to help his fellow-men. Need flies to him, and if he had a hundred hands, and each day were a hundred hours long, he could not satisfy the opportunities for doing good which crowd themselves tumultuously upon him. And then, right in the resounding echoes of his busy work, you will find that other sight—always so sad!—of one who wants to help his brethren, and round whose life there shuts a wall of uselessness, within which he can only sit and feed upon himself.

Or think of health. The well man breathes it in from every breeze. The sick man feels every touch of the life-giving nature stealing what little life he has away. And so of healthiness of soul,— that cordial, fresh, and kindly interest in things which makes the joy of living. All the complications of life, all the touchings of life on life, are always pouring more of this red wine into the cup that is already full, while they make more morbid the soul that is filled with suspicion and discontent already. And so of enthusiasms and devotions. Your mind is full of an idea, your soul is given to a cause, and inspiration and encouragement flow in to you from every side. You find assurances that you are right and will succeed everywhere. Nature and man both become the prophets of your strong belief.

But to your friend who, working with you, has no such faith as yours, all nature and all men have only voices of discouragement. All that comes to him frightens him.

We might go on and catalogue everything that there is good and fine in human life. We make our theories of compensation and of equal distribution. We go on expecting that somehow, some time, everything will be adjusted and equality proclaimed: the conditions are to be reversed; the outs are to come in and the ins are to go out. We try to make it appear that everything is mechanically adjusted by what we call "impartial justice" every Saturday night, or at that great Saturday night of all which we call death. And all the time, underneath all our theories and expectations, breaking up through them constantly with its contradictions, there runs this vast law with its countless illustrations,— the law that the happy always tend to become happier, and the good better, and the wise wiser, and the rich richer, and the bad wickeder, and the fools more foolish, and the poor poorer. All the while to him that hath it is being given, and from him that hath not is being taken away that which he seemeth to have.

And now what shall we say about this law? In the first place, there can be no doubt that in the operation of the law there is wrought out the greater part of the picturesqueness and interest of human life. That which some amiable theorists delineate, and try to establish as the actual condition of things, would certainly make a very tame and monotonous world. The strong, emphatic characters and careers which, having much, are always drawing to themselves more and more of the things which make life rich,— these certainly give to humanity a various strength and beauty which none of us, not even the humblest and the least endowed, would really be content to lose. Do you suppose that the obscure man who finds that everything like fame or notice drifts away from his life and gathers about the lives of one or two preëminent men of his time would really wish, in all his discontent, that all the world of reputation could be rolled level and no man be thought more of than any other man in the great, flat expanse of average existence? I think not. There are—and it is one of the signs of goodness that there are—new emotions and sources of pleasure which come out and exercise themselves when a man finds that his is not to be one of the privileged points of human life. The pleasure and growth which come by admiration of what is greater than himself; the unselfish joy in helping to complete the good work of some one who is supremely qualified to do it; the growing conviction that the world is richer for these concentrations of power which at first only excited jealousy,—all of these, which are among the truest and most cultivating pleasures which a man can have, become available to him who accepts and rejoices in the law which makes some lives supremely rich, even though his be not one of the rich but of the poor. The valley may wish it were the mountain up to which it gazes from its humble depth, but it would rather be the valley with the glorious mountain towering above it, and drinking in its sustenance from the mountain's side, than to have the whole earth rolled smooth, mountain and valley obliterated together in one indistinguishable level of dreary, barren plain.

Believe me, my friends, there is something better for you to do than to accept the patent inequalities of life with forlorn resignation. There was never any champion of individuality like Jesus, and yet He recognized and found no fault with the law of privilege, the law by which wealth and culture and the patent forms of happiness flow together and collect in the rich lives of certain men. It is possible for you, though a poor man, to take so wide a view of the world, and of your race, that you shall be thoroughly glad that some other men are rich. In conscious ignorance and inability to learn, you may delight to know that some man whom you see is very learned, and learns more and more every day. Nay, you may be very wretched, and yet have your wretchedness not deepened, but lightened, by the sight of some brother's life, into which happiness seems to have poured its most profuse abundance, and who goes singing under the windows of your sorrow.

You have anticipated me, I know, in thinking that the perplexity and difficulty come when we apply our law to moral life, and find that goodness and badness also have the same principle of accumulation. Then it is often very bewildering. There is a man who has the love of goodness in him. Something of the divine passion of holiness has touched him. He is very far indeed from perfect, but he is a good man as distinct from a bad man. The direction of his life is set toward righteousness. To him come trooping all good influences from all regions of the earth. Everything he reads and sees and does, everything that other people do to him or around him, seems to give him some new opportunity of good. The very temptations that beset him seem compelled to render up to him their strength, and help him to grow better. The world of things seems to have taken his goodness into its charge, to bring it to completeness.

Close by his side, it may be, is another man, whom all the world calls bad. He does a good thing here and there, but the choice of his life is wickedness. The deeper dispositions which run under all the casual events are deliberately set toward sin. What is it that makes that man's life terrible to watch? What is it that makes gradually gather in his own eyes a hopelessness that sometimes enrages him, and sometimes only serves him for an excuse? Is it not the way in which everything that happens to him seems to increase his wickedness. The evil element in everything seems to fly to him. Out of the quietest scenes there rise up voices calling him to sin. If there is a bad man, he meets him. If there is a combination of circumstances which can bewilder faith and shake responsibility, it seems to gather around him. This is the way in which life easily comes to look to us like a great machine for making good people better and making bad people worse. It matters not that round the good man there do gather manifold temptations to be wicked and round the wicked man come crowding the persuasions to be good,—nay, the very subtlety with which goodness draws out of the worst temptation some ministry of grace, the dreadful ingenuity with which sin draws out of the best influences some provocation of evil, only makes the truth more manifest of how easy it is for the good to grow better and for the wicked to grow worse in this great, mysterious, fertile world.

You wonder sometimes how men can believe in heaven and hell. My friends, the wonder is how, with this sight before them which I have described, men can help it. The belief in heaven and hell is but the carrying out into the long vista of eternity of what men see about them every day,—the law of spiritual accumulation and acceleration, the law by which sin and goodness increase each after its kind. The more clearly a man believes in the life to come, and thinks of it as under the same great moral forces that pervade this life, the more impressive grow to him its spiritual necessities. He believes in a mercy which runs beyond the grave; but unless it be a mercy which does what mercy never does now, and *compels* to goodness the soul refusing to be good, there still stretches out the possibility of a wickedness forever obstinate, and so forever wretched.

But think of it, if you will, only as it concerns this present life. It would be impressive enough even if there were no life to come, this tendency of everything to make the good grow better and the evil worse. If the fact is as clear as I have stated it, then it must stand as one of those things, like the wind or the sunshine, of which it is quite unnecessary that we should spend our time in asking whether it ought to be, as we can see very plainly that it is. What we do need to ask is the value of such a truth, so fundamental, so pervasive, set right into the midst of our life. How will it affect our living? What good effects is it intended to produce? The answer to that question seems to me to be twofold. It will emphasize individuality; and it will keep ever vivid the difference between right and wrong. Let us look at these, and see if they are not what the world very much needs.

The emphasis of individuality, the conviction of a man's self as having a personal character and living a personal life, is not this the thing the lack of which has made the weakest moments of all our lives? There are two classes of sins,—those that come from our feeble yielding and those that come of our wanton obstinacy. Of the latter class we may say sometimes that they result from our exaggerated individuality. Really they come of our distorted and diseased individuality. But the other class comes surely from the absence of any strong sense of individual life at all. From the boy who catches his first oath from the lips of the boy three years older than himself, whose impressive age and experience swallow up the personal responsibility of the admiring youngster by his side, on to the old man who dies rich, with a fortune that he has made by some of the conventional unrighteousnesses — where is the trouble in it all? Is it not in the feebleness of the boy's and the man's conception of *himself*? Duty, duty, that great, personal idea, something that he owes to God, something that he must do, whatever anybody or everybody beside him in the world may do, — that has not taken hold of him. He knows nothing about it. If he gets deep enough to have any philosophy about it all, his whole philosophy will be this, — that goodness and wickedness, like happiness or unhappiness, come by chance, that neither is to be struggled after or avoided.

Oh, it is terrible to think how full our streets and houses are of that philosophy! The man you do your business with, the friend you take your pleasure with, the brother or sister with whom you live in the same house, it is terrible to think how all moral life seems to him an accident, that it is as perfectly uncertain whether he will be noble or base to-morrow as whether the wind will blow east or blow west. There can be no strong sense of personality there. There personal life resolves itself into a bundle of tastes, and the man recognizes himself only by what he likes or hates. But now suppose that man can come into our law. Growing cognizant of moral life, trying to be a good man or coming to know himself a bad man, he finds all the world declaring a disposition towards him, helping him on in the way which he has chosen. He has called it a world of accidents, and thought himself its puppet. But the minute he makes any moral declaration of himself he finds the world all devoting itself to the fulfilment of that declaration, all tending to make him more and more what he has set out to be. He has been floating on the waves, tossed where they pleased to toss him, but the minute that he says, "I will go thither," and begins to swim, the water under him becomes his helper; it lifts him up and floats him; it answers to the beating of his hands; it bears him on and lands him where he wants to be. Now that is thoroughly personal. It cannot be anything else. A man setting a moral destiny before himself, and feeling the whole current and power of things immediately bearing him on to it, *must* come to the certainty that he is a self-determined being and that God helps his self-determination.

Oh, my dear friend, this is what you want. In your parlor, at your club, you are losing yourself, you are losing your soul, you are getting to seem to yourself the mere creature of accidents. What do you need? Go and undertake some duty. Go and be moral. Go and be good. Go and find the soul that you have lost. Go, and in the midst of your self-indulgent life surprise yourself by doing what perhaps you have not done for years,—by doing *something that you ought to do because you ought to do it*. As you enter that moral region you have no idea of the revolution that will come in all these accidents and their relation to your life. It will be as if a general had forgotten his generalship, and gone to playing games and running races with his soldiers, who have forgotten it, too. But by and by the bugle sounds, and he recalls himself. He

flings his play aside, and arms him for the battle.
And then they, too, reverence him again, and cry,
"Oh, let us help you, for we are only your servants
as soon as you have really undertaken to be worthy
of yourself." So all the world will help you as soon
as you try to do your duty. When you claim your
manhood it will own your manhood, and you, who
have counted yourself a mere playfellow of the
blind chances of the world, will find yourself recognized by the world as a true moral creature, to
whom it is commissioned, by the God who made it,
to render its humble help in working out your
moral life.

I said, again, that the truth which Jesus emphasizes so, and on which we have been dwelling, is of
value because it keeps ever vivid the difference between right and wrong. The idea that out of the
mass of influences about us the good character appropriates the elements which belong to it, so that
it grows ever better, and the bad character appropriates its own elements and grows ever worse —
that seems to me to be one of the most profoundly
impressive declarations of what essentially different
things the good and evil are. I take two seeds
which look so much alike that only the skilled eye
can tell the difference between them. I plant them
side by side in the same soil. Immediately each of
them sends out its summons. Each demands of the
ground the elements of growth which its peculiar
nature craves. The earth hears and acknowledges
the summons, and renders up to each what it demands. So two men, who seem just alike, are set

down in the same city. Instantly to one there fly all the influences of good; to the other there gather all the powers of evil that pervade that city's life. Or, into a man's life is dropped a purpose. That purpose instantly declares its character by the way in which it divides the forces of his life. If it is good, it calls all that is good within him or around him to its aid. All that is noble gives its strength willingly to this new, feeble plan. All that is sluggish, base, selfish, in his nature or his circumstances sets itself against his new desire.

It is in such discriminations that the essential differences of the qualities of the good and bad display themselves. In the least atom of good there lies a power to attract goodness and repel wickedness. In the least atom of wickedness there lies a power to repel the good and to attract the bad. That is the qualitative power of moral natures. Ah, when we think how everywhere we are imposed upon by *quantities*, do we not need, do we not welcome, this strong statement, that the real power of things lies in their *qualities* — in what they really are, whether there be much of them or little? See how we are deluded. We take some vice which, in its larger manifestations, we know is flagrant and destructive. We make it small. Without changing its character in the least, we bring down its dimensions. We turn the great public cheat into the little personal deception; we transform the large, insulting slander into base, personal, gossiping detraction; and what was acknowledgedly bad on the large scale is accepted as graceful and venial in its smallness. Or, just the opposite: we take some action which in its petty forms everybody owns to be bad and mean, like the bullying of the weaker by the stronger, and, lifting it to a higher degree, we crown it with dignity and honor, as when we glorify the oppressor and the tyrant. Oh, we do need everywhere more of that conscientiousness which looks at the qualities, less of that superficialness which is overcome by the mere quantities of things.

The other side of this is to me even more impressive. If we lose sight of the essential nature of evil very often by dwelling upon the increase or diminution of its size, so that the very great or the very little evil seems to us to be almost absolutely good, the same is true about the quality of goodness. There, too, we are imposed upon by quantity till we forget that quality alone is vital. If we could all see, and always see, the essential force which is in every good act, however slight it is, and in every true belief, however meagre it is, how different our lives would be! But our goodness and our faith grow very small; and, instead of valuing all the more intensely what is left, our ordinary impulse is to throw the remnant away. It is so little, we think, that it is not worth the keeping.

Suppose that out of the world there should be slowly or suddenly destroyed all the seed of corn except one handful, just so much as one man could hold in his palm. Can you picture to yourself the care with which that handful would be guarded? Can you imagine the interest that would gather about it, the poetry and dearness that would be in it; how men, looking at it and knowing it to be the real thing,—true, real corn,—would see in it the assurance of days yet to come when all the fields should wave once more with harvests? That is the way in which you ought to treasure your faith if there is not much of it, if little by little it has slipped away from you. You say it has grown to be very little. You say that many things which you used to believe seem to you no longer to be true. You stand holding in your hand the remnant of a faith. What then? Is it real? Is it true faith? Whether it be little or great, do you really believe it? If you do, then surely that belief ought to be very precious to you. A little, a very little, belief it may be,— nevertheless treasure it because it is belief, instead of despising it because it is little. Value it for its quality, instead of dishonoring it for its quantity. As you look into it behold its possibilities. See in its meagreness the promise and power of a great and manifold belief that may yet some day cover your whole life with verdure. Put it where it will be safe; and the only place where a faith ever can be safe is in the shrine of an action. Put it there. Do what that belief would tempt you and command you to do; and trust to its true quality to grow under the care of God, who knows in heaven every particle of true faith that there is scattered about the earth. In His sight it is all too precious to forget.

What a great many people need to-day is to forget for a while their care about the quantity of their belief, and to give their anxious attention to its quality. Not, *how much* do I believe? but, *how* do I believe? It is well worth while for you to learn to ask that deeper question. Seek reality, even though it be by casting aside much that you have carried about with you that was unreal. It is a glad day for a true man when at last he plucks off and casts away a faith which he has not believed, or a hypocritical habit which has not been truly his. " Coming down to reality," he calls it. It really is coming *up* to reality. The fresh, strong, hopeful future opens before him.

Of every other experience that is true which I have been stating thus about belief. You need to learn, when you hear Christ your Master insisting on repentance, on love for Himself, on love for fellow-man, on devoted work, that His desire is, first of all and deepest of all, for the qualities of those things. He wants a real repentance, a real love, a real devotion. If He sees reality, we can well understand how He can be infinitely patient with littleness; for where He stands eternity is all in sight. He sees forever. He knows through what summer of cloudless sunshine the least grace will have time to ripen to the richest. He knows in what rich fields the seed will find eternal lodgment. So there is time enough, if only the seed is real. If it is not real, eternity is not long enough and heaven is not rich enough to bring it to anything.

How impressive this is in the story of Christ's earthly life! How patient He was with imperfection! How intolerant He always was of unreality!

He could wait for a publican while he unsnarled himself out of the meshes of his low vocation, but He cut with a word like a sword through the solemn trifling of the Pharisees. He never was impatient with His disciples. Their graces were very small, but they were real. Eternity was long, and He could wait till the graces which He saw to be real opened into all the possibility which He discerned in them; till the Peter who paraded his genuine but feeble resolution of devotion at the Supper grew to the Peter who could die for Him at Rome, and live with Him in some high doing of His will in heaven.

It is good for us if we can treat ourselves as our Lord treats us. Try to find out whether your repentance for sin is real — a genuine sorrow for a wrong life. If it is, no matter if it falls far short of the complete contrition which you picture to yourself, still keep it, hold it fast. Do not let it slip away and drop back into the placid content which you felt before you were penitent at all. So with your love to your Saviour, — do not throw it away because it is not that large-winged devotion which soars up into the very sunshine of His closest company. Keep it. Feed it on all you know of Him. Never trifle with it, or surround it with any unreality of profession merely to make it seem larger than it is. Reverence it, not because it is great enough to be worthy of Him, but because for such a being as you are to love at all such a being as He is, is a sublime act, — the glorification of your nature, and the promise of infinite growth.

I long for every Christian, especially for every young Christian, to see this first Christian truth of the value of the essential qualities of things set deep into his life. Christ was full of it. Christ showed us how full God is of it. In it is the secret of endless patience. In it is the power of enthusiasm at every stage of growth. Can the soul just come to Christ, just trembling with its first love, its first hope, lift up itself and sing enthusiastically? Yes, if it can know indeed that " to him which hath shall be given," that it is in the very essential nature of the life it has begun to go on, and never stop, until it stands in the glory which is before the Throne of God.

In the truth which Jesus taught, then, in the proverb which was so often on His lips, there lie still the warning and the inspiration which He put there. It is the truth of a live world, a world so full of life that into it nothing can fall without partaking of its life, a world that makes the good grow better and the bad grow worse always. If the world is making us worse, then not to change the world, but to be changed ourselves, is what we need. We must be regenerate by Christ, and then the world shall become His schoolroom, by all its ministries bringing us more and more perfectly to Him. May He give us His new life, that the world may become new to us!

II.

HALF-LIFE.

"Truth shall spring out of the earth, and righteousness shall look down from heaven."—PSALM lxxxv. 11.

Do not these words suggest the way in which one part of every life stands related to another part of the same life? There is a heaven and an earth in every man; first in his nature, then in his experience; and it is on the cordial working together of these two parts of his life that the healthiness and completeness of any man's existence depend. Think what these two parts are. The earth of every man's life is what we are apt to call, in our loose, superficial way, its practical part. It is that which has to do with the methods and machineries of his existence. It is made up of numberless details. The house in which he lives, the food he eats, the business he pursues, the places where he travels, the dress he wears, the amusements in which he finds recreation, the daily plans by which his living is conducted,—these make the earth, the lower and terrestrial level of his life. All these would be altered to something different if — the same man still, with the same purposes and standards which he has now — he left the earth and went to live on some star of other conditions than this familiar one of ours.

And then, always over and around this world of methods and machines, as the sky is always over and around the earth, there is the world of purposes and standards,—the reasons why the man is doing these things, as distinct from the mere way in which he does them. To this world belong all the affections, all the calm or tumultuous passions out of which actions are fed, as the cornfields are fed out of the brooding or the hurrying clouds. To this world belong religion, all lofty and inspiring ideas, all great ambitions, all desire for culture,—everything which, unseen, is yet the motive and the force by which the visible activities of our lives are set and kept in motion. These make the heaven of our life. These would go on essentially the same in any other star. They are not dependent on the conditions of the earth. They would inspire other conditions if these present ones should be removed.

Are you not aware of these two regions in your life? As, standing on some great mountain, you feel the solid ground under your feet, and see the sweep of landscape, mountain, and lake and plain and river all around you; and then, over all, the sky, separate from the earth, yet making one system with it, living in closest relation with it, and meeting it all round at the horizon,— do you not know these two worlds in your life, the world of method and the world of motive, the world of deed and the world of thought, the world of embodiment and the world of inspiration, the world of what and the world of why—the earth and the heaven, may we not call them?—which make up together the total system of your life?

And now the suggestion of our text is that, in order for a human life to be complete, both of these two worlds must be active and both of them must be true. If either of them is inactive, or if either of them is false, the life is a failure. Truth must spring out of the earth and righteousness must look down from heaven. The different failures to which men's different lives do really come are the result of the different ways in which these two worlds do not work, or work falsely, or do not work in harmony. Let us study this a little while, and I think we shall see that it is no mere theory, but the simple story of what is going on always in the world.

The easiest and most obvious illustration of our truth, that which must let us see immediately what it means, appears in what we call the fine arts. There the two worlds are most distinct, and the need of their harmonious coöperation is most manifest. You go into a sculptor's workshop, and how evident the lower world, the world of method, is! The tools that lie around, the hard, clear block of marble, the model in the clay, the evident need of technical skill which can only have come by practice with the most concrete and tangible of things,—all that is clear. But how the whole place loses its character, and is nothing but a mechanic's factory unless, behind what you see, you are clearly aware of the unseen; unless the place is full of presences, of visions and ideas, of thoughts of beauty which are to be embodied in forms of beauty through the means of all this visible matter and this technical skill. Here are two worlds; and evidently both of them are necessary, or you have no sculpture and no sculptor. Leave out the world of method, and you have only a dreamer left, who thinks of statues and never carves a stone. Leave out the world of motive, and you have only an artisan, who cuts statues as another artisan cuts doorsteps, with no vision, no meaning, no idea to make them live. Both worlds must be there and both must be true. Falseness in either ruins the result. You must have purity, loftiness, and truth in the conception which you want to embody, and you must have simplicity, straightforwardness, and reality, freedom from artificialness and trick, in the technique by which you work, or you make nothing worthy of the name of statue. Given these two,— truth in the world of imagination and idea, and truth in the world of execution,— and then the Venus of Milo or the Dying Gladiator comes.

We have not, most of us, to carve statues, but we have all of us to live lives; and so I turn at once to see how this our truth applies, not to a special art, fine or coarse (though it does apply to them all), but to the general conduct of a life. And it seems to me that the result to which our thought about it brings us is this: that there are four kinds of men — four kinds of characters, three of them weak and imperfect, one of them complete and strong — who may be conceivably produced by the imperfect or the perfect relations of these two worlds to one another. All of these four kinds of men are actually produced and live among us. Let us describe them to ourselves, and try to learn some of their lessons.

I said, then, that both of the worlds, the world of *motive* and the world of *method*, as I called them, must be active in every man, and that they must work in harmony with one another, to make the perfect man. You will see at once where the imperfect kinds of men will come from. There will evidently be: 1st, the men in whom the world of motive is alive, but not the world of method; 2d, the men in whom the world of method is alive, but not the world of motive; and 3d, the men in whom both worlds are at work, but work on different principles and keep no harmony with one another.

1. How common the first kind of defect is, we all know, I am sure, only too well. We see it in our brethren; we feel it in ourselves. Wherever a man lets himself be satisfied with ardent aspirations which never go forth in deeds, or with admiration of goodness which does not utter itself in some struggle for the increase of goodness in the world, have we not got exactly this: Righteousness looking down from heaven, but no truth springing out of the earth to meet it? How long she may lean over the golden walls, and look and look in vain down to the dull, unresponsive earth! You let your mind dwell upon the misery of poverty, the wretchedness and terrible temptations of the poor,— how dreadful, how mysterious are these inequalities of human life; the advantages of one, the disadvantages of another! How rich the opportunity, how pressing the neces-

sity that they who *have* should give not merely money, but time and thought and sympathy, in help of these others who *have not;* that the rich and happy should freely bestow themselves on the poor and wretched! Your soul is filled with these ideas. It not merely is filled with them; it glows with them. The theory is perfect. The conviction is complete. And then comes the demand for action. The poor man stands before your door. The special problem clamors for solution. And where are you? You have stopped short upon the borders of your theory, and are loitering in the mists of your enthusiasm, and all the need of vigorous action cries out for you in vain.

Or take a case that concerns only your own personal life. You have some vice, some bad way of living, and who is there so clear and cogent as you are to reason about it? Who will so clearly show its evil origin, its mischievous result? Who will be so earnest in praise of the man who with a manly resolution breaks the chains of this bad habit, and in spite of all the pain which the struggle costs him goes out free? And yet you go back over and over again to your abused and detested habit, and the new years as they come one after another find you still its slave.

I am telling a most familiar story. It is what we have all seen and felt all our lives. It is the old story of unfulfilled purposes and enthusiasms that disappear like dreams. The world is ready with its explanation. It always makes its easy explanations of complicated situations, and is quite sure that they are right. The world cries out, "Hypocrisy!" It believes that the enthusiastic purpose which failed before it came to action was unreal. It laughs at the brave young reformer who was going to renew the world, and whose sword is missing when the battle morning breaks, and says, "You see there was nothing in his boasting. He meant nothing. It was all insincere."

The world is wrong. The problem is by no means such an easy one as that. There is such a thing as hypocrisy, of course; but the chance is that this is not hypocrisy. It is half-life. It is life only in the world of motive and not in the world of method. It is righteousness looking down from heaven without truth springing out of the earth. These high enthusiasms are thoroughly real, perfectly sincere. It is simply that these men live in the region of emotion and idea, and very probably the lower world of action seems almost contemptible to them. They almost despise it. It belongs to lower souls. Their part in life is loftier.

No doubt, in time, this partial life tends to become unreal even in the part of it which does exist. An unused conviction always tends to insincerity. But it is real enough as it glows upon the lips of the young enthusiast — this outcry of high motive which never lays a finger to the tasks it paints so glowingly. The experience of how much there is of it in the world is what makes sad and pathetic the sight and sound of the college, full of high thoughts of life, and the hosts of brave young thinkers there, kindling with the reading of great books and looking as if they could not wait for graduation day to save the world.

2. With this sort of failure in your mind turn suddenly and look at another which is just its opposite. Here is the man who lives only in the other world, the world of method. As he of whom we have been speaking never came forward out of the region of enthusiasm into the region of action, so this man never allows the region of action to have any background of enthusiasm. That the thing should be done is everything. That there should be a fine, high, spiritual reason why it should be done is nothing. Such men, I sometimes think, have grown most common in our time. They are of every occupation. There are professors very learned, very faithful, very skilful in all the technical details of teaching, who will grow silent or grow scornful if you suggest the higher, the religious, purposes of learning, the duty to one's own nature, to society, to God, which constitute the ultimate reason why one should be learned at all. There are business men, honest and charitable and intelligent to a degree which fills the whole business world in which they move with light, who are utterly bewildered if you bid them think of the relation of business to the Brotherhood of Man and to the Redemption by Jesus of the earth into completeness as the Kingdom of God. There are philanthropists the inspiration of whose philanthropy never gets above the economics of alms-giving and the wastefulness of poverty. There are politicians enough to whom the state is a great machine of wonderful

complexity and fineness, but with no divine purpose, no possibility of character. Nay, strangest of all, there are religious men and women who, above all things, would guard religion from becoming overspiritual. Ask them why they are religious, why they go to church, why they say prayers, why they send missionaries to the heathen, why they read the Bible, and they will give you dry and dreary answers about religion being a natural craving of the human soul; or, drearier still, about its being so helpful to the order of society. Not one word of eager and impulsive utterance of the child's yearning for the Father's love, or of the sinner's gratitude for the Saviour's glorious salvation! All is of the earth: nothing is of the heaven. It is faithfulness, intelligence, truth, springing up from below, not looking down from above.

I know and I think that I value fully the better feeling which is mixed up with all of this. I know the dread of vagueness and sentimentality. I know the impatience with tiresome gush and enthusiasm that fail when it comes to work, the contempt for the mere pretence of lofty purpose, which by and by cries out, "Let motive go, and simply do your work. What the world wants is that the students should be taught, the asylum founded, the railroad built, the Church service maintained." All that is very natural, and also very shallow. Because there is sentimentality, no man has a right to disown the power of true sentiment. Because there is hypocrisy, what right has any man to say he never will be enthusiastic? Because the sky breeds fogs, does that give any man the right to build the low roof ten feet over his head, and live in his poor cabin as if there were no mystery of sky beyond? Because fanatics have had their heads turned by the Book of the Revelation, must you abolish the vision of the New Jerusalem from the vistas of your life?

The danger which comes with such a fault and folly is manifest enough. Let it grow to be the habit of the world; let great, enthusiastic motives cease to be felt as the inspirations of the world's activity, and sooner or later that activity must lose its quality of faithfulness; and even while it maintains that quality, and while men keep on working hard without any supply from the most profound depths and the loftiest heights of their natures, still their work must lose its breadth, and degenerate into tricks and artifices. This is what, I think, we have to fear more than anything to-day:— not a loss of the intensity of industry, but a loss of the nobility of industry; work done upon the lower and not upon the higher plane, and so not rendering the best result to the worker, nor giving the largest inspiration to the progress of the world; business done sordidly, government conducted mechanically, learning gained and given mercenarily, religion practised formally, life in general relying for its impulses upon the needs which spring out of the earth, not upon the inspirations which come down from heaven. May God save us from these things, and preserve for us and in us not merely the activity, but the nobility of labor and of life!

3. I have depicted two kinds of failure. Let me

say a few words about a third, which is less simple, more subtle than these two. I have spoken of the man who lives only in the region of his affections and enthusiasms, in the world of motive, and leaves the world of method and action unattempted; and then of the other man who lives only in the lower world, and will not meddle with enthusiasms and high impulses at all. There is another man, as I suggested, in whom both worlds are active, but in whom they work contradictorily and will not keep time with one another.

Have you never known the man with two consciences? Have you never known the man with the higher and the lower conscience? One of the consciences was active in the region of his speculations and emotions, the other in the region of his practical, active life, and they were hostile each to each. They were both consciences. They both were based on the idea of duty, but they were set in opposition to each other, and confusion was the result. One or two instances will illustrate my meaning.

Here is a man who, in the higher region of life, has accepted the duty of Humility. The more he reasons, the more he sets himself in the presence of the sublimest truths, the more he always is aware that to be humble is the only worthy position for a man all full of weakness and defect. He has stood in the sight of God, and felt how insignificant he is. He has looked the possibilities of his own life in the face and been ashamed of what he *is* beside what he *might be*. " I must be humble," he has said;

"what right have *I* to boast? My only chance for any comfort is in owning frankly to myself and everybody else what a poor thing I am."

Now, that is perfectly honest and sincere. The man in his closet says that to God and to himself with all his heart. And then he goes out from his closet to his business. The world lays claim to him. Tangible things to do, concrete questions to answer, meet him on every hand. Do you not know how often a new sense of duty comes up in the street, which is different from that which filled the closet? What can a humble man do in scenes like these? Has a man a right to be humble here where self-confidence is the first element of strength? Does not humility mean self-obliteration? And so the man who, when he thought abstractly, philosophically, and religiously, accepted the obligation of humility, when he comes to act practically and concretely, finds it his duty to be proud. In the same way, the duty of trust and confidence and cordial faith in man seems to be met in common life by the counter-duty of suspicion. "I have no right," says the confiding man, "in this world of wickedness, to indulge a faith in man which will only make me the victim of his wiles." In the same way, the man who, in the higher region, bids himself hope, forces on himself in common things the necessity of fear. So he who knows in general that man is meant to be tender and sensitive hardens himself with some base alloy when he goes among his brethren, as if so only he could be of any use. So the obligation of perfect truthfulness is met by the practical necessity of a limitation of candor which really is deceit, and which pleads for itself in the sacred names of pity and justice.

You see what all this means. It is not simply that high motives melt and weaken when you try to put them into action. It is that the world of action seems to have different standards of duty from the world of thought. Those which seem imperative in one appear impossible in the other. There are plenty of cases where we do not carry our religion into common life because we are cowardly or indolent or selfish. The real trouble comes when, being perfectly ready to carry our religion into common life, we dare not carry it there because it seems as if our religion there would do not good, but harm; because it seems as if that common life bred its own duties, and would not tolerate these that come down to it from above. There comes the deepest confusion. That is the real perplexity in which multitudes of business men are struggling on year after year. When they first met the difficulty as young Christian clerks, it filled them with dismay. Since that they have long ago settled down into a dull hopelessness of its solution, and take it as a thing of course. But it is still the oppression of their lives. The heaven and the earth which are in them will not harmonize, and neither of them can they cast away, or bid to yield in absolute subjection to the other.

4. And what then? Is there any solution? Is there any harmony of these two discordant parts of this one life? Is this third failure a hopeless failure?

Must a man escape from partialness only to fall into confusion?

And this brings us to the positive which stands over against all these negatives—to the description of the sort of life which is not a failure, to which the study of these failure-lives must have been helping us. I wish that we could fill our minds at once with a picture which will bear witness to us of its own possibility of being realized. It is the picture of a man alive all through, from the summit to the foundation, in the celestial and the terrestrial portions of his life. It is the picture of a man who never thinks a high thought without instantly seeking to send it forth into its fitting action; who never undertakes an active duty without struggling to set behind it its profoundest motive. He is one total man. The heavenly part of him is not vague because it is so high; and the earthly part of him, the lower part, is not counted wicked or contemptible. It knows its place, and, filling it completely, is full of dignity and peace.

I say that such a picture, when we set it before our imagination, in some true sense proves itself. Our human nature, disappointed with many failures, recognizes its true idea, and says, "That is what I was meant to be!" And then, when we look earnestly around to see how we, in our personal life, may indeed come to be that, we find ourselves at once in contact with a truth to which we always are returning. That truth is, that whenever man thinks of himself as a composite being, a being made up of parts and therefore liable to inconsistency, liable to fall apart, he finds that he needs God for his power of coherence, he needs God for the element in which his inconsistency may be reconciled with itself and the whole nature find its harmony. Here, here alone, is where our three failures must disappear, and the only true success of human life come in their place. "The heaven is His throne; the earth also is His footstool,"—let those words come to mean for us that there is no highest thought or emotion which is not subject to His will, and no least plan or action which does not rejoice to put itself at His feet; and then, in common obedience to Him, the discord between the higher and the lower life must disappear, and the whole man, as the child of God, be all one, and all alive.

I turn to the character and the career of Jesus, and all of this is plain. That wonderful character and career may be summed up in many ways. It shapes itself ever into a new orb of beauty as one sees it ever from a new side. In our summary of it, may we not say that it represents the higher and the lower life of man, harmonized within the obedience of God? It was because Jesus was always perfectly consecrated to His Father that the most exalted enthusiasm was never dissipated into a dream, and the simplest task was never degraded into a drudgery. We love to think how Jesus never intimated the least contempt for common things. Contempt for common things is apt to be the feeble and desperate resort of men who cannot keep them from intruding into an importance where they have no right, and so would tread them under foot and out of existence altogether. He who is in no danger of overvaluing them is prepared to give them their true value, and finds it easy. "These ought ye to have done, and not to leave the other undone." "Your Father knoweth that ye have need of these things." "Seek ye first the Kingdom of God and His righteousness, and all these things shall be added unto you." What a poise and balance there is in all those words! What an entire absence of contempt for common things! "The common is not wicked," they declare, "only less and lower. Therefore it is not to be abolished, only kept in its true, second place."

How different this voice is from that which has come from many of the seekers after spirituality in all religions and in every time! All asceticism tries to increase the exaltation of the higher life by defaming and as far as possible abolishing the lower, which is as if you tried to make the sky loftier by destroying the earth and doing away with the horizon. Or if asceticism recognizes that the total man must be made up of heaven and earth together, it finds the fulfilment of this necessity in the general humanity. Let a few men and women, priests, monks, nuns, what we will call Religious people, live the spiritual life; and let the rest of men do the plain duties of their ordinary stations; and so the race, as a great whole, will be complete. Each part will see fulfilled in the other part that which it cannot fulfil in itself. To think that each man can live in the heaven and the earth at the same time is a delusion. Against all that, Christ's life and words and work are a perpetual protest. He bids each man be entire. He says to every one: This you must do and yet not leave the other undone. All His New Testament is full of that. Strange, that with the great Christian Book so clear about it, the old false division — the assignment of the heavenly life alone to one set of men, and of the earthly alone to another set of men — should have so fastened itself in Christianity!

You say, indeed,— how men are always saying it! how terribly familiar it has grown!— you say, "I am not spiritual; I cannot be. My possibilities on that side are very small; somebody must do my spirituality for me. Enough for me if I can creep through the common tasks of common life with decency." Of such talk from anybody let us make little account. We make less and less account of it, I think, the longer that we know our fellow-men. At any rate, however much it may mean when a kind man uses it about his brother-man, making for him such excuse as seems possible, any man ought to be ashamed to use it in self-excuse about himself.

The truth is, my dear friends, for any man in this short fragment of a life of ours to dare to think or say that he has understood the limits of his possibilities is worse than folly. It is almost blasphemy. What do you think of the boy that stands up at the age of ten, and looks you in the eye, and says that, as he has found he has no faculty for language, he proposes to deal with his language-books no longer? Do you not bid him learn a little self-respect and modesty together, and send him back speedily to his grammar and dictionary? And we are not children of ten yet in our long life of immortality! Before us stretches so far away the long experience, so dim, so calm, so certain, so certainly full of richer conditions and a perpetual development of this mysterious humanity of ours. What will you say to the pert little man who stands up sharp in the midst of the concrete trifles of his busy life, and says, "Oh, I cannot be spiritual. I have no faculty of prayer. It is impossible for me to find God, or even to seek after Him." Will you not say, " Be more modest, and so have more respect for yourself! Go back to your closet and your Bible, and do not dare to say what possibilities God has put into that nature of yours, which He made, till you are older, a great deal older than you are now; yea, till you are old as eternity!"

Think of the other tone. Think of the man who says, " So long as I live, until eternity shall end, I never will cease to hope that out of the depths of my nature, hopeless as it seems, may open the power to be that which, as I have seen it in the best souls among my race, is the best thing that a man can be — a lover of God, and a dweller with Him among heavenly thoughts and motives." When a man is saying that with all his heart, then how ready he is for the words of Jesus: " He that hath seen Me hath seen the Father." " No man cometh unto the Father but by Me." Then comes, " I will go to Him, to Christ, and find God! How long, how slow, how hard the journey through Him, through Christ, to God may be, I do not know; but henceforth, in this world and in whatever world may lie beyond, I will go on and on and on through Christ to God." With that determination made, with that journey begun, eternity is not too long; nor has this world, nor any other, the temptation which can turn the man aside from his eternal search.

O, you who have begun that search, be content, for at the last it must succeed. O, all of you, be sure that life is not really life for you until you have begun that search for God through Christ! Be sure that when through Christ you have found God, then, and not till then, will the harmony of your whole life, totally submitted in all its parts to Him, be perfect; then in you shall this great text which we have studied now so long be perfectly fulfilled: "Truth shall spring out of the earth, and righteousness shall look down from heaven!"

III.

THE POWER OF AN UNCERTAIN FUTURE.

"Watch therefore, for ye know neither the day nor the hour wherein the Son of man cometh."—MATTHEW xxv. 13.

JESUS spoke these words at the close of the Parable of the Ten Virgins. The people were still under the impression that the parable had made upon them. It is the air of expectancy that pervades it which gives the parable its character. It all looks forward. It is busied with the future, not the past. The waiting virgins, the sleepless eyes, the well-filled lamps, and then the hurried stir, the rustling garments, the passing voices, and the opening and closing doors,—all the movement is expectant, and is full of one idea: Be ready, for a future is coming —new issues—new destinies—new duties. Forget the past! Look forward!

That is the tone of the parable, and it is the tone of the Gospel always. Stretching out into an infinite distance, it shows the endless future of human life. It lays its hand upon every soul that is asleep and says, "Wake, for your work is not done yet." New developments of truth, new perfections of character, and infinite plans of God in which we are to take part,—these are the burden of the Gospel, and of the spirit of these the Parable of the Ten Virgins is full. It is all alive with expectancy. It is a parable of the Future. "Behold the Bridegroom cometh!"

There are times, I think, when this character of the Gospel seems hard and almost cruel to us. There are times when the thought of expectancy is oppressive. Sometimes the soul is simply weary, and wants to lie down and go no farther. It seems to have done enough, to have lived enough. There is much in the past which is precious to it, but the thought of going on and making new history for itself is dreadful to it. Life seems behind it. To turn and see that life is yet before it seems very hard. But always the Gospel keeps its character. It will allow no resting in the past or in the present. It is always holding up its future and insisting that its disciples should live in "the power of an endless life."

But this verse of warning which comes at the end of the parable has one special point. It brings out one kind of power in the anticipations of the future which is very striking. "Watch," Jesus says, "not merely because there is to be a future, but because you cannot know what the future is. Watch, for you know neither the day nor the hour wherein the Son of man cometh." Here is a sort of life enjoined—watchfulness. I hope we shall see clearly enough before we are done that watchfulness is not a single act, nor a special habit, but a whole new character of a man's life. And this character of a whole life is represented as coming out of the fact that the future of the life is uncertain. There is one sort of life that a man will live who anticipates no future at all, who lives wholly in the present. There is another sort of life for the man whose future is all clear before him, all ticketed and dated. There is yet another life for the man who knows that larger and stranger things are coming than he comprehends, who expects surprises. I want to speak of this last kind of life. Our subject is "The Power of an Uncertain Future." "Watch, therefore, for ye know neither the day nor the hour wherein the Son of man cometh."

We have one illustration of our subject always before us in the life of childhood. I suppose that it would not be possible to get a better idea of what Jesus meant by the watchfulness that would become the character of one who was always looking for His undated coming, than we should have if we could understand perfectly the strong and subtle influence which the uncertainty and apparent infiniteness of the life before him has upon a child. The alertness, the receptivity, the modesty, the eagerness and easy enlargement or readiness for great things, which belong to the best childhood, seem to me to be the very qualities which the Gospel is always trying to make in Christians, and all these qualities belong essentially to the uncertainty with which a child's future hovers before his eyes. If you could take a very high average of human attainment, something considerably beyond what the majority of men have reached, and fix that as the uniform level of men's accomplishment, if you could decree absolutely that every life should go just as far as that and no life should go any farther, you certainly would have taken the spring out of the ambition of very many young aspiring souls. You would have taken away the uncertainty, and so you would have destroyed the romance and attractiveness. Probably not half of them will reach that line, but probably those who do reach it will go beyond it if you do not set them a limit there, but leave them all infinity to aspire into. One will certainly shoot his arrows higher if he shoots them out-of-doors, with all the sky to shoot them into, than if he sends them up against the ceiling of a room that seems just as high as he can reach.

And so it is the child's uncertainty about his life that gives it all those characteristics that I spoke of. He does not know which way it will go. It is full of wonderment. Every door tempts him to open it, to see what lies beyond. Every corner tempts him to turn it. And so, just as you or I, going to Paris or London, will walk more in a day than any Londoner or Parisian in three, because our curiosity is always kept alive by the uncertainties of the unfamiliar streets,—so the child will make more character in a week than we grown people will in months, because life, not having yet hardened itself into routines and certainties, is always vividly interesting to him and is always enticing him a little farther on.

There must be grown men, old men, here to-day,

who look back to nothing with such wistful longing as to the interest that life had for them when they were children. Can it be, indeed, that this dull and faded thing is the same that once flashed and sparkled with such bewitching colors? Living has disenchanted them with life. And if they look into it they will see that what has gone out of life is simply its uncertainty. They have solved all the problems. They have opened all the closets. Once, when they got up in the morning, they wondered what they would do that day; they thought of a thousand things that might happen before the sun went down. Now, they know just what will happen and just what they will do at every hour of the day. Once each New Year's day was a pinnacle on which they stood and looked out into an enticing splendor of vague possibilities. Now, on New Year's day they balance their books, and, presuming that they will make and spend about the same amount of money in the next year as in the last, settle down to the dull content of a certain competence. So the interest of life, you see, depends upon its uncertain futures. It will not do to solve the problems of life, unless in solving them you open new ones. If you can do that, then you can keep the interest of living. If you can open a new prospect, with all the splendor of vague distance about it, yet farther on, then you can afford to go over and examine in detail and so lose the romantic beauty of the prospect that has already opened to you.

My dear friends, all this seems to me to lead to

very serious truth. It seems to me to show that life is certain to become dull and uninteresting and weary to an old man, to every man as he grows old, unless some future beyond life opens before him, which shall be to his old age all that the yet untried life was to his boyish dreams. The boy dreamed of the infiniteness of life, and there was color in his cheek and brightness in his eye and a dewy freshness in everything he said and did. That is all gone with you, perhaps gone so far back that it seems as remote as the book of Genesis when something calls it back to you. Is there any possible thing that can replace it for you? Only that opening of another future, with new uncertainties, which has turned many an old man into a child again as he stood at the gateway of the Everlasting Life. When this life is exhausted, when its crooked streets have all been trodden to the end, still the interest need not have gone out of living if only from the hilltop of experience new and untrodden ways can open themselves before us, rolling on into the mystery of eternity. Then one may die with as true vitality, as eager curiosity, as he has ever lived. To him the interest of life is still preserved, as alone it can be preserved, by the power of an uncertain future.

There are some touching instances of this feeling that an unknown future is necessary to any real pleasurable interest in living. Have you never heard people ask one another whether they would be willing to live their lives over again, and has it not sometimes seemed sad to see how almost everybody said " No "—almost with a shudder, as if the idea was almost dreadful to him? It is not really that men's lives have been so unhappy—that is not why they would dread a repetition so. There have been portions of their lives that they would dread. There are places, if we had to live our lives over again just as we have lived them, where we should set our teeth in grim misery as we came in sight of the old blunder or the terrible catastrophe which we had almost forgotten; but on the whole there has been more of happiness than wretchedness in all our lives. But the main reason why people shudder when you ask them to live their lives again is that the proposition seems to them so utterly dreary. A life with no surprises! A life where you knew just what was coming! There is no succession of terrible blows that can fall upon a man that could begin to be so wretched as the dulness of such a life would be.

Or take another question: You ask yourself, " Would I have lived my life, if I had known at the outset just what it was to be? If all the picture could have been set before my baby-brain, would my baby-hands have been reached out to welcome it, or would they have thrust it impatiently away?" I am afraid there are a good many people here who, either from general temper or from some temporary mood that they are in, would think the answer to that question only too plain. " Never!" they say. " Never would I have lived if I had known beforehand what life was!" And yet how good it is for these people that they have lived! How much they have added to the world's stock. How much happiness they themselves have had in spite of all. They have been tempted on, spared the worst misery of anticipation, and never wholly deserted by eagerness and hope, through the power of an uncertain future.

My dear friends, if we feel this, what can we say? Is there one of us that dare complain of God because He keeps our futures uncertain? Does it not put something like a reason underneath these endless changes by which our plans are always being broken up and our best hopes disappointed? Is it good for a man to grow gloomy over that which is the only source of interest, hopefulness, and joy in life?

These words are very general; let us take our text somewhat more closely. This future in whose uncertainty the power resides is spoken of as the " day and hour wherein the Son of Man cometh,"—what day and hour is meant? The Son of Man is Christ Himself. His coming is certainly not a time when He draws near to the world, for He is in the world always. It must be, then, some time or times in which His presence becomes manifest. Such comings there are several of. Men discuss which of them the text refers to,—whether to the final coming for judgment, the coming to every man at death, or the coming of the Spirit at a man's conversion. Let us not try to settle which it means, but let us take all three. It is good for us; it cultivates the life called " watchfulness " within us, not to know when Christ is coming to judge the world, when He is going to call us to Himself by death, when He is coming by some great experience to our souls,—the unknown coming for judgment, the unknown time of death, the unknown spiritual experience.

1. Take first the coming of Christ to judge this world. Clearly the Bible tells of some such time. Clearly there is to be some close of the present state of things and some new dispensation, to begin with some peculiar manifestation of Christ to men. Forever in these chapters of the Bible runs the prophecy of the opened heaven and the Son of man sitting there throned among His angels. "He cometh, He cometh to judge the world, and the people with equity." But yet the time is all uncertain. "Of that day and hour knoweth no man." Perhaps for cycles upon cycles yet this tangled web of forces may move on as it is moving now. Perhaps already the great wheels are trembling on the brink of stoppage. Science no more than revelation ventures to guess the *time;* though science, just like revelation, catches glimpses of the coming *fact*.

And then, when we ask what the effect of this uncertain future on the world's character is, we are struck first of all by this,—that every attempt (and men have always with a strange persistency kept making their attempts) to fix what God has left uncertain has done harm and not good to those who made their guesses. Certainly such attempts have not helped the religion on which they tried to fasten themselves. The Apostles evidently, after Jesus had gone away, believed that He would come back while some of them were yet alive, but that was not the religion that inspired the zeal of Paul and John. Again, as the thousand years after Christ approached toward the end of the ninth century, you know there was a strange and widespread impression that when the thousand years were over, Jesus would come. The people waited. From many a housetop, as, in the night, one century gave the world over to the next, eyes must have watched the heavens for the coming Lord. But we do not find that such a confident expectancy made the world better. Certainly there were few centuries darker than the ninth, the century of wars among the nations, and gross corruption in the Church, and ignorance and misery in private life. Again, many of us are old enough to remember how, forty years ago, a vast number of our people believed that on a certain mentioned day the world would end and Christ the Judge appear; but certainly, among the multitudes who looked for such a crisis, no one ever heard that virtue or religion came to any wonderful development, that life was purer, holier, profounder, than among their unbelieving neighbors. Nor will the most enthusiastic supporter of any of the Millenarian theories that have attempted to tell what is to be the end of things with more or less exactness, venture to say that his theory has established for itself any right to be called necessary even to the highest Christian life.

No; history shows us that where men have thought they knew the end, it has not been good for them. It is better that they should not know. And certainly we can see why. Can we not understand that the best culture for the world is just in that idea under which God has kept the world living,—the idea that all these things were temporary, and yet an entire ignorance as to the length of their endurance? If the world has been saved from entire sordidness, if its heart in every age has aspired after loftier things, if it has been able to keep in its remembrance that *character* was the one permanent thing, if thus it has been able to sacrifice other more manifest things to the invisible majesty of character, the reason in large part has been that in all ages men have believed that the time would come when all these things would pass away. The " eternal hills " were not eternal. The calm heavens were some day to part in fire, and the Judgment Day of the world to come. On the other hand, if the world of men, believing in the coming Judgment, has still worked on, toiled on the substance of this perishable earth as if it were imperishable, developed its resources and so made it a fitter instrument for their own development, it has been because no *day* for the catastrophe stared them in the face, paralyzing their healthy activity, and blighting their courage. To live in one's work, and yet above one's work, is what one needs. To be a servant of the earth, and yet superior to the earth, where it has been put by God, is the lesson that the human soul always has been learning; and that lesson it has been taught by the power of the world's uncertain future.

I think it is just the way in which a wise parent

treats his child during the preparatory years in which he lives still as a child under the parent's roof. He lets him know that that home-life is temporary. He opens windows through which the boy can see the life that he must live for himself out in the world, when this first dispensation shall be over. And at the same time he draws no line, fixes no date, makes the child-life as real as it could be if it were to last forever. So God trains this world for the next. So He keeps Time full of solemn watchfulness for Eternity. So, in the ears of a humanity which is to be educated by the ministry of perishable things for those which are imperishable, He seems to be always uttering those unutterably solemn words: " Seeing that all these things shall be dissolved, what manner of persons ought ye to be in all holy conversation and godliness, looking for and hasting unto the coming of the day of God?"

2. If we can see much reason why the world should be left in ignorance about the time of Christ's coming to be its Judge, we can understand even more of how good it is for every man not to know just when the word of the Lord will come to him, as it does come to every man, to call him out of this state of being to a higher. I suppose that we have all thought, sometimes, what differences it would make in all our life if we all knew from the beginning just when we were to be called to die. Certainly we do not know, men do not know themselves, how much the certainty that they must die some time influences and controls them. It is not often on their lips. It is not often consciously upon

their hearts. But there is something in the life of every man that would be changed in a moment if he suddenly were made aware that he were to stay here upon the earth forever. We say sometimes that men live here just as if they never were to die; we think that all this hurrying crowd upon the street has utterly forgotten death and hurries on as if it were to pour up and down these thronged avenues forever; but it is not so. Every man has in his nature the influence of the fact that he always knows, though it is not always consciously before his mind. The traveller in the city is always different from the citizen, though he has no time fixed for his departure, and even prolongs his visit to many years. So the pilgrim-and-stranger feeling is somewhere in all of us. It differs in us all. It is an awful sense of brooding mystery in some, a tireless and hurried energy in others, and in almost all it is a certain tenderness and dearness gathering about the earth which we are certainly some day to leave. But just consider what the consequences would be if this vague certainty were brought down and made definite, and each man knew from the beginning of his course just when to him would come the summons that no man can disobey.

The first thing that I think of is the great decrease of physical energy and work that it would probably make in the world if every man knew just when he was to die. One of the strongest springs of action among men is the desire for the preservation of their life,—perhaps it is *the* strongest spring of action. It is this, the desire to prolong their life, that has in large part broken up the forests and opened the mines and bridged the rivers and built the cities. This, in large part, is what one hears through all the clatter of the world's machineries and the hoarse roar of business,—the personal desire for life. It is the clangor of the hammers with which men are building walls between themselves and death. This, too, is at the root of almost all our institutions: society, government,—they are all to secure men in life, liberty, and the pursuit of happiness; and of these great ambitions *life* stands first and lies deepest of all.

And, then, consider how, in the uncertainty as to the time of death, every man's labor lasts almost— some men's last quite—up to the time of death. Almost or quite up to the very last they still contribute to the wealth and progress of the world. No sight of the approaching end unmans their courage and makes them drop their tools before the time. Think, if you please, how many men, if they knew that their dying day was only one year off, would feel no spirit and no call to work during that year, the hope of self-preservation being definitely taken from them. And, then, think how much the world would have been robbed of, if all the labor that her millions of great and little workers have done within a year of the time when they were called away were taken out of the aggregate; and we can see already some reason why the cloud is not lifted, and men walk on, working and living and hoping, up to the very door of the other life.

And when I think again, not of what the world

would lose, but of what the character and culture of the men themselves would lose, if the day when they were to leave the earth were known to them from the day when they first entered on it, then it seems clearer still. You train your little child for all the duties of his manhood. From his very cradle the thought of "when he is a man" is before you as your inspiration and your guide. God takes your child, still in his childhood, to the higher education of the perfect world. The training for this life that you gave him, if it was really sound and true and godly, was the best training that he could have taken to the Eternal School; but could you have given it to him if you had known that he was to die so young, that he was never to mingle among men in all the ministries and competitions of the world? Or, again, could a young man train himself to prudence, self-constraint, truth, and all the qualities that make the best successes of men's middle-age, if he knew from the start that just upon the threshold of that middle-age the angel would touch him and he must go away? That eager student,—would he have studied so if he had always known that his knowledge would never be used here, that with its new richness all about him he was to lie down and die? And then the happiness that comes to hearts that look forward into years of friendship,—could it have flowed in so abundantly and cloudlessly upon the soul if that soul had foreseen the coming separation? Still, indeed, there would be left the highest values of knowledge and the highest sources of happiness; still the student might have known that he could learn nothing that was really true, for which he would not be the richer in whatever world he lived; still the friend might twine his friendship all the closer that it might be strong enough not to break even with the strain that carried it beyond the grave; but all the inferior sources of culture and happiness, which, though inferior, are pure, on which we all so much depend, must surely suffer a blight. Surely it is a good, kind God, a blessed Father, who lets us know that He is coming, but does not tell us when. We are like children off at school, to whom the father sends word that he will bring them home, that so they may study all the harder and be ready, but does not fix the day lest they should drop the books altogether and merely stand looking for him out of the window, wasting their time. God will bring the shortness of life home to all of us so as to make us say, "We will work the harder," but He will not let it weigh upon any of us so as to set us thinking, "It is not worth while to work."

And we must think not merely of what such a certainty about the time of our death would take away from us, but also of what it would bring into our lives. It would set us all to preparing for death in a narrow and special sense. It is not good for a man to devote himself to preparation for dying. It is preparation for living that you need. When, in mediæval times, men, feeling that death was near them, used to give up their work, lay down their arms, and, like the cloistered emperor, put on the cowl and go and live in monasteries,—nay, build their coffins and keep their epitaphs written on their cell-walls,—we know that it was a mere makeshift. It was better perhaps than nothing, but it was an attempt to crowd into a year or two what a whole lifetime should have done, to force by unnatural means that intimacy with the God to whom they were to go which should have been healthily gathered out of the daily experiences of a long, devout, obedient life. You cannot so make the perfect friendship any more than you can make the lower friendship so. To take away the uncertainty about the time of death would have a tendency (which the best men would resist, but to which multitudes of men would yield) to give the bulk of life up to indifference and recklessness and crowd the last few months or days with an artificial religiousness that would have little power to prepare the soul for its great change. The only real way to "Prepare to meet thy God" is to live with thy God so that to meet Him shall be nothing strange.

So, surely, it is better for us as God has appointed it. So, surely, the picture of a faithful man, by every duty of his life preparing himself for the next duty, and so at last finding that living has prepared him for dying, and laying his life back into the hands of a Father in whose strength he has lived it all,—this is the highest illustration of the power of an uncertain future to influence and ripen and prepare us for more than we foresee.

3. And now, but little time remains for me to speak of the last of the three comings of the Son of Man. Christ comes to all last for judgment, Christ

comes to each of us at death, but Christ comes also in the hour of conversion, when He claims a man for His servant and bids him take up his cross and follow Him. In the religion of our day, conversion is made a less prominent and separate moment in a man's life than it used to be considered in the religion of other days. If this change means that all the life is recognized as being more full of God, and so lifted up nearer to the level of the conversion-hour, then it is well; but if it means that the supernatural power of the conversion itself is being disallowed, and so the whole life brought down to the level of every-day worldliness, then it is bad. All Christian experience bears witness that there are times when that Saviour who is always present and always seeking us makes Himself peculiarly manifest to our souls and asks us to be His. It may be in connection with some great outward change that comes to us; or it may be something wholly of the inner life, unseen, unheard by any one beside ourselves; but do you not know that such times surely come? I speak to any servant of the Saviour here: Were there not days, perhaps years, when you went on in your own way, Christ by you always but you not seeing Him, Christ speaking to you and you not hearing Him? But at last there came a time when He looked on you with a new face and you did see Him; when He spoke to you with a new voice and you did hear Him! That is the time—be it a moment or a day or a year—of a man's conversion,—the beginning of a new life.

And now, can you not see that it makes a great

difference whether that supreme meeting of your soul and God, which must come and which is fraught with such stupendous consequences, is to come at some fixed time, when you have reached some special age, when you are ready for some special study; or, on the other hand, whether it may come at any moment—*at any moment* between the solemn moment when you first find that you have a soul and that other solemn moment when you give your soul up to your Master and your Judge? If the first, then you may wait, wait unexpectantly until you hear Him coming. If the other, then any time in the ever-turning journey of life may bring you into sight of Him; any sound close by your side may be His footstep. This next moment may be His moment to bless your soul. Nay, this moment, *now*, may be His time, and you may be letting it pass just because you are not knowing that it may be any moment, and so are not listening every moment for the slightest indication of His coming.

More and more the law of the Christian life seems to me to be this—that Christ the Saviour comes to every man, and that they that are watching for Him and expecting Him know Him when He comes, and enter with Him into some higher life. "They that were ready went in with Him to the marriage"; these words of the old parable tell the whole story. Ah, yes, as we look back over our life, how sudden always have been the comings of the Son of Man! We looked for Him off in some distance, and suddenly His voice spoke to us close at our side. Again we said to ourselves in some proud moment of self-exaltation, "Now He must be near me; now He will speak to me," but that proud, selfish moment has gone by, utterly cold and dead, without a sight or sound of Christ; and then, when we had just passed down off from the mountain where we hoped for so much, into a valley of humility where we expected nothing,—then everything around us has been radiant with His presence, and He has spoken to us words of wisdom and a Brother's tenderest love. We have expected Him, and He has not come; we have forgotten Him, and He has been with us. The deepest experiences of our life have taken us unawares. In such an hour as we thought not the Son of Man has come.

Every man knows this of his life, and so what is the law of life that it ought to make for us? It is not hard to see. It must be always useless to prepare oneself against this or that moment, to make up conditions for what we fancy are to be the most critical times of life. That is spasmodic and unreal. But to be so possessed with the conviction that God is around us always, and may show Himself to us in any commonest moment, that we are always alert and ready to receive Him,—that is the true condition of the soul. Sometimes from mere expectancy you may be deceived; sometimes it may seem as if God spoke to you when it is only your own longing that He may speak that makes you think it is His voice; but I think it is better to be mistaken so a hundred times than once not to be ready, and so say, "Oh, it is nothing!" when He really does speak. It is better, after all, to be so superstitious that we find God where He is not, than to be so sceptical that we will not find Him where He is.

Have we not, then, come at the end to something like a clear tangible notion of what the watching is to which the Saviour urged His disciples long ago, and to which He still urges us? It is not an act, not a habit, but a character. It is a constant alertness of soul which, believing that Christ does come near to people, is determined that He shall not come near us and escape us because we are asleep. It has no plan for the future, and so is always ready to catch any intimation of His plan. It is profoundly conscious that the world is full of Him, and so is ready to hear His voice from any unexpected corner. It believes, just as those disciples believed, that Jesus never died for men and left them to their fate, but that He will certainly come back to claim the souls He died for. It lives in prayer and work, both of them keeping it open and dependent; and by and by He comes, and they, being ready, enter in with Him to His home and their home in God.

One would like to speak to all these young people very earnestly. Do not think that the life you are beginning has shown you yet all its mystery. Do not think you have got to the height or the depth of it when you have just found it pleasant and sunny. It is more solemn and profound than that. It will bring vast experiences. To you, more wonderful by far than you know yourself, and capable of far greater intercourses than you have imagined, the Son of Man will certainly come. Do not manufacture experiences. Do not pay too much regard to those who shout to you, " Lo, here is Christ!" or, " Lo, He is there!" but be so expectant of Him always, keep so in the pure way of His commandments, pray so earnestly for Him to come, that when He does come you will know it; when He calls you, you will answer; when He says, " Come to me," you will leave all and follow Him. Let your life be that, and then one hardly dares to say which is the holier, the time here while you are watching for His coming, or the Eternity hereafter when He shall have fully come and received you to Himself. May God grant you first the one and then the other!

IV.

THE SPIRITUAL STRUGGLE.

"For we wrestle not against flesh and blood, but against principalities, against powers, against the rulers of the darkness of this world, against spiritual wickedness in high places."—EPHESIANS vi. 12.

IN this world wherever there is life there is struggle. We grow so used to it as a perpetual accompaniment of life that we do not always give it its true name. We give the name only to some forms of wrestling with difficulty, and think that other lives are easy and struggleless. But always when we come to know these other lives and to examine them with any kind of care, we find that they too are engaged in strife, that the difference is merely one of form. Sometimes one strong man's struggle shakes the world and makes the nations look. Sometimes it wears the man's soul out in silence, and cannot be told, however the struggler longs and tries to tell it to his dearest friend. Sometimes it writes itself in haggard lines upon the forehead and the cheek; sometimes the darker the strife that rages behind, so much the brighter is the smile upon the face. Sometimes the struggle is the joy of the life, making it like a perpetual field of trumpets and banners and marching hosts; sometimes it is all the blackness of darkness, as if a man wrestled day and night for years in a dark dungeon underground with an enemy whom he never saw and only came to know by the untiring persistency of his strength and cunning. Sometimes it is the saint struggling with the last temptation that seems to keep him from perfect peace; sometimes it is the poor wretch struggling with what seems to be the last effort of the Spirit of Goodness to rescue him from perfect satisfaction and content in sin;—whatever, however, it may be, in this world there is struggle wherever there is life. The only way in which some souls seem to escape from struggle is by lowering the tone of life, by making themselves half-dead.

No man in this world need ever seek after struggle. Let him seek after life, and the struggle will come, healthily and naturally, by the law of the world we live in. When a young man or young woman, with a Byronic impulse, seeks directly for struggle, tries to reproduce in one life those signs which have told of the deep movement which has stirred some other life, the result is only an artificial and unpleasant affectation; the contortions do not move our sympathy, but our disgust. No, do not try to struggle, but try to live, and the struggle will open before you surely. Do not seek it, and do not shun it, but let the increase of life deepen as it will the seriousness and solemnity of your contact with those things which your growing life will have to touch. It is one of those things which puts heaven past, outside of, our comprehension that *there* there is to be the fulness of life, without struggle, in unhindered ease and peace. We cannot understand that now, for in this world wherever there is life there is struggle.

And then, another thought which follows immediately upon this, and which is also abundantly confirmed by the experience of men, is that with every change in the character of life there will come also a change in the character of the struggle that goes with it. As men come to a new and higher life, so will they find themselves in the midst of a new and higher struggle. It is as when a soldier storms a citadel: with each new chamber into which he presses as he comes nearer to the central room which is the key and core of all, where the choicest treasures are guarded, he meets always a more and more watchful and formidable enemy. Only beside the very treasure, only when his hand is laid upon the prize which he has come through all the perils thus far to seek, does he meet the strongest enemy of all, the stoutest heart and strongest arm that the whole citadel can furnish.

The illustrations of this are endless. A man has been trying to be rich, and he has met the enemies and hindrances that beset that search,—the fickleness of the market, the competition of his brethren, his own temptations to indolence or to extravagance. But by and by, perhaps, the man *is* rich, and then he presses forward into an inner chamber of ambition. He aspires to be wise. He wants to learn. With that wish opens a new life, and with the new life opens a new struggle. In his newly built study he fights a fight which his store could never give him,—no longer now against the chances of the market and the opposition of the street, but against prejudice, against bigotry, against intellectual selfishness, against pride, against all in himself and other men that dislikes and dreads the truth; against all this he fights the moment that he becomes a scholar. A man who has been selfish learns to love. Instantly he is struggling not merely for his own self-respect which it was so easy to conciliate, but for the respect and confidence of his beloved, which can be won only by magnanimous devotion. A man mounts to the thought of charity, and he is wrestling with other men's woes and sorrows, no longer only with his own.

Or take St. Paul. Think over his life. Think how, as he opened one door after another into the successive chambers of his long career, he always met a new fight in each of them, and his growing life was marked and recognized by his growing struggles. His life began with that mere struggle for a place among the physical things of the physical earth, which all human lives must encounter first —the struggle for existence,—by success in which he made himself a standing-ground for all his other fightings. Then, as a scholar of Gamaliel, came his fight with ignorance and with all the enemies of the ideas that ruled in that master's school. Then, to the fiery young Pharisee, riding to Damascus, persecuting the upstart Christians, there came the new life of national enthusiasm, and with it the new struggle against what he thought his nation's enemies. Each of these lives, with its new struggle, was nobler than the one before it.

But then this Paul became a Christian. To the spiritual truth of a spiritual Master he gave up his soul. The life hid in an unseen Christ opened before him. He was drawn into it as if by a great, unseen arm put out around him. And once in there, once living not for himself but for his Lord, the new life thoroughly begun, behold the struggle was all new! No longer now with disease and physical dangers, no longer now with the scholars of other schools who fought wordy battles with the young Gamalielites, no longer now with seditious followers of One who seemed a traitor to his nation and his church, but now with all the spiritual enemies of his Spiritual Lord,—with sin, with his own selfishness, with lust, with falseness, with unspirituality. The whole battle is drawn inward. On another field, with other weapons, inspired by other hopes, led by another watchword, now it rages. Hear him tell of it himself. "We wrestle not against flesh and blood, but against principalities, against powers, against the rulers of the darkness of this world, against spiritual wickedness in high places."

This was the way in which St. Paul came up to this great utterance of my text. The spiritual life had brought the spiritual battle. We cannot read the words carefully, indeed, without remembering how much there was in Paul's mind which has grown unfamiliar to these modern minds of ours. Paul was a Jew. To the Jews the whole idea of beings outside of our race, who were in continual contact with and influence upon our race, was one in which they had been bred and in which the whole history of their nation had been lived. They believed in angels, and almost looked for their daily presence and help. They believed in spirits of evil, and traced the evil works which they saw in the world to unseen spiritual hands. Man's sin consisted not simply in yielding to the persuasions of his own worse self, but in giving way to the temptations of those external powers of wickedness of which the air was full. When St. Paul, then, describes his battle, it is of these powers that he is thinking. The "principalities and powers," the "rulers of the darkness of this world," the "spiritual wickedness in high places," that is, in the upper regions of the sky,—all these are not figures of speech with him; they are real beings, true objective enemies of the human soul.

It is hard for us to realize how far we have departed from that whole conception. Man's look then was turned outward, and all the universe was conceived as fighting for the possession of his soul. Man's look now is turned inward, and his soul is fighting with itself, tossing in the fermentation of its own internal passions, its own enemy or its own saviour. They are different views of human life, the objective and the subjective view. Both views are true, but they give us different sides of truth. Probably no century has been so one-sided as ours in its intense acceptance of one aspect of life and its almost complete rejection of the other. No century has had its eye so earnestly fixed upon man's struggle with himself. No century has made so little of the thought of any evil spirits outside of us, trying to harm our souls. And we are all men of our century, and must look on truth from the side from which our time regards it, but yet we never ought to entirely forget its other sides, from which it has most powerfully appealed to other times. I am willing enough to talk after our modern way, to represent the struggle of man as a struggle with himself; but all the time I want to remember with St. Paul and all the great objective thinkers and believers, that the universe is large, that it is full of beings who must send forth influence upon each other, and so that, while the spiritual enemy with which I fight to-day meets me immediately as a lust of my own soul, it has its sources and connections farther back in the world of spiritual being which stretches far, far away past my sight, but not too far away to send forth forces from its farthest depths which shall touch and tell upon my life.

We want to bear this in mind, and see that Paul's way of feeling and our modern way are really one. The underlying idea is the same,—that he who tries to live a holy life is beset by a new kind of enemy and lives in the midst of fears that he never felt before. Paul sees those enemies gathering out of the realms of space. Range beyond range, world beyond world, back into the most mysterious distance of the universe, he sees their hostile faces bent upon him, he feels their far-sent breath upon his cheek. We know our enemies, as they gather from the depths of our own nature, as they attack us from the newly stirred regions of our own tumultuous selves; but in both cases the meaning is the same; we have begun to live a new life and we have found it beset by new enemies and fears.

Indeed, this was what Jesus said to His disciples when He invited them to a higher life. He described and characterized the new life by its new fear: "Fear not them that kill the body, and after that have no more that they can do, but fear Him who hath power to destroy the soul in hell. Yea, I say unto you, fear Him." These words really agree with and fulfil the words of Paul. Paul says that as a man grows nobler he will wrestle not with men, but with devils; Jesus says that as a man grows nobler he will fear not men, but God. They really amount to the same thing, which is, that as a man grows nobler he will fight and fear not for the body, but for the soul, will fight the soul's enemies and fear the soul's Lord,—just as when a soldier is raised to the command of a great army, he is filled at once with a new fear of the enemy that is set against him, and a new fear of the king who has raised him to such responsibility.

Let us look then at this struggle of the higher life, the new battle of life which a man begins when he for the first time undertakes to do battle against his sins. It is a profoundly solemn moment. The man who heretofore has tried to do what the world called right, because he thought that it was decent or because it would make the world think better of him, gets a new idea. The right is right because it saves the soul. The wrong is wrong because it spoils the soul. The soul, the real spiritual self, the soul capable of a celestial whiteness, in danger of perpetual ineradicable stain, the soul whose purity is precious and delicate beyond anything on earth, —that soul becomes the touchstone and test of everything. Oh, my friends, with that new passion in the soul everything around you changes; expediency, fame, pleasure,—every other wish,—is swallowed up in the desire to keep that soul pure. Is it any wonder that Christ called it a new life to which men could come only by a new birth? Let us see what some of its characteristics are.

And, first of all, there is a certain strange and very delightful sense of dignity and exaltation which runs along with and continually blends into the fear with which the new life is beset. I think that this is always so. That which makes responsibility tolerable, that which supports a soul when any higher duty surrounds it with more pressing and dangerous dangers, is always the deep satisfaction, springing up with the fear and filling it and glorifying it, at finding that the manhood is capable of such a fear, that it has in it the power to dread that which it has now discovered to be its enemy. For natures might be graduated by the fears of which they are capable. And to come to a higher fear declares a higher nature and sends a thrill of conscious dignity all through the life. Man glories to find that he cannot play, "unconscious of his fate," like the "little victims" who are only brutes. And in all the weight of danger which the man carries who has learned to care for his soul, there is a sober joy which makes his life the happiest in all the world. I think we can have no idea of how the inspiring sense of human dignity would fade out of the life of our race if man came to really think himself a creature of no spiritual capacity or peril, with a chance of no spiritual heaven, in danger of no spiritual hell.

This is the first quality of the struggle with sin— the struggle after goodness. I would always mention this first. It is a solemn and noble exhilaration to the soul. And the next striking thing about it is the *silence* with which it goes on. When a man begins to fight his sins he does not sound a trumpet to tell the world that the battle is begun. The world rightly distrusts any such parade, and, if it hears the trumpet, believes that it is no real battle which is so vociferously announced, but only a sham fight, with an understanding all the time made between the man and his sins which he pretends to wrestle with. The essence of the real spiritual fight is its silence. A man is stirred to the depths in some great revival meeting, and with an impulse which he does not try to control, he lifts up his voice and shouts his hallelujah to the Lord. He declares his new allegiance. He gives himself to Christ with "solemn noise." But by and by he begins the fight that he must fight under his new Master. His old sins hear what he has done, and gather up their power to reclaim their servant. They meet him in the old familiar places. They find him in his shop, in his study, at his table, in his church. There he must fight with them. The other,—the meeting where he shouted,—that was not the fight, that was only the enlistment. This is the fight and there is no noise; all is silence here. Men see some sign, it may be, in the face, a new light in the eye, a pressure which speaks both of pain and power in the lips, but no word is spoken. The fight is too personal. It is for the man's own soul. The fighters are the man's own sins. Oh, how it sometimes transfigures the dull street as we are walking in it and suddenly remember that a very large part of these men and women whom we pass, are fighting in silence battles with temptation, with falsehood, with lust, with scorn, with doubt, with despair, with cruelty, which make their lives heroic! We cannot see their fight. They could not show it to us if they would, and would not if they could. The battle is "above the clouds." But the clouds of men's lives, the dull and dubious and foggy sides which they turn to us, cease to be dreary when we allow ourselves to think that behind and above the dreariest of them the real soul of the man is fighting silently with its sins, and winning certainly a better life.

It is this silence of the spiritual struggle that easily lets one who is not a sharer in it become sceptical about it. I do not doubt that there are men who honestly think that there is no such thing, that it is all a matter of nerves and dreams. That a man should fight with other men to win from them what is theirs—*that* they can understand. They are doing that themselves every day. But that a man should fight with himself for himself, with his own sins for his own soul,—that is incomprehensible. It never can be made credible to such a disbeliever till he himself undertakes it. When he does, when, on some great, new birthday of his life, he feels his soul claiming him, sees it beset—poor thing!—with all its enemies, and gives his life up to saving it,— when that time comes, then he will understand the spiritual fight of all these other souls. The mists will scatter from before his eyes, and that fight will seem to him to be the one real thing that is really going on in all the world. The earth will seem to rock with it. He will feel it all about him when he once carries it within him.

And this suggests another characteristic of the spiritual struggle, namely, its *companionship*. Silent as it is, it is not solitary. Have we not all felt sometimes that silence, with those who are in genuine sympathy with one another, brings men nearer together than any talk can do? Talk necessarily obtrudes details. Talk compels me to feel the special form of a brother's life, and so, in the differences which there must be between the form of his life and mine, obscures the identity of spirit. But two souls side by side, doing the same essential work in different forms, but doing it in silence, feel one another's companionship perfectly, and get the best blessing and help from one another. So it is in men's fight with their sins. Let every man shout aloud the story of his battle, and the impression will be of infinite difference. Let every man fight on with earnestness, but with no foolish attempt to tell the details of his struggle to his brethren; and the truth of the identical spirit that pervades them all will come out clear, and each will get the inspiration of all the rest. A world full of men who fight their several battles in their several circumstances is like one of those old eastern towns where there is one single fountain, out of which all the people of the town have to draw all the water that they need. They live their different lives; they use the water which they draw for various uses,—one in one trade, another in another,—but once a day they all meet at the fountain to refill their pitchers for their several works. The fountain is the centre of the town and gives it all its unity. So the souls of all earnest men are in their different struggles, but they all meet, all rest, in Him who is the supply, the fountain of them all, the God to whom they are all dedicated. He who is the fountain of goodness is the centre in whom all men who are struggling for goodness find unity with one another. How true, how deep, that union is! You have not learned its deepest quality if you require that men should tell you what their struggles are, and tell you that they know of yours. You have not fully learnt it unless, without a word, you live in company, through God, with every soul, known or unknown, whose life in its own way is seeking Him.

Yet one more thing about the spiritual struggle which gives it a large part of its character is its *perpetualness*, its persistency. It is to run on through all our life. We always do differently those things which we do temporarily and under some special demand, and those other things which we do continually as a part of our life. The first are spasmodic and take force out of us. The others are calm and determined, and put life into us. There is always a difference between the taking of occasional medicine and the taking of regular food. And some men fight their sins as if they expected to conquer them all and to be perfectly good by tomorrow night. Other men look calmly forward and see the work they have to do stretching on solemnly to the very end; and, with complete dedication, accept struggle not as the temporary necessity, but as the perpetual element of life. Oh, what a repose comes to a man's soul when he has once done that, — the repose not of idleness, but of accepted work. No longer does he tire himself in trying to shirk what he knows is as true a part of himself as the drawing of his breath. He wakes every morning to his struggle, not with weary surprise, but with glad recognition that his struggle is still there. He plans for it far ahead as a thing which, he is sure, will still be with him. And his greatest wonder about death and heaven is how he can ever leave behind that which is such a true part of himself, and what it will be to grow in goodness against no resistance, how it will seem to do right when there is no temptation to do wrong which must first be trodden under foot.

The *dignity* of spiritual struggle, then, its *silence*, its *companionship*, and its *perpetualness*,—these are the positive qualities in that fight with unseen sin in which every true man is engaged, and in which his deepest life is lived. I want still to suggest to you what are some of its negative qualities, what are some of the freedoms into which a man is liberated by it, at the same time that it gives these endowments to his life. When St. Paul says that we wrestle " against principalities and powers," he says also that " we wrestle not against flesh and blood." The more that the battle *with* the unseen *for* the unseen takes possession of a man, the more the battle *with* the seen *for* the seen must let him go. You may put it to yourself either as a necessity or as a privilege, either " you may " or " you must." But at any rate the two are inconsistent with one another, the eagerness for the spiritual and for the temporal victory. They cannot live together. This liberty from carnal passions and struggles will be the best test that the higher spiritual struggle has really entered into us. When the passion of our life is to conquer sin and be good, we shall let men beat us in the race of business; we shall let men overwhelm our wishes with their arrogance, or drown our good repute in their slanders, wherever the great fight of our life, the fight with sin, would suffer a moment's hindrance by our effort to refute the slander or to right the wrong. This is a noble liberty. The true struggler with sin will no more turn out of his way to punish a man who has wronged him than the captain who is leading his army into deadly fight will stop to chase a fly that stings him on the way. The battle with " principalities and powers " puts us above the fight with " flesh and blood."

Again, this assurance of the Apostle, that the true man's battle is not with flesh and blood, has another meaning. It contains that old truth which it is so hard for all of us to learn, but which, when we have learned it, cuts for us the knots of so many difficulties,—the truth that the moral trouble of our lives does not lie in our circumstances, and that it is not our circumstances that we have got to conquer in order to be better men. Fighting with poverty, fighting with ignorance, fighting with allurement, fighting with bad health, beating ourselves against the narrow walls in which we have to live,—those may be fights that we cannot escape; but none of them is the great fight of our life. We may be defeated in them all, and yet be conquerors in the fight to which God sent us. Not with circumstances but with spiritual conditions is the struggle that makes us men; not with the things the tempter uses for his tools, but with the tempter; not against flesh and blood, but against spiritual wickedness.

But still more Paul's view of life shows us the folly of substituting personal hostilities for the war with wickedness. It is so easy to hate a wicked man! It is so hard to hate a sin! And men have always been letting one slip into the place of the other. This is what has made those dreadful things called religious wars, and the persecutions of heretics, which have stained the pages of Christian history with such unchristian blots. Three hundred years and more ago two knights stood before the great Emperor Charles the Fifth, one asserting and the other denying the doctrine of the Immaculate Conception. The Emperor bade them fight their battle out with spears upon the field. They fought; and the champion of the disputed doctrine unhorsed his adversary and compelled him to confess his error as he lay helpless on the ground. What a strange, deep twist there must have been in men's minds before such a performance could have meant anything to them. Imagine the brave young victor standing with his foot upon his prostrate foe. He has conquered him. He hears the words of reluctant and insincere confession groaned forth between his tortured lips. And then, suppose, in all his flush of victory there start up in his own soul, as well there might unless he is merely a splendid animal with an arm that is invincible and a mind incapable of thought,—suppose there start up in his own soul doubts about the dogma in whose behalf he has fought and conquered. Suppose it seems to him, all of a sudden, to be incredible,—this for which he has risked his life. How worthless this battle which he has just fought with his brother knight must seem to him! *Now* the only real fight is just beginning in his own troubled soul. The shouts of the people tell him he has conquered, and the doctrine is sustained. He knows that the battle is yet to fight, that it lies between him and these unseen doubts. The victory over flesh and blood withers into worthlessness even as he takes its laurel. The true wrestling is to be with doubt and unbelief; and for that he goes to the silence of a cloister or the venerable peace of some altar in the Church.

We do not set our knights on horseback any longer for the faith, but oh! the cheaper, tawdrier way in which we set denomination over against denomination, and count the majorities of church over rival church, and think that that has anything to do with the answering of the question over which the soul of man is anxious,—What is truth? We do not any longer kill one disbeliever, but we think that in some way by hating and abusing him we substantiate our own belief. Only when in a man's own soul the real strife comes, does it appear how worthless all that which we called fighting for the truth really was. When the " powers of the air " are up in arms against us, when our own hearts fling their doubts in our faces, when we are wrestling for belief with the devil of unbelief who has taken possession of our own souls,—then is the moment when we are least likely to revile the unbeliever. The fight with " principalities and powers" frees us from the struggle with flesh and blood. That is the human charity and patience which belong to all deep life.

And just once more, the law that the deepest struggle of life is spiritual gives us, when we have realized it, the power to separate between the special forms and the essential spirit of the wickednesses that are around us, and always to fight against the spirit, not against the form. To denounce dishonesty not because it is dishonest, but because the cheater happens to be cheating *us;* to abuse impurity because of some offensive aspect which for the moment it has taken; to upbraid slavery not for the absolute wrong that it does to the slave's manhood, but for the blood that a specially cruel master draws from the slave's back,—all of these are fightings not against the spirit but against the form of sin. Christ set us nobly an example of the fight, not against the form, but against the spirit, when, instead of rebuking the single bad acts which He saw about Him, He laid the strong and tender hand of His Redemption on the essential badness of the human heart, and so has changed the world.

O friends, that we might know—I hope that many of you do know already—the privilege and joy of that profoundest struggle, in which a man, full of the passion of holiness and faith, wrestles with sin and doubt; and, coming by Christ who is our Brother to God who is our Father, finds eternally in Him the goodness and the faith which are well worth all the struggle through which we may have to reach them, and without which no man really lives.

V.

THE BATTLEMENTS OF THE LORD.

"Take away her battlements, for they are not the Lord's."—
JEREMIAH v. 10.

IT seems to be a hard and cruel cry which the Prophet Jeremiah utters in these words. Jerusalem was the City of God. Over the choosing and winning of the picturesque site where it was to stand, over its gradual growth, over the building of its temple, over its fortifications and embellishments, over its fortunes in peace and war, God had watched with peculiar care. Its enemies had been His enemies, its friends His friends. And now His city was beset by foes. She stood, almost visibly trembling, upon the rocky height where God had set her, almost as if she were a frightened deer which had taken refuge there from the dogs of war whom she could hear all round her, howling for her blood. The Chaldeans were pressing upon her and thirsting for her life. And the poor city was getting comfort out of the single thought that she was well protected. Harassed and frightened, she looked up to her walls and there were the battlements which she had built. They surely would protect her. To be sure they were her own, not God's. He had not bade her build them. She had built them even against

His will. But now, how strong they looked! How well it was that she had ventured to put them up! How the enemy would tremble at them! Only to picture herself without them made her shudder. And just then rang the stern voice of her prophet through her streets, "Her battlements are not the Lord's, take them away!" The very thing she trusted in! Her pride and strength and hope and confidence—take them away! Was this the God who loved her, who had promised to protect her? Was this His prophet whose voice now cruelly commanded the destruction of the only thing that could save His city? Well may the people have trembled in the streets and thought that their God had forsaken them indeed!

This is the picture which stands out in the prophet's verse. Of what that picture represents and stands for in our modern life I want to speak this morning. Every human life is dear to God. Every human life, when it thinks of how God has blessed it and shown to it the tokens of His love, must seem to itself to be a sort of Jerusalem, a city built and furnished and glorified by God. Such a resemblance between the life which God loves and the city which He used to love so dearly has been often suggested. The picture of Jesus weeping over Jerusalem, for instance, has been always appropriated by souls which wanted to depict the sorrow of the Saviour over the wasted opportunities of any life. Souls are Jerusalems which God has built and which are perpetually watched and protected by His love.

And then the parallel seems to go on. As God by His prophet bade the defences of old Jerusalem to be swept away, and would not tolerate any attempt to save the city by means which He had not ordained, and with what seemed severest cruelty stripped her bare of the very things of which she had been most proud and in which she had most trusted, so there are many souls which seem to have been treated by God in the same way. They too have built themselves defences and decorations which He has broken down. They too have been left desolate and bare just at the time when it seemed as if they most needed luxuriance and fulness. They too have seemed to find God cruel and stern as, with a hand which appeared to have no pity, He tore their dearest things away; and they too have had at last to learn, just as Jerusalem did, that their God had never been so kind to them as just in those days when He took away the battlements which were not His and left them naked and exposed, with nothing to trust to but His help. It is of this treatment of lives by God—the taking away of the battlements which are not His—that I desire to speak.

The distinction which the words imply is one that every man who is aware of God at all can easily understand. God is so universal, so complete, that the life which He occupies and guards He claims entirely for His own guardianship and occupancy. He wants it wholly for Himself. That which the man who lives in the life does, he must do as God's tenant, everything that he does being embraced and surrounded by God's ownership. All that the man does to make his life safe and strong and growing, he must do as the tenant of God, completing and strengthening God's life—the life that belongs to God—in God's way. Thus every good effort of a man to perfect his life, every right and healthy culture which he gives to himself in reverence of and obedience to God, is one of God's battlements —one of the methods by which God through him develops and protects this city of His love. But when a man forgets his tenantry and tries to strengthen his life as if it were no property of God's, as if it were no sacred, holy thing, but merely a personal possession of his own; when, then, he defends it by mere earthly policies and plans, or even by deeds which are wicked and base,—then he is putting on God's city battlements which are not God's; and it is these which God often pulls down because the strength which seems to be in them is weakness. All that a man does to make his life safer and better and stronger, in obedience to God, are the battlements of God; all that a man does to strengthen his life in selfishness and disregard of God are the man's own battlements; and however for a time these last may stand, and men may trust in them, at last they must come down, and it is the mercy of God that calls for their removal.

Indeed, no man has compassed and gone around the mercifulness of God on every side, who has not discovered this kind of mercy in Him and felt its richness and beauty. A child has certainly known only part of his father's love who has thought of his father as loving only in his indulgence. There is a whole other region of his father's love which he has never entered,—the region in which his father, with a profounder care for him and also with a completer trust in him, shall show his mercy by denial. We can all remember, I suppose, how once if men had asked us how we knew God loved us, the answer that leaped to our lips would have been the glowing catalogue of all that He had given us, all the incentives which He had put into our lives, all the securities by which He had surrounded us, all the successes by which He had shown us that we belonged to Him. These still remain. These still are on our lips when we sing His praises; but if we have at all compassed His love as the years have swept along, there is another side of it which has grown also dear to us, and which has in its dearness a peculiar depth and strength and sweetness which are all its own. There is a profound strain in our thankfulness which sings of the many times in which it has been through the exhibition of our own weakness that God has shown us His strength; of the plans and purposes which He has brought to failure in order that out of their failure He might build success. It is a poor and wretched life which has not such consecrations of its disappointments and its miseries. A life which has not these carries as a burden what it ought to be hugging as a treasure; and one whole side of the perfect sun of God's mercy, which burns with a glory all its own, this life has never seen.

Let me come to more special illustrations of what

I mean; and just in passing I may note how true our truth is of the history of the great groups of men, of states and churches,—the truth that God often in seeming cruelty tears down what seems to be a life's strongest protection and most beautiful adornments, in order that He may make the life really safe and really beautiful. The groups of men, the nations and the churches, often seem as if they were men seen through some sort of lens which magnified their size, and, while it blurred many of their more delicate details, brought out in broader exhibition the great fundamental features of human character and tendency, and so gave us a chance to study some things concerning man and them in a way which the individual man did not make possible. And what can tell the story of the breaking down of old and treasured institutions in the state, what can put a meaning behind the terrible convulsions or the slow growths by which autocracy and feudalism have disappeared from half the world, what can read to us the grand and simple secret of the destruction here in our own land of slavery which to so many men seemed to be the very palladium of our liberties and the very battlemented crown upon our nation's head, but this, that God saw in each age that what the nations called their strength was really their weakness, and out of heaven He sent forth His voice crying: " Take her battlements away. They are not Mine."

And in the Church's history, who does not know how church members have always been setting their heart upon something, some statement of doctrine or some expedient of organization, and then piling up all the most sacred interests of their religion behind that; as men in a besieged town bring their most delicate and precious possessions and heap them up in the one bomb-proof that they think most absolutely impregnable. Often they were not wholly sure that the doctrine on which they staked everything was absolutely true, or that the expedient to which they trusted was wholly righteous; but their pride and their fear united to make them treasure it and raise on it their brightest banner, and think that in it the Church's safety lay. And what are all the Reformations, with their fearful convulsions, but just the thunder of the voice of God shaking these false defences, which make His Church not strong, but weak; what are His commissions to His great Reformers, His Luthers and His Cromwells, but the same old message which He sent by His Jeremiah—the message which always sounds so cruel, and really comes out of the heart of His tenderest and most divine compassion—bidding them take down the battlements which are not His.

But I do not want to dwell upon the nations or the churches. I want to come more close to you. What I have been saying may serve for illustration; and now, turn to the way in which God treats our lives, the way in which, I think, some of you will recognize that He has treated you.

1. The blankest, plainest, and most common case of all is that in which a man tries to secure prosperity by fraud or some kind of unrighteousness. The forms of such attempts are numberless. The

essence of them all is one. If I could issue a summons and subpœna the experiences of you business men, I should not lack for testimony or for illustrations in the very lines of life where you are most familiar. There is no line of life wherein men seek success in which there are not men who believe that they can get success, and protect success when it is got, by fraud. The petty shopkeeper who misrepresents his goods, the great capitalist who misleads the market, the office-seeker who defrauds the polls, the doctor trying to impress men with pretensions which he knows are not true, the lawyer pretending to believe what he does not believe, the writer making men read what he writes by flavoring it with impurity, the leaders of society who degrade its purity that they may add to its attractiveness,— where should we end the catalogue! It bewilders us when we think of the amount of labor which has been expended, which is being expended every day, in building these false defences of men's wealth and comfort.

And then what comes? God does not want you to be poor; He does not want you to be wretched; and yet, in spite of countless exceptions and delays, how the conviction has grown rife among men that there is some power whose tendency it is to break down every battlement of fraud and iniquity, and leave exposed to ruin the prosperity which tried to shelter itself behind such feebleness. "A power not ourselves which makes" *against unrighteousness*— that is the impression which many men's experience, conspiring with their own misgivings as to what ought to be the world's construction and government, has given them of God. Has God shown Himself so at all to you? Have you seen any of your tricks for the support of your prosperity fall into ruin? Have you looked up, ready to curse God for His cruelty? And then perhaps have you seen something in the face of God which made you stop, which put a new question in your soul, which called up the deeper perception of a deeper love, and at last, as you thought and thought and thought about it, has let you see that God never was so kind to you as when He broke down the wrong and the sham behind which you had sheltered your budding hopes and compelled you to trust those hopes to Him, that He might first make them over into such hopes as should be worthy of a child of His, and then might ripen them into fulfilment in His own time and His own way? If you have known any such experience as that, you have been taken into one of the richest rooms of God's great schoolhouse, one of the rooms in which He makes His ripest and completest scholars. Oh, if our souls to-day could mount to the height of some such prayer as this: " Lord, if I am building around the prosperity of my life any battlements which are not Thine, any defences of deceit or injustice or selfishness, break down those battlements whatever pain it brings, however it may seem to leave my hopes exposed," —if we could go up into some mountain of aspiration and pray that prayer, how earnest and calmly ready for whatever God chose to do to us our souls would grow!

2. Again, see how God deals with men's efforts to secure for themselves peace and repose of mind, freedom from disturbance and anxiety. The way that a man first tries to secure that precious treasure is often by the studious culture of his self-complacency: "Let me be able to think well of myself, and then behind that wall of self-esteem my soul may sit down undisturbed." And so a man goes to work to cultivate his satisfaction with himself. He tells over to himself his own good qualities. He shuts his eyes to all his own defects. He keeps in the company of the men who are most sure to praise him. He shuns any rough, honest soul who will remind him of his faults. He does the things he can do best, and so keeps conscious of his powers. He avoids the tasks which it is hard for him to do, and which will expose his weakness. So he tends his self-complacency. He feeds it and pets it and makes it grow, and behind it he sits down in the peace of self-content. But then how often, when a man has just got his self-complacency built up, there comes some dreadful blow that breaks it down. Some terrible mortification comes. Some shameful exposure breaks out. Men find out as it seems by diabolic instinct where your weak spot is. Or, without any blow, any attack or open scandal, there just comes creeping in upon you misgivings about yourself, visions of your own meaner and smaller parts which you have tried to hide and to forget, and you find that your whole bulwark of self-complacency is riddled and honeycombed with doubts and suspicions about yourself; and your

well-sheltered peace shivers and shudders behind its useless barricade. It is a terrible condition unless it can be but preliminary to another, unless where the worthless barrier of self-complacency has fallen the true protection of humility can be built up, and the soul can come to that only true peace and repose which is attained by the absolute distrust of itself and the hiding of itself behind the great, wise, strong, loving guardianship of God. This was what Jesus did for Nicodemus. This is what He wants to do for all our souls, which He first exposes and fills with shame, and then shelters in all their conscious nakedness behind Himself.

3. Then take another of the precious things of human life which a man may try to keep safe behind false defences. The esteem of our fellow-men —no standard of life is true and healthy which does not count that a very precious thing indeed. Not the most precious,—on the contrary, a thing to be always held with a certain looseness, as a man in shipwreck holds the box in which his property is contained, ready to let it drop at any moment when it must be dropped to save his life. So a man ought to hold his fellow-men's esteem, ready to let it drop the moment that he cannot hold it and yet keep with it his own self-respect and his loyalty to God. But while it is not the most precious, it is a very precious thing. All true men desire it and value it. And now suppose that that esteem, your reputation among men, is guarded and kept safe behind some false conception which they have formed of you. They think some act which you have done was

brave when it was really cowardly, or unselfish when it was really full of selfishness, or the result of deliberate intelligence when it was really nothing but a happy blunder. It may be that you have falsely claimed these merits for yourself, or it may be that they have chosen to attribute them to you. In either case there sits your reputation behind its false defences, its battlements which are not truth's and are not God's. I think that very often a man is genuinely impatient with such a misconception of his merits. He even hates it. The reputation which is shielded behind it seems to be a mean and sickly thing. But very seldom has a man the strength of soul to put up his own hand and pull that misconception down. It is a hard thing for a man to speak out and say: "I am not what you think me. Here is what I am. Judge me truly, and hate or praise me as I genuinely deserve.'" In our nobler moods we may do that; but often God, kind to our feebleness, spares us the effort and does it for us. Very often He tears away our false repute and shows us as we are, lets men behold us at our worst. And many and many a man, I think, who would not have the strength himself to tell men that he was not all they thought him, is profoundly glad when God in some way sweeps the cloud aside and, reducing the exaggerated reputation to reality, gives him a chance to win men's truer, even though it be far more moderate, honor for what he really is.

4. I shall take only one illustration more, but it is perhaps the most urgent and impressive of them all. Every one of us has been tempted—and most of us

have yielded sometimes to the temptation—to guard the truths which we hold dear and sacred, and the faith which we have in the truths we hold, by battlements which, if we questioned ourselves, we knew were certainly not God's. I believe some truth of my religion; I believe it really; I know that it is true. But I know also that there is a great deal in the world which is in conspiracy against my truth. I know that I hold it against enemies. I know that my faith in it is constantly in danger; and, knowing that, it is only too natural that I should try to build around it every possible defence, and even tolerate and help to build defences which I know are not strong and sound. See what some of those false defences are. I may put forward arguments, not merely to other people, but to myself, which I know are fallacies and do not really support the faith I hold. I may defame the character and the religious life of men who do not hold my truth, trying to make out that disbelief in it makes a man wicked, and so hoping to strengthen my faith in it by all my dread of sin. I may put forward the authority of men who have believed what I believe, and who have been very good and noble men, but whose goodness and nobleness I know had no inherent and essential connection with their having believed this truth. Or I may try to intensify my sense of its preciousness by making it exclusive, talking of what ought to be the world's possession as if it were my own peculiar privilege, or by narrowing the truth to my form of it so as to think that no man holds it who does not hold it just like me. Or, finally, I may build up around my faith the sheer, dense wall of bigotry—that gross, coarse, thick, unreasonable mixture of pride and fear and obstinacy and hesitation, all mingled and kneaded together into a stubborn mass, through which men flatter themselves that no arrow of doubt can penetrate, but through which it is also absolutely certain that no light can come.

These are the false defences which men build about their faith, and when they are built they seem to their builders to be not merely part of the faith which they assume to protect, but often its most precious part. The very fact that it is of the man's own building, and not of God's, makes the cabinet in which he has enshrined his faith even dearer to a man's soul than God's jewel it enshrines. Sooner or later, to every man who builds such battlements about his faith the hour of their destruction comes, and it is very terrible. The false argument is triumphantly refuted. The slandered heretic does some noble act that refutes at one stroke all my slanders. The authorities on whom I have relied desert me. And, so far from accepting my faith in the narrow and sectarian way in which I hold it, the world makes it evident to me that my faith never can become *its* faith until it has broadened itself to meet needy humanity with the entire truth. And, finally, my bigotry displays its essential stupidity and hatefulness so that not even I, the bigot, can give it any longer reverence or love or trust. These are terrible blows to a man's faith, when its trusted defences fall. The faith, stripped and exposed, frightened and bewildered, halts and thinks that everything is gone. It sees the sceptic standing and shouting on the ruins of its battlements, with his sword drawn, all ready to leap over the wall and take its life.

And just then it is — then, in the moment of its apparent failure — that to many a frightened faith the revelation of its true strength has come. It is just then, when it seemed as if what he had believed was at the mercy of every unbelieving enemy, that many and many a believer has to his wonder learned that the only real strength of a belief lies in its absolute truth; that, in the long run, no weight of accumulated authority and no sacredness of organized institutions can keep a faith safe which is not true; and likewise that no faith which is true can ever perish for the mere lack of the weak battlements of human authority or institutional support. There is no confidence or real belief in that which he believes for any man till he learns that. Until he learns that, you will see him out upon the walls after every gale of unbelief, anxiously counting his authorities and setting up his pasteboard battlements which have been blown down. When he has learned that, he trusts his faith and lives in it. Driven back to the fundamental questions concerning it, enlarging it into its most majestic simplicity, finding the witness of its truth in God's Word and his own soul, finding every day new strength and new simplicity in his faith as it meets each new attack, there is no gratitude in all his grateful heart so deep, so earnest, as that with which he thanks the God who let him be bewildered and frightened by the destruction of the weak, unreal protections of his faith. "Now, at last," he says, "I know what it is really to believe."

Oh, there are many believers among us for whom God has done all that. As they look back over their lives, there are days whose memory still makes them shudder, days when it seemed to them as if all faith were gone and all the world of truth were but the very blackness of darkness of despair. And yet these very days are the days out of which came the light that now makes their life a perpetual song and joy. For then God showed them that for His child there can be no final witness of His truth except Himself and the immediate testimony of His Spirit, and that whatever hinders or restrains the giving of Himself to His child's soul, however sacred or necessary it may seem, it must be His wish and His child's best blessing to have swept away.

I turn back from these illustrations to the general truth which they all illustrate. I hope that they have made it clear. Failure, the breaking down of men's confidences, the going to pieces of men's plans,—failure means many things. One of the things which it means is this: that God will not let the soul hide behind any protection which He knows is insecure. His whole love binds Him to let the soul know its blunder before it is too late. The general goes through the field where his army lies full in the face of the enemy. He sees each soldier building his little section of the rampart which, all together, is to protect the army. What shall he do when he comes to one poor fellow who, instead of piling up stones, is twisting bits of straw together and making an ingenious, pretty fence that the wing of a flying bird might knock away? Is it cruelty when the wise general with his drawn sword cuts the flimsy fabric down, and leaves the silly soldier ashamed, perhaps angry, but convicted and exposed and ready for better work? So a young man lays out his plans; says, "I will be this, I will do this, I will think this"; devises how he will construct his fragment of the long wall that all true men are building, which is to stand between human nature and its enemies. He thinks his plans are perfect, and then they all fail. What does it mean? It may mean many things. It is blessed, indeed, if the young man can learn, there at the very outset of his life, that one of the things which it means is this: that his Father loves him so, and has such great things for him to be and do, that He wants him to trust His love completely—His love and nothing else,—so that He may be able to give Himself completely to His child. In such an early failure of his first bright hopes has been the light and salvation of many a man's life.

Sometimes it is an old man and not a young man to whom the failure comes. When, as the evening gathers in, a man for whom life has seemed but one long success looks up, and lo! much that has seemed success has changed its whole aspect and is evidently failure; when, not because he has had enough of them and is tired of them, but because he has come into the fuller light and sees them as they really are, the ambitions, and pleasures, and occupations in which he has spent his days look empty and dreary and worthless to him; when the old man stands and says of his long life, "What a long failure!"—is there no meaning of love and kindness in that revelation which has come to him, at the very last, from his patient and loving God? Blessed, indeed, it is for him if, at the very last, standing among the ruins of the battlements which it has been the business of his life to build, he can in utter despair of himself give himself penitently and absolutely up to God, and look forward to the joy of testifying by the long obedience of eternity his thankfulness for the mercy which, before his life here was wholly over, has scattered its delusions and shown him his weakness and his sin.

I hope that I have not seemed to preach to you as if God were a mere destroyer, jealously taking away out of our lives the things He did not like, tearing away the poor defences that we had patched up for our prosperity, our peace, our reputation, and our faith, but giving us nothing in their place. I have tried to say all along that all of God's destructions are only to make way for stronger building of His own. Let me tell you that as earnestly as I can before I close. For everything human and weak that God tears out of your life He has something strong and divine to put in it. He takes away the battlements of selfishness only that He may defend you with Himself. Everything which you have a right to do at all, and which you are doing now in self-reliance, it is possible for you to do in direct reliance upon Him; and our lives so belong to His life that it is only when the healthy activities of life are based upon and built around by trust in God that the noble capacity of those activities comes out and the whole life shines; and the old Jerusalem which sat upon her earthly hill becomes the New Jerusalem which is hung down from heaven by the golden chains of God's love.

If the work of Christ for a man's soul is to fill it with complete humility, and then, when it is utterly humbled and made distrustful of itself, to bid it stand up upon its feet and bravely begin the new life with trust in Him,—then is it not Christ, the Lord to whom we must be always coming back, of whom I really have been preaching to you to-day? Oh, that from all our souls He may tear away every falsehood, every shelter of sin, no matter what it costs us, no matter how it seems as if He tore our heart out with it. And then, where these used to be, oh, that He may set Himself, knitting His life into our life by the meeting of repentance and pardon, of grace and gratitude, making Himself our tower, hiding us safely forever and ever behind the battlements of His love!

VI.

CHRIST OUR LIFE.

"In the name of Jesus Christ of Nazareth, rise up and walk."—ACTS iii. 6.

EVERYWHERE power is seeking opportunity, and fulness is seeking need, throughout the universe of God. The teeming hills send their streams down into the thirsty plains. The winds rush in to fill the vacant fields of space. Knowledge is always trying to widen its field and fill with its abundance some new emptiness of ignorance. The search is mutual and, going on everywhere, it makes the unity of the vast world. The mighty globe is bound together by these cords of power running out in help, and need running out in appeal, all over its surface.

Add to this another truth,—that all the power and all the richness in the world are really one, are really God,—that, take what form they will, come through what channels they may, they all proceeds from one great central Love and Abundance, which is God,—and then the unity is more complete and more impressive. Then the study of the endless variety of the channels through which the power and supply of God flow into needy places becomes supremely interesting. The schoolmaster is teaching his scholar in the school. The philanthropist is freeing the slave out of his bondage. The father is feeding the children at his table. The artist is painting his picture on the wall. The farmer is turning the forest to a fruitful field. The merchant is making the world the master of its wealth. How various are the activities! How the earth quivers and sparkles with their abundance and their difference! But if we believe and if we say that they all come from God, that, in a sense, they all are God uttering and giving Himself in many ways, through many channels, is not the sight then far more wonderful and beautiful? It has gained loftiness and unity without losing distinctness and variety. And each one of the channels through which flow the power and abundance of God, no longer counting itself a spring of original supply, must find a profounder dignity and interest in itself and catch infinite visions of what may be accomplished and attained through it. The schoolmaster opens his books and says, "Here is God's truth." The emancipator says to the slave, "Go forth into God's freedom." The father invites his children to come and eat the bread of God. The artist feels thrilling through his soul and his brush some of God's beauty. The farmer and the merchant open the field or the ocean that the bounty of God may flow through them. Has not each found its nobleness? Is not each full of dignity? May not each think of itself as incapable of comparison with any other, because, whatever of God's power any other channel may bring, there is something of God which must come through this and this alone?

I am led to these thoughts as I consider the disciples of Jesus when, after their Lord had passed out of their sight, they found His power beginning to use them for its channels. Peter and John went up to the Temple and at the gate they found the lame man lying. He called to them for alms, and though they had no money which they could give him, something began to stir within them. How they must have wondered at themselves! A thought, a dream, a hope that possibly they might do something more than drop a penny in his outstretched hand,—a strange, unreasonable wish that they might actually lift him up and set him on his feet, and give strength to his poor, tottering ankle-bones and make him walk. How they must have wondered at themselves! Deep feelings were stirring in their souls—not merely pity for the man's misery, though that was there, but other feelings,—a sense of the sadness of weak limbs and defective life, a longing for the completeness of vitality, a perception of the mysterious unity of life, so that he who had most of it ought to be able to give it to those who had least,—all of these emotions the disciples must have found moving tumultuously in their hearts, and they must have been amazed. Was this some new-discovered quality and power in themselves, something which had been sleeping unsuspected in them ever since they were boys in Capernaum and Bethsaida? Why was it that they had never dreamed of any such capacity before?

And then they said to themselves: " This has come to us since we had to do with Jesus. It is since we were His disciples that this new power began to stir within us." And then they must have said: " It is the same which stirred in Him. Do you not remember how we used to see the same in His face which now is in ourselves ? He too was full of pity, and loved life, and counted the loss or the defect of life a woe, and tried to give of His own life to others." They remembered all this in Jesus; and then they came back to themselves and all was clear. All this was in them as they belonged to Him. It was in them because it was in Him. This desire and power to heal was His, not theirs. He was the spring and fountain out of which the divine water flowed. They were only the channels down which it poured to its result.

Everything must have become credible to them when they understood that. They could believe in the power when it was not theirs, but His. The channel could open itself freely when it felt the stream behind it. And so they looked into the lame man's face and said: " In the name of Jesus Christ of Nazareth, rise up and walk." And he obeyed.

The critical moment which came then to the disciples is always coming to whoever is called to exercise power in the world. He who is moved to do something is either a fountain and source of power, or else he is a channel of power through which comes the efficiency of God. Which is he ? Which are you ? According to the answer to that question comes the whole nature and degree of the man's efficiency. Very silently, often very unconsciously, the answer to that question is being given. Everywhere men, who are doing the same outward work, part with each other when the answer has been given one way for one and another for the other. He only enters on the highest life who decides fully for himself that he is but a channel of power, and thenceforth feels behind himself the movement of the infinite life, and does all things in the name of Christ.

I want to trace out with you what some of the consequences in life will be of such a fundamental conviction with regard to the source of power. But first I want you to feel how absolutely universal is the possibility of that conception. It applies to everything. Whatever a man does, no matter how secular he chooses to call his action, he may do it in the name of Christ. The divine power working behind him, using him for the channel of its utterance, *that* is what does everything. Not merely the acts which we call sacred, but everything is done by God, and the man only opens his life to God's efficiency. Not wickedness, indeed,—and there wickedness seems to appear as that which it has so often been described to be,—negation, death, the ceasing of activity. It is the ceasing of the activity of God, interrupted and interfered with by the will of man; but all good action, all healthy activity, however secular it seems to be, is really God, declaring Himself and uttering his power through the appropriate channel of the life of man. And the acting man who is aware of this, claims it and declares it as he does His action, " In the name of Christ."

1. I ask you to notice, in the first place, how such a conception as this establishes the nobleness of life. Our life feels everywhere the lack of nobleness. Very pathetic, almost the most pathetic thing we see, I think, is the effort which men make everywhere to compel life to look noble,—when in their hearts they feel deep suspicions that it is not noble, but ignoble all the while. They make artificial motives for it which are not its real ones. They make fellowships with other men who are living the same life as themselves, as if that would look dignified and precious in the multitude which was base and petty in the single worker. They declaim about the dignity of all labor. Or, if they have to give up in despair the effort to glorify their own vocation, they take some avocation, some outside work which seems to deal with nobler things, and try in that to find some nobler color for their lives. How many men, pressed by the bondage of necessity, driven each morning to their work, are thus pathetically, sometimes very beautifully, trying to find or feign for their lives a nobleness which all the time they feel is lacking.

And now, what is there which can really do for men what they are thus pathetically trying to do for themselves? What can take your life and ennoble it, O my friend? If really Christ could be felt behind it, and it could all be really an utterance of Him, would not the work be done? If you could genuinely know that it was His will which was finding fulfilment in what you did, whether your work were the writing of state papers or the building of bricks into the wall, so that as you shaped a new sentence or spread a new layer of mortar you could say, "In the name of Jesus Christ of Nazareth," would not the spell of sordidness be broken, the suspicion of pettiness be dissipated from your life? We are dominated and confused by two things—the accidents of our surroundings and the opinions of our brethren. Many a soul really doing brave and useful work struggles and writhes under the burden of these two oppressions. They are both gone, they disappear, they crush us down no longer, just so soon as our work becomes Christ's work and not we but He is really doing it, and we are doing it only in His name.

Be sure, O, my young friends, that you are doing something honest, human, useful—no matter how humble or useful it may be—and then this nobleness waits at your doors. Be doing something of which it is conceivable that a man can say, "In the name of Jesus Christ of Nazareth I do this thing." A man can say that who drives sheep or digs a ditch. A man cannot say that who sells liquor to make his fellow creatures brutes, or who forces his dollars out of the crowded tenement where men's and women's and children's souls are ruined. Be something, do something, of which you can say, "Christ does it! I do it in Christ's name," and then nobleness waits at your door. Any moment it may enter in, and sordidness and pettiness give way at its coming.

This which I am preaching is, I think, the full, real meaning of that phrase which fascinates us with its sound, but whose exact definition some of us perhaps have found it hard to give. "In the name of Jesus Christ of Nazareth rise up and walk." It is the idea of all power finding its source in Him. It involves all the various thoughts with regard to the disciple's relation to his Lord, which come to their combined consummation in the complete dedication of the disciple's life, making it altogether the servant and expression of the Master's will. Gratitude is in it, admiration is there, love which desires communion, the sense of oneness of intrinsic nature,—all these press the man-life on the Christ-life and make it aware that its true glory and effectiveness is in uttering Him. All this I take to be wrapped up in those rich words: "In the name of Christ."

2. And notice, in the second place, how in what these words express there lies the true secret of the unity of various lives. There are two notions of unity in men's minds. One of them is really the notion of uniformity. It has no place for diversity. It wants almost complete identity between the things which it compares. The other rejoices in diversity, and finds its unifying principle in the common motive or purpose out of which an infinite diversity of many actions may proceed. How vain the search for any unity but this! It is the unity of nature. The budding, bursting spring is full of it; a thousand trees all different from one another are all one in the oneness of the great life-power which throbs and pulsates in them all. And souls the most unlike, most widely separated from each other, are one

in Christ. Christ is their principle of unity. The thinker pondering deep problems, the workman struggling with the obstinacy of material, the worshipper lost in his adoration, the men of all centuries, the men of all lands,—they are all one, if all their lives are utterances of the same Christ. It seems to me to be beautiful, the way in which each new Christian strikes into this unity and becomes a part of it immediately. A man has been living by himself, seeming to find all his sources of activity in his own life. By and by the change comes and he is Christ's. The pulse of universal Christian life begins to beat through him. Now he is one with all men who, anywhere, are doing anything *by* Christ *for* Christ! How he lays hold of and comprehends the ages! All the past is his; he knows what men were doing in the days of Abraham and David. All the future is his; he knows what men will be doing in the millennium,—not the forms of their activity, but its heart and soul, its meaning and its spiritual experience. All this he knows the moment that he has begun to do his special work " in the name of Jesus Christ of Nazareth." He is set into the living system. The star is taken up by the chorus of the stars and joins their music. Still the man goes on at his little work,—adding up figures, selling goods, driving his little machine,—but he is one with the greatest; he is one with the least. O, that the children might learn that, and feel their lives from the beginning set into the unity of that utterance of Christ which is the complete activity of the world! How much conceit among those who thought themselves great, how much complaint among those who thought themselves little, such a conception of life would save!

3. It is time for me to touch another question which may have been suggested to you as I have spoken. "What effect," you will ask, "will this absorption into Christ have upon that development of personal distinctness, that character, that individuality which all men who are anything desire to possess? To do everything, to be everything, in Christ's name—will not that blur everything into indistinctness and keep your life, my life, from standing out vigorous and clear? Nay, in my own name let me live my life and do my work!"

But surely this implies a narrow and crude thought of individuality. What is the Individual? A being distinct not only in himself, but in all his peculiar relations to the Infinite and Total Being. It is in the relation to that mass of being upon which every individual being rests, and to which it belongs, that individuality asserts itself. Wycliffe, Howard, Napoleon, each of them is a distinct, distinguishable figure among men. But how? By the way in which he manifests our universal human nature, and by the effects which he produces on it. Take any one of them out of all connection with the universal human life, and while, no doubt, his distinctive personality would still be there, it would be a crippled, ineffective thing. It would find no opportunity either of exhibition or of education. Put Wycliffe, or Howard, or Napoleon into his true place, and he shines with his own radiance and does his own work because of his true own place in which he stands. You see to what this tends,—that the true and natural relations of a human life bring out and strengthen and do not destroy or hide its individuality. You put a solitary man into a family, or into a warm friendship, and how his personality comes out! How much more of a man, how much more of *this* man which God meant for him to be, he is!

Now, Christ is the most natural home of man. He is the human manifestation of Divinity. Where then as in Him shall man naturally implant himself and be at home? And because the implanting of man in Christ is natural, and not unnatural, therefore the individuality of him who is set in Christ is developed and not destroyed, and the Christian becomes more and not less himself the more truly and devotedly he is a Christian.

And the true Bible figure of the Church is also the home. It is the family of God. And so, while it keeps the great sense of comprehensive unity, it will never blur or stifle the freedom and variety and spontaneousness of individual life.

Indeed, all true conception of originality and individuality must include the truth of the necessary belonging of the individual in the great whole. No self is its whole self which is itself alone. Part of the selfhood of everything is its share in the complete being of which it is a part. Will you take the man and uproot him from all his belongings? Take him out of his fatherhood, his business, his scholarship, his citizenship, his church, and then tell me, have you got him in his true personality? Has not his personality disappeared with all those separations? The time may come when, loosing himself from all these associations, leaving them behind as outgrown things, the man's soul, pure and personal, shall soar away to some existence where they can have no place. But who can say into what new sceneries and societies of a celestial city, and a perfected human family, and a triumphant church that freed soul shall unite itself, claiming anew its personality in its associations? And, however that may be, it certainly will come to pass that there the soul will fix itself in God, and realize its individuality and know itself in Him.

If this be true, then men will become not less, but more themselves as they all feel behind their lives the Power of Jesus, and do all things in His name. It will be like the pouring of the sunlight on the earth, giving to everything a radiance which is the sun's and yet is the thing's own. It will be like the pouring of the brook down the dry channel, making each pebble shine with its true color. So acts burst into radiance when the great glory burns behind them. You are doing things with lower motives, and so with lower powers (for the motives of deeds are the powers of deeds); and this change comes, the great love of Christ takes possession of you, you love Him with the overwhelming gratitude which acknowledges His love. Your life presses itself in and occupies His life. His power fills you. "Not I live, but Christ," you cry, in Paul's great words. And then every act is yours with wonderful and new distinctness. You and Christ are the unit of this new, strange life. Strange life? Yes, but only strange as the absolutely natural is strange when it strikes into the midst of the unnatural which has possessed the world; only strange as the whole is strange when, surging up from the depths, it takes possession of and overwhelms and harmonizes the parts! In that strange life each act, each thought, each word, flashes with light, glows with color, quivers with power, distinctive and unique, as it is done, or thought, or spoken in the name of Jesus Christ.

What shall we say of our poor, colorless religion? What shall we think of our Church, which often seems to swamp and drown instead of bringing out lustrously the characters of those who live in it? What can we think except that it has not really filled itself with its Master's power? It does things which He could never do. It turns away from tasks which His soul longs for. It is not because they have given themselves to Him, but because they have given themselves to Him so partially, so feebly, that the members of His Church seem often to have lost instead of gaining personal distinctness and the full power of their own true life. You must go deeper into the stream which now only the tip of your foot is touching. You must be more of a Christian, not less. You must give yourself up heart and soul to Christ, that Christ may make you all yourself. Has not He Himself told the story? You must lose your life utterly in Him that you may find it.

Let me say only one thing more. The defect in a man's life is double. It is in the things he does not do, and it is in the things he does do. I have been thinking mostly about the things which a man does not do, and of how his activity would be stimulated if he felt behind all his life the Power of Christ. But consider the other side. Think how the soul which lived by Christ would become incapable of many an action which, if he thought of his life as having no deeper sources than himself, he might freely do. He thinks of himself as an utterance of Christ. What Christ is He will be—nothing else. What Christ does He will do—nothing else. "In the name of Jesus Christ of Nazareth" shall be the stamp which he will set on every action. Is not the range of his action limited at once? He can do nothing which will not hold that seal, nothing over which those words cannot be said. He raises his arm in passion to strike some defenceless creature a cruel and vindictive blow. "In the name of Jesus Christ of Nazareth," he says, and his arm falls powerless. He cannot strike. He sets out on some career of reputable deceit. He has his approved lie all ready on his lips, but before he utters it, he says, "In the name of Jesus Christ of Nazareth," and the lie is as impossible for him as for Christ Himself. Ah, how everywhere it is true that higher power means also more restraint! To be able to do one thing means always not to be able to do something else. Let any man here in society accept Christ's power as his moving principle, and what then? A hundred old familiar doors must close.

But one great door opens, and through that he goes in to another life.

Here, then, my friends, is the whole doctrine which I wished to preach. It is the great redemption from a blank, narrow, and lonely thought of life, if there is behind us a vast Power of life by which we live and in whose name all that we do is done. Moses stands by the rock, about to smite it and bid the water flow. All God's omnipotence is behind him. All the love and care, all the infinite nature of God is waiting to utter itself through this poor Hebrew who stands, rod in hand, before the mountain. What opportunity there is for him to glorify his life! How he may become like a very right arm of the Almighty! If he will only lift up his voice and cry, "In the name of God, let the water come for the thirsty people!" But listen, What is it that he says? "Hear now, ye rebels! must *I* bring you water out of this rock?" How the man shrinks and shrivels as we look at him and hear him speak! Just he, and nothing more! his little, narrow personality. Just Moses. Nay, *not* Moses! for the true Moses is Moses full of God, and this Moses who speaks has cast God away, and so he is not really his whole self. No wonder that that losing of his chance to be his best was the beginning of his death! We all begin to die when we let go the chance to live our fullest life.

May God help us to give ourselves to Christ, who, as St. Paul says, "is our life," so that He may flow freely forth through us. May we do all things "in His name." May we do nothing which we cannot do " in His name." So may some of His work get done through us, and we, in doing it, grow strong and pure and unselfish and like Him, becoming so our own true selves.

VII.

MY BROTHER'S KEEPER.

"Am I my brother's keeper?"—GENESIS iv. 9.

THE first chapters of the Book of Genesis still keep their hold on human life. Indeed, it sometimes seems as if the difficult and puzzling questions which have been raised concerning them had tightened that hold instead of loosening it. Many men at least have come to see that, whatever may be the fact with regard to the historical nature of the record which is written there, the narrative has a spiritual truth as a description of man's perpetual experience, which is most valuable and never can lose its power. Much in those chapters may perplex us, but yet its pictures never fade out of our sight nor lose their meaning for our consciences.

The new-made garden with its freshness of sparkling stream and waving tree and bounteous grass; the man, first alone and then with his life richened and deepened by the woman's presence at his side; the mystic catastrophe of the disobedient eating of the apple; the gateway with the angels and the flashing, flaming sword and the poor man and woman terrified and desolate outside; then the new poetry and pathos that came into the world with the first family life; the birth of the first children, the first boys the world had ever seen; and then, all of a sudden, bursting like a thunderbolt out of the sky, hatred and murder! How that picture has fastened itself in men's hearts! The dreadful, forsaken plain where one brother lies dead beside the smouldering altar, while the other brother wanders far away with the irrevocable deed burning at his soul, trying in such hopeless despair to make himself believe that he is not the wretch he knows himself to be, answering the voice of God which speaks to him from without and from within with this angry and helpless and passionate rejection of responsibility, "Am I my brother's keeper?"

I take this last picture out of the old Book of Genesis to-day. Very different indeed is this wild son of Adam, roaming desperate through the primeval earth, from the decent and reputable citizen of our modern world on whose lips to-day we can almost hear the same question which came forth from the mouth of Cain. But the words are the same. To-day the same disclaimer of responsibility shows how disordered is our world. Still men who ought to know and care how it is faring with their brother-men refuse to know, refuse to care. We may leave Cain in his far-away remoteness and, turning to our own present days, ask ourselves the meaning of man's indifference to his fellow-man, ask what the meaning is of that which so many men say in their hearts when they are bidden to hold themselves responsible for the lives of other men, "Am I my brother's keeper?"

And, first of all, I think, we ought to remember how difficult it always is for men to imagine themselves into a way of life of which they have had no experience or trial, and not to let that difficulty impose on us. It may be the very way of life for which they were made. The life which they are living may be most imperfect and unnatural, but when you say to one of them, "Come here! Be this!" he turns upon you in unfeigned surprise. The whole thing looks impossible. You say to the idler, "Come, be a scholar. Taste the fascination of great books"; and he replies, "I cannot. Other men were made to study, but not I." You say to the selfish man, "Come, here is need, relieve it"; and he looks you in the face as if you had asked him to climb to the stars. You say to the undevout man, "Come, be religious. Come, love and worship God"; and he replies, "You do not know me. You are taking me for another kind of man. It is as if you asked an eagle to swim for you or a fish to sing." All the time, in each man lies sleeping the power whose possession he denies, and in the use of which alone can he attain to his true life. Do we not come to feel how almost absolutely worthless are men's descriptions of their own impossibilities? Whatever is of the general substance of noble humanity, every man may be in his degree. For a man to stand up and say, "I cannot learn"; "I cannot be generous"; "I cannot be devout," proves only how little he knows himself.

Once, I think, I used to be imposed on by such statements. Once, when a man said any of these things about himself, it seemed as if it might be true, as if here might be a man in whom this one capacity of manhood had been left out; but so constantly the flowers have broken out of such unlikely soils, so often the darkest heavens have burst forth in unexpected stars, that it has come to seem as if no man's assertion of his own deficiency were trustworthy. "God knew things of him that he did not know of himself," we say when some new life opens upon a man who thought he had exhausted his capacity of living.

Let us be taught by such sights. Let us apply to ourselves the lesson that they teach. Let us beware of drawing hard and fast the line of our own limitations. Trust the impulsive leap of heart which tells you, when you read the life of Agassiz or of Livingstone, that you too might be a devotee of science or an enthusiastic missionary. Expect surprises out of the bosom of a life which God made, and which you whom He has set to live in it only half realize,—as a tenant who came but yesterday into a palace only half knows the mystery and richness of the great house where he has been sent to live.

Now all of this applies, I think, exactly to the subject of which I want to speak to you. Here comes the demand that every man should be the keeper of his brother-man. That means, that whatever may be the care which a man takes of his own life, however he watches it and tends it, he has not done his duty, he has not filled out his existence, unless he also has, just as far as he possesses the ability and chance, watched and protected and helped the lives of other people.

Now what shall we say of that demand? It seems to me that until we think carefully about it, we have no idea of what multitudes of people there are to whom such a demand, made definitely of *them*, must and does seem absolutely preposterous and absurd. They may feel that somebody ought to do it, that there are people for whom it is possible and altogether right that they should go burdened with the care for others, just as there are people to dig the ditches and to build the fences, but for them it is totally out of the question, as totally unreasonable as to ask them to take the shovel in their hands.

Meet one of our gilded youth upon the street, one of those boys who was born and has grown up in luxury, and has never had any self-control asked of him except that he should not complain of the monotony of luxury in which he lived. Stop him an instant and point him to a poor, wretched cripple toiling along under a heavy burden, with poverty in every line of his poor, haggard face. Ask your bright, glittering young friend what it means that that poor creature is so poor, and why he should not in some way help him? and there is something infinitely sad and touching in the transparent honesty with which he looks you in the face and tells you that it is no affair of his. Perhaps he does remember that somewhere there is a charity bureau to which the poor creature might be sent. Perhaps he vaguely fumbles in his brain to find some remnants of what he distantly remembers to have been taught in college about the political economy of pauperism; but that it is his business to undertake personally, with thought and care, the relief of that poor sufferer!—you might as well tell him that it is his place to go and find the sources of the Nile.

Stand at the door of a fashionable club-house and call for recruits, earnest and self-sacrificing, in the work of political reform, or the freeing of slaves, or the repressing of intemperance,—why! I can hear even now, as I stand here, the empty, noisy laughter that comes back in answer to your summons. Nay, lift up your voice in a much nobler place. Cry aloud in the halls of learning, talk to the student at his desk and tell him how hosts of his fellow-men want the crumbs from his table, want the inspiration of his teaching presence; and what a blank unconsciousness is in his eye as he turns back to his problem, wondering how any man could dream that he ought to even feel, in his sublime search for absolute truth, the base and elementary needs of this ignorant multitude, whose very crude craving after knowledge shows how little they really know of what learning is.

Do you recognize these people whom I thus describe? Are they not real? Are they not common? Are they not specimens of many others? And what does the existence of such people mean? Does it not mean that there are in the world very many intelligent people who do not in the least believe that they have any responsibility for other people? Somebody has, they think. There are the ministers. There are the managers of philanthropic institutions. There is the "benevolent public." But they have no such responsibility. They are nobody's keepers but their own.

Such a condition of things, such a wide-spread conception of life which robs the world of so much strength and helpfulness, is certainly most significant and demands our thoughtful study. And the first thought which it suggests is this: that men have been too apt to think of helpfulness to their brother-men as an accidental privilege or an exceptional duty of human life, and not as a true and essential part of humanity, without whose presence humanity is not complete. See what I mean. A beautiful voice is an exceptional privilege of a few extraordinary people among mankind. He who finds it in himself thinks of it, according as he is devout or undevout, as a gracious gift of God or as a happy accident. In either case it is a personal and special thing. It does not belong to this man because he is a man, in very virtue of his manhood. Other men are destitute of it, and cannot sing any more than the stone upon the hillside, and yet they are as truly men as he. But a man has two arms, and the feeling about them is immediately and intrinsically different. They are not the exception. They are the constant human rule. It is not a privilege to have them. The man who is without them, the man who has one arm or none,—he is the exception. He is, just in that degree, just to that extent, deficient in his humanity. He is not a total man; he is a fragment or a monster. The loss may have come nobly, by some great self-exposure which it was glorious for him to make; nevertheless, he has suffered a detraction from the completeness of his humanity, and is partly not a man.

Here, then, there are two kinds or classes of possessions, and you see the difference between them. One of them is a peculiar privilege. The other is a test and proof-mark of humanity. Not to have the beautiful voice is to lack a lovely ornament and decoration of the life; not to have two arms is to lack a portion of the life itself.

And now is it not true that a large part of the trouble, in this matter of men's helpfulness to their fellow-men, has come from the fact that helpfulness to brother-man has been put into the wrong class? It has seemed to be like the beautiful voice, a special, splendid privilege and gift; not like the two arms, a test and proof-mark of humanity. The man who had it has seemed to be something more, instead of the man who did not have it seeming something less than man. Often and often the man who never dreamed of anything for himself except a selfish life has gazed with honest admiration on the men who could not rest until their brethren's need had been relieved; but it has been as the snake might watch the eagle soaring in the sky, or as you and I might listen to the singing of an angel,—never stirred either to shame or emulation by it, because it all came by a power which we did not possess.

Suppose all that were altered. Suppose you and I really knew that in us, too, as a true part of our humanity, there was the angelic power of song; suppose the selfish man really believed that for him to be selfish was as true a loss of the completeness of his manhood as it would be for him to be lame or dumb; would not the whole aspect of the case be different? Would not the rule and the exception have changed places? *Now*, not the wonder and the praises and the garlands for the rare servant of his brethren, but the pity and the shame and the sense of loss for him who dared to live for himself alone, and leave his brethren unhelped. Now, not the mean and stingy question, "Why?" but the generous demand, "Why not?"

Sometimes, when we think how some one change would regenerate the world, we grow buoyant with hope, for it seems as if that one change might come to-day. But then, when we think how vast that one change is our hearts almost despair, for it seems hopeless. But this change is not hopeless. That men should come some day actually and practically to believe and feel that a man who takes none of the responsibility of other men's lives upon himself is a fragment of a man—that is not hopeless. There are some men, and not a few, who believe and feel that to-day, and who are trying to complete themselves, —not to win an extra-human ornament and grace, but to complete their human selves in sympathy and brother-help. I think that very often, in the most selfish man, there must sometimes come, with the recognition of his uselessness, a blind thrill of dimly realized imperfection, as sometimes the man born without arms must feel the arms to which he has a human right trembling and craving life in his poor, maimed shoulders. And I believe that the constant impossibility of thinking of God without thinking also of the necessity of care for man as a true part of His nature, does keep alive in some degree the sense, and does prepare for the time when the sense shall become universal, that man without the acceptance of responsibility for his brethren is only a fragment of a man.

How we always come back to the same truth! Man must think better of himself, not worse,—must see the essential glory of his human nature to be more and not less rich and splendid than he sees it now, before he can be his best.

It seems to me that one of the great indications of the fact that helpfulness of man to man is a true part of our human nature, and not a mere addition to it, appears in our constant experience of the impossibility of avoiding some sort of influence upon our brethren. "Am I my brother's keeper?" you say, when some one points out to you that another man beside you is going to his ruin, and begs you to save him,—"Am I my brother's keeper?" you reply and turn away in scorn. There might be some small show of reason in it if you *could* turn away entirely, if it were possible for you to shut a wall around your life so that it could have no possible influence on his. But when you try it, you find how impossible that is. Little by little you learn that you *must* have something to do with your brother, with your brethren.

The sense of that, when it has once taken possession of a man, makes life so solemn! There is nothing that you can do which does not make it either harder or easier for other men to live, and to live well. The little circle which your eye can trace is such a small part of your influence! Deeds which you seem to have nothing to do with are really the results of the things you have done and been.

Here is a poor suicide, who, in a frantic moment in some wretched room to-day, does that most cowardly and miserable sin, and with the pistol or the poison flees from the post where God had put him. You never saw the man. He never heard of you. Have you anything to do with his miserable dying? If you have cheapened life; if you by sordidness and frivolity have made it seem a poor instead of a noble thing to live; if you have consistently given to life the look of a luxury to be kept as long as it is pleasant, and to be flung away the minute it becomes a burden, instead of a duty to be done at any cost, with any pains, till it is finished; if this has been the meaning of your life in the community and in the world, then you most certainly have something to do with that poor wretch's death. You helped to kill that suicide.

Here is this poor soul in its trouble feeling about for God, unable to find Him, almost driven to despair for lack of faith. Have you anything to do with that? How can you have? You never tempted or disturbed his faith. You never talked scepticism to him. You never told him what a childish superstition you thought it to believe in God. But what then? If you have lessened and lowered the world's faith by your base worldliness or wanton refusal to acknowledge spiritual forces in your own life, then you have poisoned the air which this poor soul has breathed, and it is dying of your poison.

Here is a social tragedy,—one of those awful crashes which come to a household when purity, which is the soul of household strength, is gone, and the poor wretched body it has left goes all to pieces at the first temptation. *You* never played the tempter there. You never struck the pillars of that house with the fire of your lustful passion. No, but you have made the atmosphere in the midst of which that house must stand a little heavier with corruption through the sort of life that you have lived. You have made it by your life a little easier for a man to wrong a woman, or for a woman to disgrace her womanhood. These are the terrible necessities by which we are all beset and surrounded. I say, "I will do neither good nor evil to my brethren. I will just live my own life." And the eternal compulsions of the universe laugh me to scorn. As well might one ray of the sunlight turn its radiance black, and think to darken nothing but itself. As well might one wave in the flowing river think that it could turn itself backward up the stream and make no confusion. It cannot be. You must do good or evil in this world. To say that you will do no good is to declare yourself the enemy of the human race.

It is also ours to accept the gracious side of the same truth. If no man can be wicked and not do harm, so no man can be brave, strong, truthful, and generous, without doing good. That we ought never to forget. We need it constantly for encouragement and strength. I said that if you cheapened life on you rested something of the responsibility of the suicide whom you never saw; and if you brought down the standard of social life, you had something to do with the mischief that comes in a household of which you have never heard. Is it not also true that, if you do anything to lift life and make it more precious, you are in some true sense the " keeper " of any poor tempted soul who is saved from his sin by virtue of the sense of the preciousness of life which gathers round him, and sustains or shames him in his need? Here is a man all in despair. He is ready for anything. Murder, suicide — nothing seems to be too desperate for his recklessness. If he had lived three centuries ago he would have taken to the highway and robbed or killed, regardless of other men's lives or of his own. Be as cynical as you will about the condition of your own time and land, you must own that there is a vast, solid influence at work to keep a man back from such desperation now. That influence is made up of the aggregate goodness of all good men. Apart from and beyond the special persuasions of personal friends, remonstrating by word and example against his sins, there is for every wicked man a great protest of all the goodness in the world, pleading, rebuking, urging, tempting him to righteousness. To that great protest every good deed of every most insignificant good man or woman makes its contribution. The boy or girl at school, the housekeeper about her quiet tasks, the laborer in his enforced obscurity, the clerk at his desk of routine, the sewing-girl, the errand-boy,—not one of them can do his duty faithfully and not make duty easier for all men everywhere; for the President in the White House and the philosopher in the midst of his great books. Not one of them but is his brother's keeper.

Perhaps that is all true, you say, but what becomes of the elements of intention and self-consciousness? Does not this last doctrine bring the whole matter back into the region of selfishness again? I try to be good and pure for my own sake, because so I best complete my own life and gain its best results and am most happy—because so my own soul is saved; and then, incidentally, without my meaning it, some other men are helped in their temptations by my struggle. I am glad to know that my life, so far as it has been good, has had any such power, but, since I did not mean it, have I not been wholly selfish? Have I been my brother's keeper in any sense save that in which the unconscious air has fed him and the song of the unthinking bird perhaps has lightened his despondency and made him glad?

It is a natural question. But what if there should come to us out of our experience another knowledge,—what if we should find that our lives are so closely bound up with our brethren's that we cannot thoroughly do our duty by ourselves unless we have them and their service in our minds? What if we learn that our personal problems get their clearest light and our personal struggles their most persistent strength when we are caring that the world should come to righteousness? What if then we should do our duties distinctly as a contribution to the influence which is to save the world? Is that impossible? I do not necessarily need to see exactly where my influence for good will tell.

Some poor wretch appeals to my sympathies, and I am a brute if I will not reach down and pluck him out of any mire into which he has fallen. But surely the great wicked, needy world is not less pathetic than the single needy soul. Even more heroically unselfish than he who offers his example to a single tempted soul is the man to whom the whole world is always calling "Be pure!" "Be true!" "Be brave!" and who is pure and true and brave for the world's sake as well as for his own. Back and forth between the world and himself flow the great tides of influence. He keeps the world and the world keeps him. He and the world make one complete system of advancing holiness. It is the experience of Jesus—" For their sakes I sanctify myself," and "The glory which Thou hast given me I have given them."

There is no subject with regard to which we feel so strongly as with regard to this—that if all men would do what a few men are doing the world would almost come at once to its salvation. It is a melancholy thing to see how limited is the working of the impulses which, if they could be made universal, would fill the world with light and power.

Look at this matter of care for fellow-man. In the community it appears as public spirit. How few men after all are public-spirited! How many men, with the best principles in the world, are just as hopeless as so many stones or trees for any great public interest! A public charity is to be established or to be put upon a strong foundation; a great improvement to the beauty of the city is demanded; a gross wrong or injustice needs to be rebuked; an old, stagnant condition of things must be disturbed and broken up;—how any of us can tell the men who are to do it! How, the moment other men's names are mentioned, we instantly turn aside, or shake our heads and say, "Oh, no! There is no use in applying to them." Why not? Are they immoral? No, indeed! Are they opposed to the public good? Are they monsters who want the evils of bad government perpetuated, and who hate progress and improvement? No, indeed! None of these things! Simply they think it is no work of theirs. They keep their own souls clean, and all besides seems to be something superfluous and extra, something which it would be a gratuitous piece of enterprise for them to undertake. What a strange delight there is (showing how exceptional that is which ought to be so familiar) when any new young man among our citizens does some notable act which shows that thenceforth he is ready to be counted among those who hold themselves responsible for the way in which things are going in their town. How few there are, when one more counts so mightily and wins such enthusiastic welcome!

The same thing is true in the Church. "The pillars of the Church," we say, as if the Church were a great mass of inert atoms held up in place by a few sturdy columns on which the whole weight rested. The ideal Church is simply winged humanity—humanity with the pinions of faith all spread and moving on with one great total impulse to the realization of the divine life for man. One's whole soul glows while he thus thinks of it; and then he turns back and sees—what? A handful of men and women who give nine tenths of the Church's contributions; a handful of men and women of intellect and piety who are willing to teach the Church's children and sit in the houses of the Church's poor; a handful of men and women who do the Church's thinking, and really grapple with the problems in which every true man who thinks honestly and seriously makes the puzzled life of other men more clear; and then a great host of men and women who never get beyond the thought that the Christian Church is made to save their souls, and that they have joined the Christian Church purely for their souls' salvation.

Your soul! What is your soul? What is it worth? Is it worth all this, all that the Bible tells us of, all that Christ has been and is? Ah, yes, no doubt it is. That soul of yours is precious beyond anything that you can guess. All that Christ did, all that Christ is, nothing less than that is necessary for your soul's salvation. But, all the more because it is so precious, what a shame it is that it is not pouring its power and value into the Church's life and finding its own salvation in saving the souls of other men!

The same is true everywhere. I go into any school or college in the land, and I know perfectly well what I shall find,—a great many good consciences, a great many boys of high standards, and of pure lives, and an almost total absence on these students' parts of any notion that they have any duty as regards the low tone, the falsehood and impurity, the frivolous or degraded dissipation which surrounds them. To keep their own souls pure, and let the college and their fellow-students go their way,—that is the most they dream of. That is where the student's faith goes, and often his integrity goes with it. They are not used, and so they grow corrupt. They are selfish, and so they are weak. Oh, if the men who mean right for themselves would only energetically mean right for the world, should we not almost see to-day the coming of the Son of Man!

Let me go back and close where I began. It is once more the earliest world, outside the gates of Eden. Abel lies dead upon the ground, and Cain is fleeing red-handed from the murder. But there is a third presence there. God is there. It is His voice that asks, "Where is Abel thy brother?" And what a right He has to ask! It is the Father asking for His murdered child!

Is not this the great final truth about it all—that within the Fatherhood of God we are to know—there only can we fully know—our brotherhood to one another? We neglect our brethren because we are so far from our God. Within His love, surrounding us like the elemental life in which alone our souls can live, may we all learn to love our neighbors as ourselves, and to forget ourselves in serving them!

VIII.

REST.

"Come unto me, all ye that labour and are heavy laden, and I will give you rest."—MATTHEW xi. 28.

I CANNOT begin to preach to you from these rich and familiar words without stopping a moment to remind you and myself what a sermon from this text ought to be. The words do not suggest or tempt any merely curious observations upon the ordinary course of human life. Nor do they seem even to allow the general discussion of abstract themes, the elucidation of great topics of impersonal theology—if there be such a thing. Let other verses from the Bible lead the preacher and the hearer in those directions—no doubt there are times when it is good that we should follow them. But this, which is beyond question one of the best-known and best-loved of all the words of Christ, has quite a different suggestion. He who would preach from it must at least try to make sound in his people's ears the sacred, solemn invitation which the words contain. There is a sermon possible (would God that I could preach it!) which should cause everything else to be forgotten, and set the Saviour in the abundance of His power, in the completeness of His love, before the faces of men weary and troubled and distressed, finding it hard to live, often overcome by what seems the impossibility of living truly and bravely; and make them hear Him say to them, "Come unto me!"—a sermon which should feel the infinite sympathy of the words and of the soul from which they came, — a sermon which should reveal to somebody that there is a heart which pities him and which can satisfy him,—a sermon which should leave the hearer, when it closed, in full communion with the soul of Christ, and with the new divine life joyously begun. Who would not give anything to preach that sermon!

Jerusalem was only a picture of the universal life of man. What goes on everywhere and always, was going on there. The streets were full of anxious faces. The houses were restless with uneasy hearts. Men were making plans and seeing them come to disappointment, and making them over again only to be still disappointed, till the heart was weary through and through, and only hoped on with the dead and brutish force of habit. Men were finding that the dearest affections, the most sacred relationships, carried misgivings and the power of untold misery at their hearts. Men were racing each other down for wealth, suspecting each other's character and motives, wondering whether the whole blind struggle were at all worth while. How familiar it all sounds! It is just what is going on to-day. And then, with perfect calmness, coming so quietly that He was there in the midst of them before they saw Him, came One who declared: "I can give you the escape from all this. I know it all, but I tell you that it need not be. Come unto me, all of you that labor and are heavy laden, and I will give you rest."

Much is it when a child comes into a household or a world of weary and distracted men, and with his fresh and unsuspicious happiness rebukes it all, and, opening some simple and elemental vision of life, bears his bright testimony that this weariness and distraction need not be. It is easy to smile in our superiority and say: "He does not know. His disbelief in our misery comes from his childish ignorance." Even while we say that, we still feel the power of his protest, and come to him with some sense that we have escaped. But this is no child who speaks in Jerusalem. This is evidently a man who has not merely flitted above, but has pierced down below, the misery of human life. He will have these men, these brother-men of His, escape not merely by forgetting, but by understanding their weariness. As He looks them in the face, and the power of His being tells on theirs, we can see certain great changes taking place within them. Behold! things which used to matter very much to them begin to show their insignificance. And there are other things which they thought that they were missing altogether of which they suddenly or slowly come to see that they are getting the essence, though they are failing of the form. And there are other things, of which they become aware that they would find more joy in having their brethren possess them than in possessing them themselves; that in some deep, subtle, and true sense they themselves had what those whom they loved possessed. These, among other knowledges, passed over as it were from Jesus into them, almost as light passes over from the sun into the diamond and becomes its light, when they felt the invitation of His presence and came unto Him. So His Rest of Soul became their rest and His promise was fulfilled even before He uttered it, as are all God's promises.

Words deepen their meaning, throb back their force to us out of a profounder and profounder heart, as we grasp them with a more and more intense experience. No doubt to "come to Christ" came to mean more and more to these men of Jerusalem, and therefore the harmony of the effect with the cause, the sufficiency of the cause for its effect, in the promise of Jesus must have become more and more apparent. First, physical approach, the finding themselves where they could touch His hands and look into His face; and then obedience, the doing of what He wanted them to do and what would give Him pleasure; and then communion, the confidential interchange of thought, so that their thinking enlarged and refined itself with His; and so, at last, likeness, the showing of His character, the coming themselves to be what Jesus was. Nearness, obedience, communion, likeness,—these were the stages of approach, these were the opening chambers, room beyond room, by which men "came to Jesus." Only when all the rooms had been entered and occupied was the coming to Him complete, but at each stage it was just so much nearer to its completion. The invitation, as each man accepted it, throbbed with a deeper meaning. At the same moment, in every mingled group which fronted Him, there were souls which each depth of the invitation reached. It was the completeness of them all together that made the fulness of the power which drew the multitude after Him as He went up and down the land.

This, then, is the old story out of which the words first came to us. Peace fell from the presence of Jesus upon the wearied and overburdened hearts of men who came to Him, who saw Him and obeyed Him, and confided in Him, and grew to be like Him. And now we want to remind ourselves of how it is that we come to have a right to transfer all that across the centuries and hear the same voice speaking in our ears. Remember we mean that in the most literal sense. I wish that I could state how literally I mean it. The summons of Christ to anxious humanity is not a memory of something which happened years ago; it is something which is actually happening now, to-day. That involves and rests upon the facts that man is the same being that he was in the Gospel days and that Christ still lives.

What then shall we say is the relation between that invitation to which eager souls listened in the streets of Jerusalem and the perpetual invitation which is always coming from the heart of Jesus to the soul of man? Shall we not say that it is the same relation which always exists between a special event of the Incarnate Life and the continuous influence of Jesus,—indeed, the same which exists between the whole Life of the Incarnation and the perpetual presence of the Life of God under the life of man? It was a particular manifestation of that which is universally true; and therefore the universal truth may be studied in and by that particular manifestation of it, while yet it does not lose itself and cease to be. It is the great fire which burns at the heart of all the earth breaking out at one volcano point. It is the sea on which the whole world floats, bursting through once in a fountain which strikes the stars. Let us not be the slaves of our senses, we who ought to be their masters and take the messages which they bring us into the keeping and interpretation of our souls. The words which the bodily lips of Jesus spoke, one day in Syria, do their full duty only when they quicken and interpret the utterance which His actually living, unseen heart is always making to our lives and souls to-day.

With this in our mind, we see how absolutely reasonable, how perfectly true, is the conviction which has possessed millions of men and women, which is possessing countless numbers of men and women to-day, that they too may come to Jesus, to a present and living Jesus, just as literally and truly and blessedly as any man or woman came to Him in the old Syrian town. The whole sky opens, and what was then is everywhere and always,—Jesus is here! We say it to each other here and now precisely as men said it to each other there and then— Jesus is here! And men in sorrow look at a present Christ and are comforted. Glad men look up and are perfectly sure that He rejoices in their gladness. Perplexed men get light from Him upon their problems. Wicked men get first rebuke, and then forgiveness, and then the power of a new life from a Christ as truly visible to their souls as the Christ of Jerusalem was visible to the eyes of the men of Jerusalem. I would that I could put in clearer, stronger words how literally and absolutely this is true. Do not be slaves of your senses,—Christ is Here! Men are coming to Him every day. He says to *you*, " Come unto me."

If we become sure of that, then all the text is ours, and He who speaks it is speaking it to us. Let us read it again and try to hear it so, with ears which know that it was meant for them, — " Come unto me, all ye that labour and are heavy laden, and I will give you rest."

The first element of power in these words is their intense and intelligent sympathy with life. He who speaks them knows what it is for men to live. Tell me, could He have known it better if He had gone down the business streets of our city, if He had sat in our anxious counting-rooms and offices, if He had stood in the tempest of noise which fills the chambers of the roaring mill, if He had gone into the squalor of the tenement house, or climbed to the garret or pierced to the cellar of the pauper? He had been in them all. He is in them all, and knows them all to-day. And the truth of His knowledge is testified by this—that it is to weariness and the sense of heavy burden that He appeals.

Ah, my friends, if there were ever days when those words of Jesus ought to be heard, and to bear witness for themselves that He who speaks them is divine, they certainly are these days in which we live. They speak to the tumult of living. And was there ever a time when the tumult of living was so intense and universal as it is to-day? It matters not what region of life you choose for your own; you live in the city or the country; you are in the heart of poverty or in the heart of wealth; you are in one business or another,—it makes no difference. Everywhere there is tumult. The street is full of furious emulation. The study is full of tireless discussion. The capitol is wild with political debate. The household is torn with social ambition and unrest. Was there ever a time when He who lifts up His voice and speaks to those who are wearied and heavy laden could so claim the hearts and consciousnesses of those who heard His voice?

We all know what it is to " take life hard." The really practical problem is: How can the vitality of the world be maintained, and the fearful wear and tear of the world be mitigated? The world rejoices in its exuberant vitality. It does not want to secure calmness and peace by death; but it is conscious of perpetual exhaustion which it believes is not a necessary part of its vital action, but a false and terrible attachment to it. The world dreams of a complete life which shall at the same time be free from friction and full of rest.

Here is a poor ship struggling through the sea. She is conquering the waves, but she is conquering them with terrible struggle. Every twist of the great water has her in its power. She creaks and groans in every strained and tortured plank. She is weary and heavy laden. And then there comes grandly and calmly sailing past this bruised and beaten vessel the great, sufficient steamer, fully competent for her task, conquering the sea instead of being conquered, going faster and not slower than her groaning sister, by and by leaving her out of sight and coming into the port which they both are seeking whole weeks before her wrenched and battered sister ship creeps in and lays herself beside the wharf. So man's dream of how he ought to live towers and shines beside and sails away past his consciousness of the way in which He is living. Whoever will speak to him and be heard must speak with the power of that dream, and tell him in some way how, without losing the energy of life, he shall still escape the weariness of life. That is the promise which he hears from the lips of Christ.

To this man Christ says, "Come to me." It is the offer, the claim of a personal presence, and the acceptance must be in the spirit of that offer. Where shall we find the illustration of that method? Let us look for it in the simplest of all places: A child is wounded in body or in mind, hurt by some of the rough things which strike our human life almost as soon as it is started on the earthly journey. He is standing with his bleeding breast, or bleeding soul, helpless and confused; and then his mother calls to him and says, "Come to me, my child"; and the poor little creature runs into her open arms and throws himself upon her pitying bosom. Does he find comfort there? Indeed he does. And how? By and by she staunches his blood and heals his wounds; or, by and by, she reasons with his exasperated spirit and sets it right; but first of all it is more personal and elemental than that. She gives herself to him. It is to *her* that he comes. A doctor might dress his wounds. A teacher might correct his blunders. Only a mother could take his heart to her heart, and, pouring nature into nature, give him strength. Why is it that you go to the friend whom you trust and love, when you are in trouble, for something which the wisest doctor or the shrewdest lawyer cannot give you? It is that not merely *his*, but *he* may take possession of you and be your healing. You sit beside him and he says no word; but the peace of his presence and the healthy soundness of his heart and the richness of his love envelop you. All that he afterwards gives you of distinct rebuke, or counsel, or suggestion, gets its character and value from this first bestowal of himself, from this possession of your nature by his nature. Alas for any man who does not have some great sacred room of a brother's life into which he many go for rest and blessing!

Now, any idea of the relation of a man to Christ is fundamentally imperfect and untrue to the New Testament, which has not, behind everything special and particular, a large and general conception of what it is to come to Him, which corresponds to that which I have thus described. We sometimes ask ourselves how Jesus would have received such or such a man whom we know, if, in the same condition and state of mind in which we know him, he had come to Jesus in Jerusalem. The real question is not that. It is how Jesus does receive that man when that man comes to Him to-day. I know the man and I know Jesus now. I see the man come into the spiritual presence of Jesus just as literally as my friend comes into my physical presence when he crosses the threshold of my room. And then, this great thing happens. All that is in Jesus, all that Jesus is, welcomes him and takes him in. Jesus beholding him loves him. That is not merely an emotion in the Saviour's heart; it is an enfoldment of the Saviour's whole being around the man, as the mother enfolds herself about the child, as the friend enfolds himself about the friend. That is the welcome of Christ. To believe that that may happen is to believe in Christianity. To experience that is to be a Christian.

Within this great conception all that the welcome and embrace of Christ may do for a man is enfolded and contained. They are the elements and constituents and methods of this rest of the soul whose essence consists in the surrounding and possession of the soul by Christ. When the great conception is thoroughly fixed and present with us, then we may look for those elements and give them their names and values. I have already enumerated in passing what they are. Let me remind you of them, and ask you to consider if you may not claim them in yourself. They are principally these four:

1. He who is the friend of Christ sees some things to be insignificant which he once thought to be most important. What a power of restfulness is there i

Some men seek it ignominiously. They say of the great and sacred things, of the things without which a man cannot be a real man: " I will not value this, because, if I value it, I shall seek it, and if I seek it I shall be in perpetual unrest." That is base. But to see, as you keep company with Christ, that He perfectly does without that which you have lived as if you could not live without,—wealth or fame or luxury,—and so to see that you can live without it and be as much, nay, be much more, a man—is there not a great rest which comes to the soul with that? There is hardly any restfulness so great as that which comes with the liberation from a false and unnatural and unnecessary desire.

2. And then, he who comes to Christ enters into Christ's eternity and so into Christ's patience. There are other things which the soul desires not less, but vastly more, when it is given up to Him. Before, it wished for them languidly and with no stir of effort; now, that those things should come to pass becomes the one passionate desire of its life. Only now, with the deeper knowledge of how great they are, the man not merely endures, but demands the necessity that they should come gradually, and is satisfied that their perfect attainment should be very far away. Christ gives him time enough. He does not relax his work for them; he works all the harder. But he works calmly. The hurry fades out of his face. The rest of Time-Enough has come to him from Christ.

3. And then, again, Christ spiritualizes and so enlarges my notion of the thing which I am seeking,

and sometimes lets me see that I may freely have, perhaps that I have already, the soul of a desired attainment, and so sets me free from the feverish pursuit of a particular form of it which very possibly I never could attain. Here am I, saying, "I must and will have happiness,"—meaning by happiness some special form of happy circumstances; and Christ, as I stand close to Him, says quietly: "Poor child, do you not see that you are happy now, or may be any moment that it is purely happiness you seek?" And in an instant all is changed for me, and I am happy; and the fever cools and dies. Is there no rest in such a revelation?

4. And then, once more, if I am really one with Christ, the whole humanity which is in Him rises around me and blends my personal life with it, so that what happens to it, in any of its least or farthest members, truly and genuinely happens to me. All that humanity has, in some true sense, is mine. I pity you if you have never caught some glimpse of what that means. I need not know everything, for my race knows. I can be unhappy, if man is happy. Nay, not that, but, I am happy if man is happy. Let all that man has be mine, and lo! I possess much which I feverishly sought; and the search ceases, and there is a great calm. The peace of Him, who because He is the Son of Man carries the whole world in His heart, is mine.

We count these elements in the rest which Jesus promises, and as we count them we are continually coming back to that which I have said at length already,—that they are only elements within the great personal bestowal of Himself which is the true and final rest which Christ bestows.

But there is more than this, which I must lead you to before I close. To the great multitude who hear the words of invitation, and to whom they become very precious, there always sounds through them one word which is not written there, which I have not spoken yet, but which really sums up and expresses all their value. That word is "forgiveness." The great burden and weariness of life, when any man has once become conscious of it, is sin. "I could bear anything if I had not done wrong," the true man says. And then begins the turmoil of self-reproach and self-contempt, and longing for lost innocence, and fear of consequences, which beats and drives the poor, bewildered soul about as the sea beats about the wrecked ship, abandoned to its power. This is the great woe of the human soul, so great that all others while it lasts seem insignificant. It is almost a mockery to talk of everything else which Christ can do for man, until we tell first what He can do for man's sin. If He cannot save the ship from wreck, it is a mockery to say that He can keep the cabins from disorder and hold the masts in place.

Therefore it is not strange that they who hear Christ's promise most of all rejoice in it because it offers them forgiveness of their sin. "He has fulfilled His word, He has given me rest," sings the released and happy soul. And what most glows in his heart, and trembles on his lips in the glad utterance, is this: "He has pardoned my sins. He has freed me from their guilt and power." Can anything satisfy you short of this? Can anything be anything to you if you have not this above, beyond, around all other gifts? Cry for forgiveness first of all,—" O God, be merciful to me a sinner."

And yet, in all the intensity of the desire for forgiveness, we must not let forgiveness come to seem too special, separate, and narrow. Forgiveness is the total giving of the Divine to the human. There is no part of that complete bestowal which is not included in it. The great salvation is not divisible sharply into periods. There is no moment when the pardoned soul stands pure and colorless, with every penalty removed, with all God's anger disappeared, but with no holiness enveloping and filling it,— naked, with all its rags torn off, but with none of the new glorious raiment yet folded on its limbs. That would be a strange, awful moment in a spiritual history. Justified but not sanctified, as the old theologies would have said. No, it is by the pressure of His gifts of grace that God drives out the usurpations of the devil. It is by claiming the soul for His own that He sets it free from every false dominion.

And so the rest which the forgiven sinner knows is one and the same with the rest which the reclaimed nature finds in its replacement in the obedience of God. The saving of the wrecked ship is one and the same act with the commission which sends it forth on its appointed voyage. Sometimes the craving for forgiveness, intense as it is, has sounded almost soft and sentimental. It has seemed to be negative. The rest which it craved has seemed to be only a release from old bondage and a luxurious repose upon the assurance that "there remaineth now no condemnation." Does not its salvation from such weakness lie in its vigorous identification with the soul's possession by the will of God? The full freedom of the slave has not come with the mere breaking off his fetters; it comes only when he has become part and parcel of the nation which has set him free. The drop of water rests in the stream only when the stream's life fills it and it moves with the great current of the stream towards the ocean.

Wrestle, O sinner, with your sin! Pray for forgiveness. Fix your eyes on the heights of sinlessness and see their beauty. Hear in your deepest soul the voice of Him who has the power to forgive calling you to come and be forgiven. But always in the depths of that sweet summons hear the call to all obedience, and to the attainment by obedience of the entire life of God. O sinner in your sin, O mourner in your sorrow, there is rest for you! The everlasting promise is for you. It is your Christ who says, "Come unto me!" You are the weary and heavy-laden one to whom He speaks. But it is all of Him that calls to all of you, and only when all of you—your obedience and grateful service resulting in gradual likeness to Him you serve—has come to all of Him,—His authority and great designs and ardent inspirations,—only when all of you has come to all of Him can He complete the fulfilment of His promise, and give you perfect rest.

This is the rest which remaineth for His people! This is the rest into which the brave young hearts and the brave old hearts who have gone forth out of our sight into His eternal world have entered. It is a rest full of vigor and activity, a rest which is the same that Christ's own soul enjoyed. It is His Peace. Behold! He offers it to every one of you. Behold! He stands before you, your Friend, your Lord, your Christ, and says to you, "Come unto me, O weary and heavy-laden man, and I will give you rest." May His voice so prevail with you that you shall come to Him!

IX.

THE MATERIAL AND THE SPIRITUAL.

"And as he went out of the temple, one of his disciples saith unto him: Master, see what manner of stones and what buildings are here."—MARK xiii. 1.

IT was the last week of Christ's life in Jerusalem. Every morning He walked in from Bethany and taught the people in the Temple, and went back again at night to the house of Lazarus and Martha and Mary. On the first evening, as they passed out of the temple between the great walls which supported its vast area, the disciples with their Jewish pride in their queenly city pointed out its massive structure to Him: "Master, see what manner of stones and what buildings are here."

It is no wonder that they were impressed with admiration. To the simple fishermen from Gallilee this superb masonry, whose remains still testify its greatness, must have seemed almost superhuman. They look to see their Master impressed, too. But here they are wholly disappointed. Jesus was absorbed in something else. He was thinking about the moral and spiritual condition of the city whose material architecture was so superbly strong. With His eye set upon those things it was impossible that

He should be overcome by the mere size of stones and skill of mason's work. "Seest thou these great buildings!" He exclaims. "There shall not be left one stone upon another that shall not be thrown down." He looked beyond these mighty works. He saw the life that lay behind them. He saw a rottenness of character which was really undermining the deep masonry. He could not value it as the disciples did. He could not answer their summons to join their admiration. He had gone beyond them, and was dwelling on something vastly more interesting and impressive. We can almost think we hear a certain yearning tone in the voice of Jesus as He felt how His deep absorption in the spiritual interests of His people had made Him incapable of finding pleasure in the merely outward signs of their dignity and strength.

And is not this the penalty of all enlightenment, —indeed, of all deepening of life of every sort? It puts out of our power the pleasures and prides that we lived in while our lives were merely superficial. We give up admiring lower things as higher things absorb us more and more. You have a child for whom, for years, you have been desiring prosperity and popular regard. You have been proud that he has won them both. He has succeeded in business and he has made hosts of friends. But in the meantime, *you* have become more of a man. You have acquired larger thoughts. You have come to the religious value of character. That a man should be pure and devoted and godly seems to you now to be the one needful thing. No wonder that your child wonders and is puzzled when, bringing into your presence his money and his fame, which used to give you so much pleasure, he finds that they do not impress you as they used to do. You are looking beyond them for something else in him which perhaps you do not find.

Or, to take a case more similar to that of Christ and His disciples, you grow up with a strong, high pride in your country,—her vast extent, her lordly wealth, her noble buildings, her endless railways, all her prosperous life. But if, as you grow up, you come to know that the real prosperity of a land is not these things, if you come to ask for lofty ideas, for brave, true men, for domestic purity, for scrupulous regard for all men's rights; and if, not finding these so plentifully as your patriotic soul desires, your enthusiasm flags over the signs of material success, will you not sometimes almost feel that you have lost something in reaching these higher desires for your country which have tarnished your satisfaction in her material success? Or, your friend waves the banner of his happiness before your eyes and cries, "Rejoice with me that I am happy." And you have to answer him, "I cannot rejoice with you as you want me to rejoice, because I see, for such as you are, so much greater and truer a happiness that you ought to be enjoying." Thus it is always. Every advance in the standards of living, while it brings a man higher satisfactions, shuts him out from some lower ones. He can no longer go on his way "like a beast with lower pleasures, like a beast with lower pains." Christ cannot glory with

His disciples over the masonry of the temple as He cannot be terrified with them over the storm at sea.

But all this introduces us to a question in answer to which I should like to offer you a few thoughts—the question of human impressibility. What ought a true man to be impressed by? What is there that is worthy of taking hold of our imaginations and really seeming to us great and wonderful? For men, as I have indicated to you already, are judged by their impressibilities; from the child who starts and leaps with pleasure when you flash a bit of colored glass in the sun before his eyes, all the way up to the philosopher who glows with joy as he perceives some new relation of idea to idea and so discovers a new truth. Find what any man is impressed by, and you have found what kind of man he is. You step into a shopful or carful of men all sitting indiscriminately together, and you tell some story of how money may be made, you repeat the story of some rich man's way of growing rich, and almost all will listen and admire. You turn from that and repeat some item of the daily news, something that only requires common intelligence and a general interest in the doings of mankind to understand and care for, and a smaller number will look up and listen. You go on and tell some tale of heroism and self-devotion that only a generous heart can comprehend, and those in your audience who are impressed are fewer still. Finally, you speak about the spiritual nature, about the soul's life in God, the blessedness of purity, the peace of trust, and only one or two or three look up and show with kindling eye and quiet, earnest face that they care for those sacred things of which you speak. The men are judged and sorted by their impressibilities. So nature impresses her own men; and Art lays her hand on hers; and both are judged by their impressibilities.

And now it stands out clearly in our story that Jesus did not care for the Titanic stones on which the Jewish temple rested. It was a superb utterance of the skill and strength by which man can control the physical world. There they are still to-day, those giant stones. The traveller may go and look at them. They bear amazing witness of the prowess of power and patience by which they have been wrought out of the mountain-side and piled into their places. They tell of man's dominion over matter as hardly any ancient sight can tell. They were crying out to the disciples of man's power over matter, and the disciples were full of wonder at it, but Jesus did not care for it. There was a higher, fuller power of man, another conquest of the world which these men had missed, and, because of their missing that, this mere material triumph did not interest or move Him. He prophesied how transitory it was all to prove, and so passed on and left it.

Now, we need to know, in the first place, that that is always true. It is something which we who call ourselves the servants of Jesus Christ have no right ever to forget,—that He never is impressed by merely material success or power any more than He was when He saw them in Jerusalem. You take the things for which men praise you,—your success in business, the discovery that you have made, the house that you have built,—nay, as one proud, exalted person of this nineteenth century in which we live, you take all our material civilization in its grandeur and superbness, and you hold it up before Christ; and what you need to know is that *of and for itself* Christ does not care for it. It was not what He came into the world to bring to pass. It is conceivable that all of it might exist to-day, and yet Christ's work be a profound and total failure. We see, indeed, that all the spring of marvellous energy, all the vitalizing power which made our civilization, has come in connection with the Gospel; and so we are apt to think that what the Gospel set itself to do was to give man this power over the material world; but when we undertake to search for it we find that not one word ever fell from Jesus' lips which told that this was what He sought. If material civilization,—that is, the accumulation of wealth, the multiplication of physical comforts, the conquering of force to man's will so that it leaps the ocean almost with a bound and speaks his messages around the globe,—if it literally could stop short there and go no farther, leave literally no impress upon character, it would make no impression upon Christ. He would care nothing for it.

And what comes next? Does it not follow that if we are Christians, servants of Christ, we too are to care nothing for material success in and for itself? We yield to it in a servile way. We let it rule us and oppress us. In our own lives it keeps us struggling and working all our days, from our earliest to our latest years, heaping up money or providing comforts for ourselves. In our brethren's lives around us we yield to its demands, and render our homage to the man who overpowers us with the bulky imposition of his wealth. If we were really, thoroughly, Christians, we could not be such slaves. We must rise up in protest and insist that these are not the true things for a spiritual being either to strive for or to admire. O my dear friends, we are not wholly Christ's until some such freedom comes to us! Now and then we see a man who does resist and rebel. We see some mortal, made apparently just like ourselves, who boldly says that he will not live for the outside of things, and who with perfect satisfaction goes his way through life, disregarding those same things that are to us the lords and kings of everything. I think that there is something very strange in the mixture of pity and respect with which we regard such a man. We look up to him and we look down on him at once. It is the curious utterance of our double consciousness about material things,—the superficial consciousness which values them supremely, and the deep underconsciousness that in themselves they have no value. Every sight of such a man stirs in us strange questionings, sets us to asking whether the secret of his carelessness is an insensibility which is brutal and has not come up to the value of these things, or a higher sensibility which is Christlike, which has gone beyond the care for them and left them behind it in its care for better things.

If we ask this question about the indifference of

Jesus, it will not be hard to give it its true answer. Indeed, we have only stated a small part of the truth when we have said that Christ did not care, does not care ever, for merely material triumphs, or for the perfection of material things. In a true sense, no doubt, He does care for them; only for Him, with His perfect perception, the whole world is only *one*, and it is impossible for Him to do what we are always doing, to take the inferior part which is meant to work as a means and to give it a value aside from its connection with the superior part which is the end to which it has to minister. Christ *does* value the material, but always with an outlook beyond it to the spiritual. If we keep this in view, I think we may believe, with the profoundest reverence, that there is no work upon material things faithfully done by man which God does not look upon with pleasure. Thoroughness and beauty are the two excellent qualities of man's work upon material things. Out of the hillside quarry are dug two blocks of stone, and one of them with patient labor is set into a wall, where for generations it holds a great tower in its place. The other is carved into a statue, which for centuries stands like a perfect flower, shedding the fragrance of its beauty around upon the lives of men. Does God have any pleasure in these two achievements? I cannot picture to myself the God entirely indifferent to them. Every being delights in seeing active anywhere the powers which embody its own best activity. Now, God is the Creator, and if in the creation we can read anything of the Creator, these two dispositions, thoroughness and beauty, must lie at the very centre of His Being; for they everywhere pervade the world that He has made. Thoroughness speaks from the lips of every compact adjustment of means to end, from every reserve of power which is revealed to us as the years go on. Beauty shines out of every flower and star and all the manifold variety of life that lies between. And when a man builds a strong bridge, or paints a glowing picture, when the constructive or the æsthetic power manifests itself in man the child, caught by direct inheritance from God the Father, the Father does not look on indifferently, but cares for what His child is doing, and proves His care by sending the forces of His creation to help the work which the child by his invention or his taste is doing. We feel sure of that concerning God, and there is no word of Jesus which implies the contrary of that. No man can read the Gospels and not catch the tone of such a sympathy as proves that wherever the eye of Christ fell upon any man in Palestine who in those days was doing thorough or beautiful work in any department of activity, the Man of men honored him for it and rejoiced in it. Oh, do not think of Him who brought our nature to its best as being totally estranged from those things which ninety-nine hundredths of our race are doing all the time. Think of Him as caring for it all, as caring for what they did and for what you are doing; but always as being preserved from the slavery of material things by two principles which were absolutely despotic and invariable with Him,—the principle that no material thing was entirely satisfactory unless it could reveal some spiritual usefulness, and the principle that if any material thing, however beautiful, hindered any spirituality, there should be no hesitation about sacrificing it. Look at those two principles. See if they did not both absolutely rule in Christ, and see if they are not just what we need to save us from the tyranny of material things.

The first principle was that no material thing was wholly satisfactory unless it could reveal some spiritual usefulness. That appears everywhere in Jesus. It was what lay at the root of His method of teaching by parables. No sentimentalist of form or color will dare say that he sees a beauty or tenderness in a lily or a sky that Jesus did not see there. No botanist will claim that he dissects an interest out of a flower which was hidden from Him who made the flower. And yet these evidently were not the things which made the sky or flower satisfactory to Jesus. Listen to Him: " The Kingdom of Heaven is like unto a king that made a marriage for his son." Then, a king making a marriage for his son must be like unto the Kingdom of Heaven; and if the marriage of a prince, then the marriage of a peasant, and all the relations of the humblest or the highest life. All was like the Kingdom of Heaven; all shone with spiritual meaning. When He had once seen that, how was it possible that He should think of them and leave that out, or that He should be satisfied with any other man's thinking about them which should leave that out?

Or take another illustration. I do not doubt that

Jesus loved the cities where He lived and worked, loved Jerusalem and Nazareth, loved their very streets, loved them as we love our Boston. But to Him a city was a sacred thing; a multitude of men gathered under the conditions most calculated to enrich and discipline life. What good they might do! How good they might grow! A city was the type of heaven to Him. If then he saw His beloved Jerusalem growing rich, but not growing good, beautiful, with sparkling palaces and domes, as it sat on its strange hilltop, but shining with no light of godliness, it was not strange that He was disappointed and poured out His whole soul in lamentation that was all the more bitter because she who had fallen was so beautiful. And the same must have been true of a man. Did Jesus care for bustling energy and enterprise? Indeed He did. Life, *life* was what He was forever calling out for. But a man full of energy who fought with everything except his passions, and desired all good things but character,—that sort of man was all the sadder to the Saviour for the energy that he possessed. Man, to Jesus who had made man, meant spirituality; and man without spirituality was to Him man without that manhood by which the body and the mind and the impetuous will are made truly human.

Now, is it inconceivable that we should come to feel about material forces and triumphs just as Jesus did? A great commercial man is ruling in our town. Men are all singing his praises. His power of making money is immense. His power over other people's destinies is awful. He can stretch out his hand and paralyze a village on the other side of the continent. Again, he can lift up his voice and bid a desert by the Rocky Mountains blossom into a city. All men are praising him. Shall you and I praise him? Let us ask ourselves what Jesus would say of him. If he is all selfish, not one word of praise would fall on him from those blessed lips. With a pity that would seal his condemnation, the Christ who saw what he might be would cry over him, "O Jerusalem, Jerusalem!" Shall you and I praise him then? Oh, for the grace and clearness to say that we will not! Oh, for the spiritual honesty which shall refuse to set such a man's life as the model life before young men! Oh, for the decency which shall refrain from belauding him when he is dead for virtues which even he would have blushed to have heard mentioned in his presence when he was alive! The time must come when Christian men shall refuse to honor capitalists for mere wealth, or cities for mere size, or their age for its mere accumulation of physical comfort. When that time comes, when every material triumph is compelled to show some spiritual gain, some contribution to human character, then how much more life will mean!

The other principle that governed our Lord's relation to the world, I said was this,—that if any material thing, however beautiful and perfect in itself, stood in the way of any spirituality, it should be sacrificed without a hesitation. We mark everywhere in the life of Jesus a perfect perception, not merely of the absolute, but of the comparative value of things, and so an easy and unquestioning postponement of the less important to the more important always. This led to a certain distinct character being stamped on the career of Jesus, which belonged to the special circumstances in which He lived and the purpose for which He had come to earth. Under these circumstances and with that purpose set before Him, He could not possibly do things which it was yet in His nature to do, and which it would have been His delight to do under other conditions.

We must guard ourselves against thinking that in the few acts which Christ did on the earth, we have specimens of all the acts which it was possible for Him to do, and so which it would be right for us to do. Some people seem to have such an idea, and it limits their notion of what it is right for a Christian to do very narrowly indeed. This applies very clearly to our Lord's whole relation to what we call æsthetics, to the beautiful in human art. There is not one sign that He was ever touched by it in the least; and any child who understands Christ could give you the reason. He was too busy; He was too earnest; He was too set on higher things; He was here to save men. The sight of their sin, their folly, their misery, was before Him every day. Behind that glowed to His divine sight the other picture of their possibility. He saw what they were; He saw what they might be. He was so set on lifting them out of what they were and into what they might be that He had no time left to think of the beauty or the ugliness with which their life chanced to be surrounded. It was not because He hated art and beauty that He never dwelt upon them; it was that He loved righteousness with the intenser love. So His indifference was not from a negation, but the whole positiveness of His soul was in it.

And how conceivable this is! How familiar some illustrations of the same thing are! The intenser and higher wish bids the lower one stand aside and bide its time. He who goes into a burning house to save a child out of the flames will not stop in the rush on which his own life and the child's depends to gaze upon the rarest or loveliest pictures that hang upon the burning walls. That seems to me to tell the story of one side of Christ's indifference to the things that occupy our taste and attention. It does not prove any absence in Him of the faculties in us to which those things appeal. A man who is fighting for his life tramples the flowers under his feet, but it does not prove that he is a brute who cannot see their beauty. A soldier gives up his home for the field and camp, but it does not show that he is a savage with no family affection. The Puritans in their fear of idolatry cast away all art, and broke the painted windows and hewed statues to pieces; it certainly did not prove with *all* of them that they did not feel the beauty of what they destroyed. With all strong men this sense of proportion, which sacrifices the less to the greater, is an essential quality. And all strong times in the world's history have compelled that same sacrifice of the æsthetic to the moral which characterized the life of Jesus. Severe and simple in His moral earnestness, nobody misses that which we yet all feel, as we compare His life with our own, to be absent,—the conscious pleasure in adornment and art, the seeking of the tastes for satisfaction.

How ought this feature in the life of Him whom we delight to call our Lord to affect our feeling about our own cultivation and gratification of the sense of beauty? Ought we to cast it aside as something wrong, and say that we will have no more to do with it than He had? Certainly not! We ought to be sure that, under different conditions from those terrible ones in which His Incarnate Life was cast, Jesus would have delighted in all true beauty that man had ever found or created, with an appreciation that no man has ever felt. We ought to rejoice in the cultivation of all beauty as the fit expression of man's joy in that life which the redemption of Christ has made so deeply and truly joyous. So the Christian has the best right of any man to cultivate the æsthetic sense. But at the same time he is bound by his Christianity to cultivate it purely, and in continual subordination to the moral and spiritual needs. The Christian may delight in beauty, but he must catch from Christ the assurance that no beauty is really beautiful which in any way hinders righteousness or weakens spiritual life; and he must be ready to strip every beautiful thing away the moment that God calls him to intenser life and duty. Does not this cast a doubt over the way in which many of your houses are adorned? Does it not convict a great deal of the unreal, impure, *dillettante* affectation which calls itself a taste for beauty? Nothing can be more essentially ugly to a wise perception than the house crowded with trinkets of exquisite form and color, and inhabited by men and women of idle or impure or selfish or little lives. The beauty with which they have bedecked their bower makes only more unpleasant the lives of the insects who inhabit it.

Here is the simple rehearsal of the whole matter. There are four classes, as concerns the whole matter of delight in and cultivation of what is artistically beautiful. There is the man who is below it all, too stupid to feel its influence—he is the brute. There is the man who loves the beautiful, but loves it either out of imitation of other people or with his senses only, having no spiritual perceptions beyond —he is the connoisseur or pedant. There is the man who allows himself all joy in material beauty but holds it always subordinate to truth and duty—he is the Christian. And there is here and there the man who is above it all, called to such serious work, fighting so fierce a battle, that he has no time left for outward beauty, but lives in the unseen beauty of devotion. At the head of all such men is Christ.

These are the two principles, then. He who insists on looking through the material to the spiritual which lies below it and which it represents and educates, he who looks beyond the material to the spiritual which is so much more important—he is the man whom mere material success and magnificence cannot impose upon. Men come to him and say, "Behold what manner of stones and what buildings are here!" They say, "See how rich this man is!" "How strong this institution is!" "How beautiful this art is!" His answer rings out clear and strong: "So far as they all mean spirituality and make spiritual men, I do indeed value them all and thank God for them; and yet I value them always with a higher value for the things beyond. I will let any of them go at any moment, if so I can reach to higher spirituality myself, or make other men better men." How free that man is! How he can walk the proudest streets and not cringe to the arrogant wealth which crowds them! How calm the judgment with which, looking at them through Christ, he dares to form his own brave, independent thoughts of men and things!

How shall one reach that freedom? I hope that I have made it clear that it is only by entering into the higher anxieties of Jesus that one is freed from the lower anxieties of men. You must care with all your soul that God should be glorified and that men should be saved. If you can do that, you are free. And you can do that only by letting God first glorify Himself in you by saving you. Let Christ be your Saviour. Then, tasting His salvation, your one great wish will be that all men may be saved, and, wishing that intensely, you will be free from every other wish that does not harmonize with that. That is St. Paul's great idea when he speaks of the Christian as "Casting down imaginations and every high thing that exalteth itself against the knowledge of God, and bringing into captivity every thought to the obedience of Christ."

X.

THE DOUBLE CAUSE.

"And his name through faith in his name hath made this man strong, whom ye see and know."—ACTS iii. 16.

A LAME beggar had sat for years at the gate of the Temple in Jerusalem, and all the people knew him well. He was part of their city landscape. They knew him as they knew the carved columns of the Temple doorway. One day Peter and John, two disciples of the Christ who had been lately crucified, had come that way and cured the beggar's lameness. The people were full of interest and excitement, and part of their excitement evidently came from the fact that the man who had been cured was one whom they all knew so well. The miracle had been worked on most familiar material. Not some strange, mysterious flesh and bone which might be different from their own had been submitted to the Healer's power; but this notorious cripple of Jerusalem, this beggar of the Temple, "whom ye see and know,"—it was his stiff and crooked joints that had been loosened and straightened; it was his feet and ankle-bones that had received strength. We can almost see his old companions gathering around him and handling him and feeling the power which always belongs to the familiar and commonplace when it is touched by the mysterious and supernatural.

The mysterious is always thus peculiarly impressive when it comes in connection with what we know most intimately. The moonlight is most weird and solemn when it shines into the room where every chair and table is well known, or when it makes strange the garden in whose well-known paths you have walked all day. The great man is most impressive and mysterious when he comes into your common room and sits among your homely furniture. In a somewhat different way this was what forced the reality of Christ's wonderful nature and works upon the people who had known His person since He was a boy. "Ye both know me and ye know whence I am," He cried. It was by hands that they had touched that the wondrous works were done. Out of a face whose every feature they knew the strange light shone.

I want to study with you this afternoon the story of the lame man's cure at Jerusalem. And first of all let us fill ourselves with this *reality* which it possessed for those who saw it first. The divine power which had touched him was all the more unmistakable and all the more wonderful because it had shown itself not on some supernal, transcendental substance, but on the dull, sordid flesh of this poor, well-known beggar. At the same time his sordid flesh had shown its inherent sacredness in being able to answer to the touch of Christ's apostles. So the great works of God's Spirit become real to us because they touch and change our common lives, and our common lives become sacred because they can be touched by God's Spirit.

The cure of the cripple, as St. Peter tells it to the people, is the work of a double cause. He says that the name of Jesus, that is, of course, the power of Jesus, has made the man whole *through faith in His name*,—that is, in His power. This faith may be the faith of the disciples who had wrought the cure, or of the lame man who had been cured. In either case, as you see, the cause is double. There is the power of Christ and then there is the condition, whether of the disciples or the cripple, which gave the power of Christ a chance to work. " His name through faith in His name,"—these two together make the total cause as the result of which the rescued beggar is even now making the temple ring with his joy as he goes walking and leaping and praising God. Neither part of the double cause could have been left out,—the exterior force or the interior condition, the objective or the subjective, the name of the powerful Christ or the faith of the obedient cripple. Either of them would have been useless without the other. As the result of the two together, there stands the cripple cured.

The philosophy which is involved here is perfectly familiar. Its illustrations are constantly occurring. Indeed, we may take exactly this formula which St. Peter uses and employ its form to describe any one of the changes which may take place in the condition of a man or of the human race. " His name through faith in His name has made this man whole," says Peter. How shall I tell the story of an ignorant child who by long study has developed into wisdom? Is there not there again the outward force made effective through a personal condition, until the result is a new quality or nature in the human being? The outward force is truth, all alive and seeking for its own expansion. The personal condition is study or devoted intelligence, and the result is in the educated man. Truth through the study of truth hath made this man wise.

And so all the loveliness of nature, finding its way in through man's power of loving nature, creates all that delight in nature and absorption of her loveliness which constitute the artistic life. Beauty through man's sense of beauty makes this man fine and rich and strong. So a commandment which is totally outside of our life, possessing us through our obedience to it, makes then a conduct which is truly our own. Commandment through obedience to commandment makes us just and kind. The commandment might thunder from the skies forever, but, unobeyed by us, it would leave us when its thunders ceased just as it found us when they began. So a great man set before our admiration makes us like himself. A great man through admiration of his greatness makes us great.

Everywhere, you see, it is the same. Some power outside ourselves unites itself with some disposition in ourselves, and so the changes in our natures come. I suppose there is no exception to the rule. I suppose no change in our natures, in what we really are, ever comes by those natures simply working on themselves, untouched by any outside force. Certainly the other statement is true. Certainly no outside force can change us until it has made itself a confederate in some will or act of our own. It is true even of our physical life. The most pestilential wind might blow across our faces and no more make disease in us than it makes disease in a statue, if it did not find in us living men and women some responsive possibility which it does not find in the dead stone. And the most life-giving gales might breathe their freshness on our lips, and make no more life in us than they make in the dead corpse, if it were not that they met in us the possibility of living and gave their strength to us through it. The vital forces of the world through our power of living make us live.

If I might dwell yet for a few moments on the illustrations of our truth, it is set forth very vividly in all the best efforts which men make to help their fellow-men. How often the experiment of man to help his fellow-man has failed, however earnestly and generously made! Here is the help abundantly, on one side,—money, knowledge, sympathy, hopefulness,—all that makes life rich. There, on the other side, is need,—a poor, crushed, broken life which wants these all. How often the effort to give them all has failed! How often help has come like the shower from the heavens, and rolled off helplessly from the hard surface of the life on which it fell! Charity, simple charity, the mere giving of what one has to another man, does not make that other man rich. There must be generous taking as well as generous giving. There must be a sympathetic soil to receive as well as a sympathetic rain to fall. And so our wiser charity is led to anxious thought about the character of the men and women upon whom benefactions are bestowed—perfectly sure that both sides must work together or only the most superficial good is done. Sympathy through the sympathetic reception of sympathy has made this poor man rich, this dreary house warm and full of comfort, this coward brave, this weak man strong. So only can the story of a complete charity be told.

But it is time now to have done with illustrations. Out of them all our truth stands clear. In every one of the instances which I have quoted, two things, the outward force and the personal disposition or readiness to receive, obey, and use the force, unite to bring the final result. The truth which issues from such an assemblage of instances must be the old, ever-new truth of how human nature and the world in which it lives belong together and correspond to one another. One thought of the world simply coördinates man with all its ordinary products. The world has made him as it has made the elm-tree and the elephant, and he is no more in it than all the rest. Another thought of the world makes it and its processes quite insignificant as regards humanity. He is so totally, so absolutely, its superior, so different from it in origin and nature, so exclusively the child of God, that he has nothing to do with the world except to rule it and to use it. It can have no power over him. The thought of our verse, the Christian thought, is different from either. Man and the world belong together. They are different in dignity, in origin, in nature. They are two and not one, and yet they are two which make one; for every result which is ultimately produced in man comes from the working of some external force with and through the coöperating will of man. Take man out of the world and you leave it full of forces which will find no worthy material to work upon. Take the world away from man and you leave him with plenty of capacities, but with no force to stir them into motion. Put man and the world—by which I mean everything outside of the personal human life—together, and then you have the total cause from which the whole result proceeds. Man as the appropriator and applier of forces through his human will and nature—that is the truth of this verse of St. Peter.

I said it was the Christian truth. Christ made these certain things evident,—I am sure that if you think over His teachings and His influence you will see how they all certainly came forth from Him. He made it evident: (1) That the great purpose of everything which was at work in the world was to make man a better man, that human character was the only worthy result to which all earthly forces were directed. (2) That human nature, or character, needs all the forces from outside itself, whether they be the forces of the world around it but outside itself, or the sublime forces and influences which come direct from God. Human character, or nature, cannot perfect itself. (3) That the world's forces come to human character only through the submission of the human will. These three things Christ made evident. They constitute the soul and heart of His religion. And these three truths are in the teaching of Peter, that it is the name of Jesus through the faith in Jesus which has made the lame man whole.

Is it not true that such a principle as this really points out what ought to be the wide range of thought and study for all earnest men? One man says, "Study nature and let man alone; science and not metaphysics ought to be your task." Another man says, "No, let nature go and study man; science is godless and profane. It is metaphysics that gives light." One theologian concentrates his thought on God, and treats man as if he were dead material. Another theologian fastens all his thought on man, as if in understanding him all problems would be solved. But if the soul of man is ultimately saved by great, strong forces of the universe,—all crowding in through the door of man's assent, eager to work upon man's spiritual life,— then certainly no region of heaven or earth, no truth which it is possible to know of man or God, can be left out by him who wishes to be completely "wise unto salvation." It is foolish and weak to think of the study of objective fact, or of the inner nature of man, as if either of them could take the other's place and make it useless; since it is fact and power through the human reception of fact and power that completes the human life.

Apply all this to practical religion. How hard it seems for many men, for many whole churches and whole ages, to keep the symmetry and completeness of the great spiritual processes by which the world is gradually being saved! What is it to you that the Church offers her sacraments, that the Bible lies open with its story of Christ, that the Incarnation is, indeed, a veritable fact in history—nay, that God lives in heaven and in the earth and everywhere? What is all that to you? Just exactly what it is to the chamber that the sunlight is pouring down upon the window-pane; just exactly what it is to the mill-wheel that the water is rushing down the flume; just exactly what it is to the ship that the wind is blowing from the west—everything, if your nature and life are ready to receive them. Nothing whatever, if the great powers of the Church and the Bible and Christ and God find nothing in you which opens to them as they lay their majestic power against your life.

A ship lies close beside a rock here on our coast. Some day the west wind blows. It comes fresh from the prairies and the mountains, and it is eager for the ocean which it loves. It blows on ship and rock alike. Why is it that two weeks from now the ship is riding in the fragrant sunshine of some Mediterranean bay, while the rock alongside of which it lay stands still, bruised and beaten by our cruel seas? Two men of you years ago were touched alike by God,—why is it that to-day one is rich in the memory of years of godliness, years in which he knows that he has been trying to do good unselfishly to God's children for their Father's sake, and the other has nothing but a life of unspiritual selfishness to remember? Is the Bible a power? Some men have held that it is, with a completeness which has seemed almost to lodge the power in the very print and paper of the Book itself. If you were to read it, even mechanically, it would save you. If you opened it, even at random, it would guide you. Are the Sacraments powerful? Surely they are; and so to a baptism which meant no consecration men have brought their children, and to a communion in which there was no spirituality men have come themselves; and they have gone away from one or the other thinking that something really had been done. Is the name of Jesus mighty? Yes, indeed; and so men say it like a charm. Is God great and awful? Surely He is; and so men rattle profanely through unmeaning and half-articulated oaths. In every case the blunder is the same. It is giving to the half the power and virtue which belong only to the whole. The Bible believed in and obeyed— that is, the Bible plus belief and obedience—*that* is power. God loved and honored—that is, the name of God surrounded with the reverence and the affection of the devoted soul,—that is strength for restraint and inspiration. The west wind plus the ship's nature makes the power of the voyage. The ground's richness plus the seed's fertility—that, no less than that—makes the tree!

We all remember how, in the first chapters of Genesis, all the beasts are brought to Adam to know what he would call them. They went out from him by and by, bearing names which he had given them. Not till their lives had touched his life were they complete and ready for their full careers. It always seems to me as if there could be no test more sure of what kind of a man that first man was than we should get if we could see into his heart as he stands there in the Garden, and know whether that submission of all the creatures made him proud or humble. Did it make him proud? Did he see them depart after his naming of them, saying over to himself, " Behold, they are all mine and all this world exists for me!" If so, he was but a poor creature, and all the misery which has come since in his race might have been prophesied. But did it make him humble? As he saw them go, did he become aware of what a great and awful thing it was to be the centre of so much life, and feel his terrible unfitness for it, and cry out for strength? If so, then he was strong, and all the good strength which manhood has displayed since then was there in its germ in that humility. Always men's qualities are shown by whether their powers and privileges make them proud or make them humble.

So you must all be judged—if you believe what I am preaching to you this afternoon—by the impression which it makes upon your soul. I have dared to tell the young man here that the Bible, the Church, the ever-pleading Christ, nay, God Himself, wait for his call before, with all their power, they can save his soul. He can say, " Go," or " Come." It is an awful power. Does it make him who possesses it bold or humble? If it makes him proud, it shows how weak he is. If it makes him humble, if the sense of what a Guest it is who stands at his door, unwilling—nay, in some true sense, *unable*—to enter until he shall bid the bolt fly back,—if all this makes him cry out with fear at himself lest he should be unfit for such responsibility; if, seeing the full depth of meaning in the words which tell that only to the " pure in heart " can come the real blessedness of knowing God, he feels how powerless he is to keep his own heart pure and cries out to God Himself to do it,—"' Make me a clean heart, O God!' O God, who wilt not enter into me unless I am such that I can receive Thee, oh, *make* me such that I can receive Thy life!"—if such humility as that possesses him, then how great he is, and what a great life opens before him! Oh, how true it is that the completest humility of man has always come, must always come, by man's knowing the greatness of his nature and his privileges!

Another value of the truth I have been preaching lies in the great hope which it unfolds to the imagination of the soul that holds it. If there were needed no coöperation of the consenting soul to the power of Christ, then Christ must have done long ago the work which He proposed to do for man. No obstacle existing, He must have pressed on at once to the entire fulfilment of His love. He would not have delayed. And then—why, then, it must be that this which we see now in ourselves and in the world is all. There would remain no hope of more beyond. Can we think that without a sad sinking of the heart? What, is this all? This half-way life—this mixture of the baser with the better way in everything—this selfishness, this sluggish-ness, this sensuality, this wearisome yielding to temptation only to repent and struggle upward for a moment and then fall again—is this all? Has Christ *done* His work in us?

But if the other thought is true, if Christ's work is not done in us, but only just begun; and if it lingers not because He is reluctant, but because, needing our coöperation, it can be done only so fast and so far as we receive it and allow it,—then, with all our humiliation there certainly comes hope. All the unknown things which Christ will do for us so soon as we are ready; all the great revelations which He has to make to us so soon as we can see them,—all these lie open wide before us. To him who thoroughly believes this truth it seems as if a voice were ever crying in those words which Jesus spoke so often to the crowds in Palestine, " He that hath ears to hear, let him hear." Perhaps no ear does hear the special message; perhaps no intelligence is yet fine and pure and clear enough to take the truth which yet some day the whole world shall know. But the cry has hope in all the humiliation that it brings. Agnosticism says, " We do not know, and because we do not know we must give up the hope of ever knowing." Our truth says, " We do not know, but the hindrance in us is not essential and perpetual. It is incidental and may be temporary. Let us be better and humbler and more unselfish and more spiritual, and we *shall* see." And so our very ignorance becomes the power of a better life.

And certainly our truth gives very interesting value to the daily incidents and little things of life.

If there is really waiting, behind the door of our reluctance and incompetency, a vast, deep wealth of blessing, of character, of knowledge, which might be ours if only there were broken down this wall of hindrance between us and it, then how important and significant everything must be which shakes that wall of hindrance and tends at all to its dislodgment. Every least incident of life may have this value. Every largest incident of life is really insignificant unless it has this value in some degree. The change from wealth to poverty or from poverty to wealth, from sickness to health or from health to sickness, the forming or the breaking of a friendship, the undertaking or the finishing of a task,—all of these are no more than the mere changes of the wind unless somehow they give occasion to such changes in our dispositions that some of the great abundance of truth and goodness, some of the great abundance of God which is waiting outside our lives, can enter in.

This touches the work that we try to do for our fellow-men, and often redeems its superficialness and insignificance. Often it must seem as if the mere exertion to make your child or your neighbor more comfortable were a very little thing. It is worth doing, for comfort is better than discomfort, and the affection which you show is well worth testifying. But if it can be more than that,—if, by the kind act, and still more by the echo which your act brings of the Divine goodness, you can open the life of your neighbor or your child to some inflow of the great goodness and truth which is all ready to invade it,—then surely it is more than worth the doing; it is worth the sacrifice of one's own will and pleasure, it is worth the consecration of one's life to do!

Little, sometimes, must it seem to the devoted worker for the poor merely to improve the dwelling where the poor man lives,—to win, perhaps, and perhaps not to win, his gratitude because his windows catch a brighter sunshine and his rooms are open to a healthier air,—little to build the gallery and open it freely to all who will come and gaze, however ignorantly, on its pictures,—little to shut a drinking shop here and there and save one wretched family from blows and starvation,—little any of these things must seem sometimes in themselves, but if they stand any chance of opening the wretched, poverty-hardened life to visions and companionships, to knowledge of God, to perceptions, however dim at first, of the divine influences which the soul of man was made to feel,—then surely they carry their own inspiration with them, and it is no wonder that the choicest men and women will so freely give their time, their thought, their sympathy, and their means to works like these.

St. Paul's sublimest, most pathetic picture is perhaps that in the eighth chapter of the Epistle to the Romans, in which he talks about the whole creation groaning and travailing in pain together until now, waiting for the adoption, the redemption, of our body. Think what that means! The world centres in and depends on man. It is what he makes it. And man is capable of being possessed by God, filled with His Spirit, echoing His character. Only the hindrance of man's own unwillingness and incompleteness delays God's occupation of his life. Behold, then, the whole creation stands by and waits! Its perfectness depends on man's. When will he let God do for him all that God wants to do, and so become the worthy centre of a new life for all the world? The whole creation groaneth and travaileth. The very hills and trees cry out in discontent; the very beasts are eager and impatient, wanting a nobler master, a master who shall more realize himself and his own capacity of being filled with God.

Am I talking too large? Am I bidding you to listen to a voice of creation which is too diffused and vague for you to hear. Then hear your own creation; hear the little circle of life by which you are immediately surrounded. Let your family, your shop, your school, your farm, your house, your garden, cry out to you in remonstrance against everything low and sensual and ungodlike in the life you live. Let them tell you how much finer and loftier they would become if you were all that you might be. It is not for yourself alone,—that were too selfish,—your whole creation groaneth and travaileth, waiting for your adoption, waiting for you to begin to live, and to go on and live completely the life of a child of God.

May I ask you to remember the course by which our thoughts have been travelling this afternoon? We saw the universal necessity that for any true change in man there must be a double cause. His own disposition must work with the force external to himself, which sought to change him. We saw how even Christ owned this necessity, and allowed His disciple to declare that it was only through faith in His name that His all-saving name could save the world. Then we saw in what profoundly interesting and critical position this put man, standing, with his power of believing or of disbelieving, between God and God's truth and God's blessing on the one side, and his own life and the world's life—so empty in themselves, so gloriously full when they are filled with God—upon the other.

Only one word more needs to be said. That name which is nothing to us unless we believe in it, has its own blessed power to tempt our belief. Thank God!—His mercy does not stand afar off waiting for us to take it. It presses itself upon us. The Guest whose coming-in is salvation not merely stands at the door, but knocks. All that is true and need not, must not, be forgotten. And yet still —still, here we stand, each with the last responsibility of his own life.

Who would be rid of that responsibility? Who would not humbly, earnestly claim—after God has done all that God can do—after Christ with all His wondrous love and patience and suffering has made His approaches to the soul, and waits and listens for the soul's reception—who would not claim then the soul's own right and duty itself to open wide the door, and say to the waiting Saviour and Master, "Even so, come, Lord Jesus!" and hear the certain answer, "Lo, I come!"

XI.

GO INTO THE CITY.

"Arise, and go into the city, and it shall be told thee what thou must do."—ACTS ix. 6.

It was the critical day of St. Paul's life. The miracle which made him a servant of Christ was just complete. He had been thrown down from his horse by the splendor that outshone the noonday, and in answer to the voice that proclaimed Who it was that thus had arrested him, he had just asked the humble question, "What wilt thou have me to do?" The stunned senses had recovered themselves; and Paul, the man who always had a purpose and a destination, was asking for the destination and purpose of the new life which he felt had begun. The promptitude of all Paul's thought and action in his conversion was remarkable. His direct, straightforward mind laid hold immediately of the new conditions. We stop to play about our great experiences. We coax them and watch over them; we hesitate and analyze. But Paul went directly to the point. "I am a new man. Now what shall I do with my new life." The fact once there it is not something to be mused and pondered over, but to be used. And God replies, "Arise, and go into the city, and it shall be told thee what thou shalt do."

The city was Damascus. Paul was just within sight of its shining walls. It was the city for which he had set out three days ago. He was on his way thither, when the miracle arrested him, going to seize the disciples of Jesus wherever he could find them. And now God says: " Still go into the city where you meant to go. Your route shall not be altered. Your new life must walk over the same road where the old life was walking. Still go into the city, and there it shall be told thee what thou must do." And so Paul started out on the old road again, a new man; and, with another spirit from that which he had expected, passed through the gate of Damascus, for which through all the hours of the long forenoon his eyes had been impatiently searching in the distance.

A new spirit always seems to demand new circumstances. It is one of the profoundest instincts of our nature. There seems to you to be something wrong when you go out full of some great experience which has changed all your inner life, and find all your outer life the same that it was yesterday. You could not help fancying that it must have altered, too, and there seems to be something almost insulting in its unchanged persistency. You carry out with you a new love, a great joy, a terrible sorrow, and can it be that this new stream, so overfull, must flow between the same old banks wherein the life, hitherto so meagre, was content to run! Can it be that with this other heart you must still meet men as you met them yesterday, talk with them of the same old things, still do the same business in the same shop, or, with the joy or sorrow burdening your heart, take up the tools of household drudgery and run the family life just as you did before the joy or sorrow came! Sometimes it even seems as if the permanence of nature were an insult. When we are absorbed in our own pain or pleasure, the hills and stars seem to mock us with their indifference. The poet cries out, petulantly, "How can ye chaunt, ye little birds, and I so weary, full of care!" We find that nature and life will not honor any such demand of ours, and we know that it is best that they should not, but it is natural for us to ask it. It is a sort of witness of our sense of the supremacy that properly belongs to spirit over circumstances. Spirit is the king, and circumstances only ought to be the robe he wears, suiting themselves to his figure and changing with his changes. We believe that some day this will come. In the new heavens and new earth wherein righteousness is to dwell, circumstances will suit themselves, freely and fluently, to the conditions of the spiritual life. They will be to the stiffer and grosser circumstances of this earth what Paul's " spiritual body " is to the " natural body " of which he tells the Corinthians. But now we come to see that only by long, slow changes and in most general ways do circumstances adapt themselves to spirit; and we learn to understand that spirit must triumph over circumstances, not by casting them away and making new ones, but by overpowering them as they are, compelling forth their richer capacities and making them serve greater ends than they have dreamed of. When the artistic spirit has filled us, we may not fling the carpenter's chisel aside—we must work with it still and make it carve our statue.

Of all the new spirits that thus enter into human life and take possession of it, the strongest and most positive beyond all comparison is Christianity. There is nothing which can happen to a man's inner life which can be so much to that life as for the man to become a Christian, for him to find and own the Saviourship and Mastership of the Lord Jesus Christ. His gentle dominion occupies a nature, and what then? One of the common phenomena of Christian experiences is this—that the new Christian, sensible of such a new life within him, looks for and expects a new life outside himself, and is surprised (if he is not almost disappointed) when he discovers that this new experience, so wonderful and inspiring, settles into the midst of old familiar circumstances. This is the feeling that has always broken out in the disposition to make a special and technical religious life. The world, with all its intercourses, seems too worldly. Its musics jar upon the new, exalted soul. Its sights seem sordid to eyes quickened by gazing into the near face of God. Let us open the gates and go away. Let us carry our new life into a new world. Let us go where the eyes and ears shall see and hear nothing but their own sacred sights and sounds. Who has not felt the impulse? And everywhere we see it taking shape. The devout Romanist covets and seeks his monastery, and so leaves the world. The devout Protestant withdraws into the little circle of the religious public and devotes his life to certain technical religious practices, and avoids the world's people among whom he used to live.

But God will not allow that impulse to find perfect satisfaction. He is always forcing the new religious life into contact with the world. The new man must still mix with the old men, and touch them closely in all the pressures of our ever-shifting life. The circumstances will not be entirely altered with the alteration of the spirit. With everything that is inherently wicked in the old occupation once thoroughly cast away, the soul then finds that it is to keep the rest and grow, not out of them, but in them, and enlarge them as it grows, and make them fit for the new work they have to do in ministering to an ever-enlarging soul.

Thus it is with the converted merchant. The mercantile life may be very large or very little. You know both kinds of it. It grows with the growing of a merchant's soul. The young man, struggling just for his own ambition and advancement, makes one thing out of business; and that same man, when his life is enlarged by the dependency of others, when he has his home with wife and children to provide for, finds the capacity of business to be something much larger. It can put on new sacredness when it is consecrated to such sacred needs. And let that same man be a Christian. Let the needs of his own nature and the claims of charity grow real to him, and then again the business life opens its new capacity, and lo! it can become so holy that the spiritual life may eat of it as of a sacrament, and charity may strike the richest water out of its rugged rocks. You may take the same truth and see how it is true of your own occupation, whatever it may be. Every occupation lifts itself with the enlarging life of him who practises it. The occupation that will not do that no man really has a right to occupy himself about. It is bad even for his smaller life if it is not capable of enlarging itself to contain his life as it grows larger.

There is, no doubt, a prevalent and very dangerous conception of the separateness of the religious life. Does it seem strange to say that? Can the religious life be too separate from the world? you ask. And the answer is easy. Certainly not in spirit. To come out and to be separate from every worldliness is the absolute duty of the Christian's life; and this separateness of spirit will of itself dictate and create certain marked separations of external life. Let all Christians once be really devout in heart, and soon enough and clear enough we shall see the marks in their external life, dividing them from the people who care nothing for what is to them supremely dear. But it is very dangerous to begin at the other end. It is very dangerous to begin by looking for external differences to denote the Christian life. It may do very great harm if we start by feeling that the sign by which we shall know that a man has become a Christian will be a change of the occupations in which we have always seen him engaged. I want to point out several of these dangers which come, as it seems to me, from all attempts to make anything like a conventional type of external religious life separate from the healthy life into which the natural dispositions of men lead them to enter.

1. In the first place it is bad for the world. It throws a mystery and unreality about the whole idea of religion, which keeps people from entering into it, or feeling that it belongs to them. One often wonders, as, after some week-day service, he goes out into the streets and finds them thronged with men full of life and intent upon their work, or as he lays down in his study some book of religious speculation and goes out into the eager and interested world, what it is really that these people think, when they give it a moment's thought at all, of this religion in which his whole life is bound up, of the Church with all her offices and exhortations. There is a great deal which makes him think that the greater number of these men and women have come to regard the Church and her religion as something apart from and almost inconsistent with the daily duties and daily life in which they find themselves engaged. The Christian acts to which they hear religious people urged are acts wholly apart from their ordinary work. The Christian people whom they hear most praised are those whose time is most occupied in certain technical religious tasks. It is not strange that they should come to think that there are two worlds, namely,—one irreligious, the world of business and of social life, the world where homes are bright and warm, where stores are busy and active along the crowded streets; and the other a religious

world, where the churches are, where the church-goers go, where psalms are sung, where life is dim and more subdued, where charity and almsgiving are the work of men and women different from themselves; and to think, too, that he who, from being an irreligious man, becomes a religious man, passes over from one of these worlds into the other, gives up the old and takes the new, so that they are surprised if afterward they meet him where they used to see him, where the glow of social joy is bright and ruddy, or where the clatter of tumultuous trade is loud. Many men's ideas about religion are all colored with this sort of strangeness. It is to pack up everything and move away. It is to cut adrift from all that makes life dear and real, and go out into a world that is really dim, however bright it may be painted.

Suppose that you could get the true idea into those men,—would it not make a difference? Suppose that you could make them see that the newness of the new life must be not in new circumstances, but in a new spirit. As I read really thoughtful men, I see them discontented not so much with the things that they are doing as with the way in which they are doing them. They feel that the things are really worth doing, if only they could be done up to the full measure of their capacity. The scholar believes more and more in the nobility of Learning, but grows very discontented with the miserable, superficial way in which he just skims the surface of her treasures. The thoughtful trader believes that Trade in its ideal is generous and beautiful. It is the reality that he makes of it by the way in which he does it that seems to him sordid. What shall Religion say? If she says, "Come away from those things. Take away your interest in your books, your interest in your store, and give them to something else," they may not scoff, they may not be contemptuous, but they are puzzled and lost. You offer them a world they cannot comprehend. It is all unreal. Can you not say—is it not all right to say: "This is the very thing religion has to do for you, to make your books and your store, your studying and money-getting, attain their full ideal, to fill them out to their complete capacity, to take their sordidness out of them and fill them with their true spirit. It is with you *in* your occupation that religion has to do, to make you in the highest sense a scholar, a trader worthy of the name."

Tell me, would not such an appeal of religion, made genuinely, made not for the sake of catching men, but genuinely,—would it not give reality to what is to men now so terribly unreal? If we could go to a man and say, "Come, love God and fear Him. Be penitent, be obedient"; and when he said, "What for?" if we would only answer—not "So that you may be something new and wholly different from what you are" (he shakes his head and is all puzzled when you say that)—but, "So that you may be perfectly what you are now so wretchedly—a true father, a true citizen, a true man";—then we should start a real ambition; and then, perhaps, by and by, having mounted up to the higher levels of these characters, he would be ready for the revelation of some higher things to be. Having been thoroughly a man by his religion here, he should be able to become a saint of some untried quality in some future life. I think of the great Hebrew people. There never was a people to whom religion was so real, and, also, there never was a people to whom religion was so little an *art*, and therefore mixed itself with all their life, flowed freely into all the structure of their state, and ran through all the family existence, and found natural embodiment in the slightest and most prosaic acts.

2. It is bad for the outsider, then, for religion to be a technicality, and to seem to belong only to certain actions. But it is no less bad for the religious man himself. Here is a Christian man who has been taught to think that Christian life consists in doing certain special things, not in doing all things in a certain spirit. He is a Christian when he goes to church. He is not a Christian when he lives among his friends in common intercourse. But a large proportion of his life must be spent in just such intercourse. The special religious actions can take up only a little part of every day. And what is the result? Why, that the larger part of every day is counted out of the Christian's Christian life.

Do I seem to make a merely theoretical difficulty? Ask yourself, I beg you. My Christian friend, is it not so? Do you not often live along, with the great part of your life just the same as it would be if you had never taken Jesus for your Master, with a few moments or an hour every day standing out apart in which you are different from what you would have been unconverted, because then you are at your public worship or your private prayers? And if some one should question you about it you would say: "I cannot be at worship all the time; I must earn my bread,"—as if being at worship were religious and earning one's bread necessarily were not!

Some one not long ago characterized "modern Christianity" as a "civilized heathenism"; and the phrase took, and people repeated it to one another. What the phrase means seems to be simply this: that here we are, eighteen hundred years after Christ, still living the same life that the heathen lived before Christ came—the same external life. The Church has not broken from the world. Men are not anchorites and hermits. They are still fathers of families, heads of households, doers of business, masters or servants, rich or poor. And these they always will be. Christianity never meant and never tried to break those first instincts which go out inevitably into those fundamental institutions which are older than the Gospel, because they are older than the sin that made the Gospel. But if the power of Christ, in all these years, has entered into these eternal relations and filled out at all their shrunk and meagre forms, if fathers are more fatherly, and citizens come nearer to the true ideal of citizenship, and masters are more full of mercy, and servants are more full of faithfulness than in the days before the Great Light shone, then the real change has come, however imperfectly, however far yet from what it ought to be. And our modern life is not a "civilized heathenism," but is coming nearer to what some day it is to be,—a Christianized humanity; a world-wide expression of that of which the Incarnation of Christ was the first great utterance—the dwelling of God in man, of the Divine Spirit in human circumstances, in human flesh.

Is it not good for us to learn that not on any sacred ground where God first speaks to us, nor on ground like that, sacred, serene, apart, unworldly, is where our Christian lives are to be lived? "Arise, and go into the city, and it shall be told thee *there* what thou must do." Where men are thickest, and these duties which come of men's relationships to one another grow most complicated and multitudinous, where experiences grow most plentifully in the hard-paved, much-trodden street,—there is the place for the Christian to feed and use his Christianity.

Oh, how one comes to love the city! With all its wickedness and misery, it is the home of life. With all its artificialness and deafening roar, with all its selfishness and meanness and brutality, how a man comes year after year to love the great city more and more, because here are *men*—men with their ever-crowding life making duties and chances for each other as the ever-crowding and unresting sea throws up its sparkles into the sunlight and its white crests of foam. It is a joy and privilege to live in a great city,—only the city Christian, above all others, needs to know that his Religion must not submit to be shut in to technicalities, but must insist on claiming all his life for her own; otherwise, so crowding is this world about him, if she consents to share at all, she will be cheated terribly and put off with very little. Her only assurance of getting anything is to claim the whole.

3. There is one way of talking about our Church activities which is far too narrow, and may do a good deal of harm. There is much talk nowadays about "Church-work." The development of Church schools and charities is manifold. The zeal of the good people who carry them on is excellent to see,—we wish that there were more of them of the best kind. But the danger, I sometimes think, is that the great number of a congregation such as this, for whom it is impossible for various reasons that they should be personally engaged in these works of the parish, should think that therefore there is no Church-work for them. Church-work has become a sort of technicality. Church-workers have become a sort of caste. The true Church-work is wider — wide as the whole activity which the Church inspires. Wherever any man of this congregation is doing anything honest or merciful out of any impulse that he has gathered here, he is about Church-work. Whenever any woman puts the spirit of the Sunday collect or the week-day meeting into her household, and does her little to purify and Christianize society, she is a Church-worker.

The Church of God we make so narrow! Some limit it by lines of ordination and some limit it by stone walls, but where does Christ see it? Wherever any of His baptized children are doing any of His work. You think that you can be of no service in the Church. Perhaps you are sorry for it and feel almost ashamed of it. But certainly you can, even the children of you. There is none too young and none too weak. Take any word that we have said or sung to-day, and carry it with you like the bread of life to some hungry heart this week; take the Christ who has manifested Himself to you to-day, and in His power do some helpful thing for some of His brothers or sisters to-morrow, and that is Church-work. The Church grows by it and Christ delights in it; and some day He will own it with these words which are the crown of all the prizes of the universe: "Inasmuch as ye have done it unto one of the least of these my brethren, ye have done it unto me." The Church of God in its complete perfection at the last will be the City of God,—so says the Bible always, and there is meaning in the figure,—the manifoldness of life all uttering the indwelling God in the city which is the Church.

Let me take time to say one last word about what we must have before the partial and technical Christian life which we live now can pass into the full and universal life which I have tried to describe.

We must have, first, a deeper meditativeness in what we do. Our life so learns to lack the habit, that we almost fear lest it should come to lack the power of meditation. There is so little rest! There is such an unreasoning passion for activity! And so we skim the surface of all things; we never look down into their depths and see the power of help and culture which they might contain. We know no more of the real depth of our own lives than a child who crosses a frozen lake knows how deep the lake is. He does not even know that it has a depth. It seems all surface. But before our life can get depth into it, it must get God into it. God is the only power that deepens lives. A life with no intention of God in it *must* be shallow. And there is no life so hard and crusted that, if God does enter into it, He will not break its crust through and deepen it to untold richness.

But the only way that brings God into our lives is first to have Him in our hearts. The soul that has Him finds Him. " To him that hath shall be given." The new man takes the old circumstances, and, bringing God into them, makes of them the new life.

Arise, then, and go into the city. It is a word for each new Sunday which makes as it were for us a new beginning of our lives,—Arise and go into the city. You will find it the old city with the old streets and houses. You will find the new weeks what the old weeks were in all their outward circumstances. But they need not be the same old hopeless, meagre, thriftless things that other weeks have been. If you will only carry into them a new light, they will be new. If you will only take some new resolution, some bolder faith, best of all, —nay, only good of all,—if you will take Christ into them, how new and ever-renewing they will be—the beginning of the new heavens and new earth for you, fresh already with the everlasting freshness of eternity.

XII.

THE HOLINESS OF DUTY.

"Wherefore the law is holy."—ROMANS vii. 12.

ST. PAUL, in writing to the Jews and urging on them the Revelation of Jesus, encountered a question which is universal, but which came into special prominence among them. It was the question of the relation which the Law of God holds to His immediate personal presence and communion. The Jews had been drilled for years to obey the Law which God had given to them by the hands of Moses. Now Christ had come and said: "I manifest to you the God who gave the Law. Look at me and see, not His will only, see Him Himself,—His qualities, His holiness, His tenderness, His love." It was a higher life of personal communion which He offered, far above the life of obedience in which they had been living.

And at once Christ's coming made two classes among the Jews. Some of them rejected Him and some accepted Him. Those who rejected Him said: "We do not need Him. Moses is enough. There can be none greater than Moses. We do not desire any such spiritual life as He offers. Let us do our duty. Let us keep the Law and all is well."

Of this class were the better and earnest portion of the Pharisees. On the other hand, among those who accepted Christ, there were some who said: " Now Moses is obsolete. A mere servile obedience to law is not for those who have come into personal knowledge of God through His Son. We are the saints. We are above the Law." There are various indications of such a perversion of the spiritual nature of Christianity, precisely the same that came, at the spiritual revival of the Reformation, among the Anabaptists of the continent and of England. These were the two classes. One class held the Law of Moses to be absolute and final, and thought that obedience to its minute details constituted all of religion. The other class believed that obedience was a mere slavery when one had been admitted to the loftiest spiritual experiences. Against both of these classes St. Paul stands up with his simple assertion of the holiness of the Law. "The Law is holy," he declares. To the first class he says: " Obedience to Moses has a spiritual meaning, and if you would allow it, it would lead you on to Christ." To the second class he says: " No perception of and sympathy with Jesus can free you from the fundamental necessity of keeping God's Law. The Law and the Gospel belong together. Not merely the Gospel, but the Law, is holy." Borrowing his figure from the sight that they all saw in the streets each day, the slave leading a little boy to the teacher's house, he said, " The Law was our schoolmaster, to bring us unto Christ."

Times have all changed, but man is still the same, and this difference which St. Paul found lies so deep in human nature that there are the same two classes still. There are men of the Law and men of the Gospel still; that is, there are men whose pervading thought is duty, the doing of what they think they ought to do; and there are other men whose pervading thought is piety, the affectionate and spiritual relation of man to God. We know them both. The first man never speaks of anything like the Love of God, never talks about holiness, never struggles for spiritual experience, but he is always looking for what is right and doing it. The other man dwells much on the soul's life, loves God, and knows that God loves him, prays, reaches out after divine communion. And each of them is liable to the narrowness of his own kind. One of them makes nothing of spiritual experience, and says: " To do his duty—that is what a man is for. Let him do that, lovingly or unlovingly, believingly or unbelievingly, and there is the limit of his nature." The other always tends to count duty as low and says: " Commune with God. Be right at heart. The outward act is of small moment." This man calls the first man " moralist "; and the first answers back by calling him " pietist." It is the oldest among all the differences between earnest men. It has its origin in deep differences of character. And it calls for a constant assertion about all duty of what St. Paul asserted about the Law of Moses— that duty leads to piety and that no piety is true which has not the vigor of duty in it. The holiness of duty is a deep truth which both the moralist and the pietist need to know.

I want to speak about that truth to-day. I want to preach of duty in its relation to religion. I think there are a great many of you who are trying to do your duty, who almost anxiously disown having anything to do with religion. I want to show you, if I can, that the two cannot be separated.

There are, then, three possible powers by which the action of mankind is governed. They are the Law of Nature, the Perception of Right, and the Love of God. Government by the first power we call Impulse, by the second, Duty, by the third, Religion. And each of these has its tendencies towards the fuller government that follows it. Impulse, proving its insufficiency, gives way to Duty; and Duty, likewise finding the limit of its power, passes into Religion. Either of the first two that refuses to lead on to its successor, and counts itself the final, perfect government of man, fails and becomes corrupt. If we insist on living by nothing but Impulse, Impulse immediately loses its sacredness and becomes passion and waywardness; if we will own nothing higher than the power of Duty, which is conscience, conscience itself fails us, either by growing weak and indulgent, or by growing so hard and rigid that the passions rebel against it and there is terrible anarchy within. The first growth, the growth of Impulse into Duty, is told in that lofty poem of Wordsworth, the *Ode to Duty*, the noblest ethical poem of our language. There he recounts his own moral history in its first stage. He tells how, beginning simply under the direction of his impulse, doing what he chose to do, he came, not to flagrant vice, but to the dissatisfaction and restlessness and uncertainty of having no master, or rather of having a master who governed by no law that his subjects could know. And then he solemnly gives himself into the keeping of the higher government of Duty, to do not what he chose, but what he knew was right, and declares the peace and light that he expects by such a change of mastery:

Stern Lawgiver! yet thou dost wear
  The Godhead's most benignant grace;
Nor know we anything so fair
  As is the smile upon thy face:
    Flowers laugh before thee on their beds,
    And fragrance in thy footing treads;
    Thou dost preserve the stars from wrong,
    And the most ancient heavens, through thee, are fresh and strong.

To humbler functions, awful Power!
  I call thee: I myself commend
Unto thy guidance from this hour,—
  Oh, let my weakness have an end!
    Give unto me, made lowly wise,
    The spirit of self-sacrifice;
    The confidence of reason give;
    And in the light of truth thy bondman let me live.

That is the first great step in moral life—from Impulse into Duty. I hope that there are many of you who have taken it. I trust, as I look into these young people's faces, that I am looking upon many who, having "tired of unchartered freedom" and "felt the weight of chance desires," have commended themselves to the guidance of the "awful power" of duty, and are trying everywhere to do what is right. And now I want to impress it upon you that this is not the end, that this Duty is not the ultimate and original governor of the human soul, that she is the "daughter of the voice of God," that she gets its holiness from her relationship to Him, and that no man has fully honored or obeyed Duty who has not seen in her the authority and beauty of her Father, God.

All this appears in various ways. And first of all, I think, in a certain struggle of duty towards personality. See what I mean. It is no doubt possible to conceive of duty as perfectly impersonal. The great conviction of righteousness may seem to seize hold of nothing farther back than a strong current which runs mysteriously through all the world, setting toward the good and away from the bad. There is a certain grandeur in that abstract, impersonal conception. To identify oneself with that current, to be borne on toward goodness by this mysterious tendency that is in all things, to be in harmony with the deepest and best movement of the universe,—I own that that is an ambition which may illumine with its clear cold light the heart of man. We see it sweeping like the power of a voiceless, invisible wind across the world. Little and great things alike yield to it. To set oneself against it seems to be monstrous. To yield oneself to it seems to be noble.

We own all this, but then come deeper questions. What is the nature of this world-wide force? All force suggests the one only primary source of force of which we know, which is personal will. The force of gravitation makes us wonder whether there be not, somewhere, some one whose will it is that every atom should seek every other atom. But the force of morality is one that it is far less possible for us to think of as entirely impersonal. It appeals to the most personal and self-conscious part of us,— our conscience. Other tendencies we can, in some moods, fancy to have their lodgment in the very material particles of which the material universe is made, but of the tendency to righteousness our imagination can never picture that. It could come only from the character of some righteous Being, uttering itself in the processes of the world He governs. Let a man own the essential difference of right and wrong, and let him feel that the great central tendencies of this world are such as to foster the right and to repress the wrong, and he can be no atheist. The fact of moral government implies a moral governor. This is the first expression of the struggle of morality towards religion. This is the beginning of the holiness of duty.

But, again, there is another fact which I would call the *spiritual suggestiveness* of duty. Let me describe what I mean by that. Every attempt to do right has a tendency to reveal to us more spiritual ways of doing right, and our need of spiritual helps in doing it. For instance, a man determines to be honest. He conceives honesty in its narrowest and hardest form. It is the mere paying of debts to which he has legally bound himself. It is justice without mercy. I do not say that many a man who sets out to be honest remains forever at that point, never gets beyond that first hard, crude justice; but I am sure that when the determination is a truly moral one, when the man means to be honest solely because honesty is right, and not because honesty is profitable, there is a perpetual and beautiful tendency of his honesty to deepen and refine itself. He is always being urged on to see that the truly honest man not merely pays his notes, but honors the unwritten rights of all his brethren, is bound to give them what they cannot claim, must have a perfect truthfulness of heart as well as of word. So the ambition of honesty grows within him until it includes all tenderness and truth. It is a condition of the soul and not a habit of the life. If it were a mere habit of the life, it might be made by drill and discipline. If it be a spiritual condition, it can be reached only by spiritual inspiration. And so the man who, seeking honesty, began by making a resolution that he would not steal, by and by, when he recognizes the infiniteness of the task he has begun, is seen with hands reached out after spiritual help, crying, "Make me a clean heart, O God, and renew a right spirit within me."

Or take the duty of charity. You begin by giving a dollar to a poor man, because you ought to. That satisfies you at first. That is the highest notion of the duty of charity which you have reached. But, bear me witness, O, my friends, how the expansive nature of that duty opens! By and by you see that, not by giving the dollar, only by giving yourself, can you satisfy its claims. A keen, warm sympathy that makes your brother's need your own —nothing short of that is really charity. And to do that charity you must have—before you know it you find yourself praying for the Spirit of Him who gave Himself for us, who for our sakes became poor. That is what I meant by the spiritual suggestiveness of duty. Every duty presses out and demands its highest motive and its fullest action. It must have, therefore, the highest help. It becomes infinite and claims God. In that tendency of it lies another element of the holiness of duty.

But there is one thing more. Duty leads men into the presence of God, is the schoolmaster to bring us to Christ even more by its failures than by its triumphs, even more by what it cannot do than by what it lacks. What Duty lacks is the power of repair and restoration. I do not know what limit there is to the career over which the power of Duty might carry a man who was perpetually obedient, and never fell. Her hands are on his shoulders always. She guides him along, and hurries him from virtue into virtue. The course in which she leads him grows more and more spiritual. He is amazed and fascinated at the new visions of goodness that she opens to him. Hand in hand the man and Duty, the man led by Duty, they go sweeping along, triumphant, almost defiant, in their strength. So all goes well, till the man falls. He is disobedient. He sins. And then how everything is changed! Then Duty's power to help him is gone. Nay, it almost seems as if her will to help him is gone. She who led him stands over him, as he lies there; she cannot raise him up; she seems almost pitiless as she looks down upon him and says: " You are not what I thought you. I did not know how weak you were. I can do nothing more for you. Some one stronger than I must help you." And then, in that weakness which Duty has made manifest, but cannot cure, the man reaches past the exacting Duty to the forgiving and restoring God. O, my dear friends, if you have ever struggled bravely, enthusiastically, and then, in breaking down and sinning, have discovered that you needed something which struggle could not give you, then you know what all this means. You look back on that old struggle, and it seems beautiful and sacred to you; but its chief beauty and sacredness in your eyes is this—that it showed you your weakness and sent you to the strength of God to get what it could not give. As Duty stands upon the farther limit of her power, and sends the soul, for which she can no longer do what the soul needs, to Christ,—there is where Duty in her failure is noblest, and shows her completest holiness.

These, then, are the holy tendencies of trying to do right. No man really enters on that struggle but before him there loom up, dim and beautiful in the distance towards which his face is set, the highest attainments of the spiritual life. They are not to be reached by the mere powers which that struggle involves. They require, as we have seen, that that struggle should show its incompleteness, and should fail, in order that other powers may be found needed and be summoned to the soul's help. But still, partly by what it is to bring itself, and partly by what, through its manifested incompleteness, it is to set the man to seeking somewhere else, the struggle after righteousness is the gateway to the profoundest spiritual life.

How shall we think about the man of duty, the moral man, as he is commonly called? First of all, we must define him clearly to ourselves. We must not give the name where it does not belong. He is not a moral man who simply falls in with right practices because they are the settled standards of the community he lives in, or because on the whole he perceives that they tend to a man's prosperity. A very large part of the confusion which, in other days more than now, has broken out in pulpit denunciations of what were called "merely moral men," came, I think, just in this way—by allowing the name to men who were not moral men at all. A man is not a good man simply because he does good things. The moral man is he who does good things because they *are* good, who loves righteousness for itself, who obeys his conscience, who is willingly and heartily in the power of the current which sets through and under all things to uprightness, the man who means and tries to be good. Of such a man all that I have said is true. He is always being led towards the thought of a personal God. He is always discovering on some new side the infiniteness and spirituality of duty. He is always finding that as duty becomes more spiritual he needs more manifestly a spiritual helper. And as his efforts fail he is always being driven to seek a Saviour, some one who can rescue and repair his life. I do not believe that any man can be truly moral and yet be merely moral. His struggle to do right *must* bring him into the Divine Presence. "I will wash mine hands in innocency," says David, "and so will I go to Thine altar"; or as our Lord Himself declared, "If any man will do His will, he shall know of the doctrine." That is the holiness of duty.

This connection between the moral and the spiritual life is the key to all the history of the Jews and gives it all its interest. We ordinarily say that the Old Testament history was a preparation for the Messiah, the Law made ready for the Gospel. That is true, but that is not all. It was not simply that for two thousand years God was preparing for an event which only came when those two thousand years were over. It was that all through those two thousand years the Law of God was leading souls on into the Gospel which all the time was awaiting them. It was that always Moses was the door by which men came to a Christ who was always present. Through all those years, as any man tried to do what was right, the doors of spirituality opened before him, and he entered into some knowledge of the spiritual redemption. David said: "O, how I love thy Law"; and straightway he was led on to all those Psalms which are full of the anticipated spirit of Christianity. Obedience and spiritual vision brighten and darken together in perfect correspondence—that is the beauty of the Old Testament. "The path of the just is as a shining light which shineth more and more unto the perfect day." And when at last the supreme spiritual manifestation came, and Christ appeared, it was because the Jews had disobeyed the moral Law that they rejected the spiritual Gospel. In the description of our Lord's own parable, it was because the laborers had seized the vineyard for themselves that they killed the owner's son who came to claim it.

I think it is an interesting and a profitable speculation to consider what would come to pass if everything we call "religion" were to disappear from the earth to-day, and only conscience, only duty, should be left behind. It is what some people seem to desire. Imagine everything that belongs to the thought of God—all love to Him, all trust, all application for forgiveness—nay, even the knowledge of His existence, to be taken away, and what is left is conscience, the sense of right, and the impulse to do right which is in the human heart. What would the consequence be? I think there is no doubt. Either the conscience would be swept away, unable to stand alone, and mankind become a race of devils; or else conscience in its sore need would reach out its hands into the darkness and find for itself religion. We fear the first alternative; we fear, with almost certain apprehension, that what would come would be the moral devastation of the race. But, if in any way conscience proved itself too strong for that, then it would be a most interesting sight that we should see. The race would try in all its best parts to obey this mysterious monitor within. Men here and there and everywhere would be found trying to do right, not for any clear reason they could give you, but because something within them told them it was the thing for a man to do. But by and by, not starting from any one man's bold guess, but growing up as a misgiving and a hope in countless hearts,—as when before the sunrise millions of half-awakened particles of air are filled with dim suspicions of the coming sun,—there would be found moving among men the thought, struggling into a belief, that all this impulse of righteousness must be the echoing will of some righteous One,—the first conception of a God. And then, as Conscience went on, she would find the duties to which she gave birth outgoing her. They would put forth wings and fly where she could not follow them. And so their new needs would begin to guess at new supplies. Since here are spiritual tasks, somewhere there must be spiritual help.

And then would come failure and sin. Conscience would prove too weak. Her power would break, and yet her will would still be undiscouraged. Unable to give up her great attempt, and yet finding in herself no power of repair, it is inconceivable that she should not with one bold leap, bracing herself for it on the divinest instincts that she found in man toward his fellow-man, *guess at forgiveness*. She could not tell its method. She could not invent for herself the divine wonder of the Cross; but somehow, somewhere, she must hope that pardon and repair were waiting, and in the dim smoke of some altar she must send up her hope towards heaven—a God, a Guide, a Saviour. These would be her dreams, forced on her by the overwhelming necessi-

THE HOLINESS OF DUTY

ties of the task she had undertaken. And these are religion.

If among such a race there stood some keen observer, some one who knew of the old religion which had been taken out of the race to make room for this experiment of " mere morality," and who had seen it go with pleasure, how familiar would appear to him these *thoughts* and *hopes* as they issued from the heart of this struggling human nature—a God, a Guide, a Saviour! "Ah!" he would say, " Here are the old superstitions back again. The eradication could not have been quite complete. Some roots must have been left below when the tree was cut down to the ground." But no! That is not it. It would be something far more significant than that. It would be the holiness of duty declaring itself. It would be the human conscience by its divine necessity claiming religion.

And why should not that be true in a man which is true in a race? If all religion seems to be gone out of a man, if nothing spiritual lights up his life, what will you do? Pray for him? Yes, pray with all your might, with all your heart. But what will you try to get him to do? First of all, most of all, to do his duty, the duty that he sees. That duty, thoroughly done, must bring him into sight of God. There are a thousand cases where the unwillingness to do some right, the clinging to some old known sin, is what hinders the man from all the richness of the spiritual life. The giving up of the sin will not make the man spiritual. It is not taking off the stone that makes the grass grow where it lay; it only *lets* the grass grow. Here is perhaps the secret of the spiritual blight that is upon your life. Oh, if you are not spiritually minded, do not wait for mysterious light and vision. Go and give up your dearest sin. Go and do what is right. Go and put yourself thoroughly into the power of the holiness of duty.

We have reached, then, what is the beginning of light in all the darkness of the moral world. That darkness meets us everywhere. It is a sign not of clear-sightedness, but of superficiality and blindness, when a man says lightly and easily that all the world is clear to him, that the thick-crowding questions do not trouble him. They trouble most men sadly. How are the evil and the good distributed? Why, if goodness is the only joy, is goodness made so hard for men to reach? Why should truth be at once so necessary and so uncertain to the human soul? What is the meaning of all the seeming failures, the attempts that never come to anything, the souls that earn a little goodness and then lose it all, the lives that start upward and are beaten back by cruel circumstances? If there is a God and He is good, why is the world so full of wretchedness? I think there is an answer to every one of these questions, taken by itself, but all together they come flocking up about us, and the air is thick with them. You can kill every separate gnat easily enough, but the whole host of them together darkens the sun.

It is when the soul's light is really darkened by such questions that the real holiness of duty is made manifest. Then let Conscience speak. Then listen to her voice implicitly. However all these questions may be answered, whether or not they have an answer, *it is right to do right*, it is right to be honest, to be kind, to sacrifice yourself for others, to be pure. *It is wrong to do wrong.* It is wrong to be cowardly, or cruel, or dishonest, or impure. Take Duty by the hand and go where she will lead you. Then you have one strong thing to hold to in the midst of the confusion.

If this were all, if it led to nothing more, it would not satisfy us. Merely to go on doing duty, with no light—nothing to which the soul might fasten its affections, no answer opening to its questions anywhere—this could not satisfy a man who is both soul and conscience. The satisfaction comes as, gradually, Duty proves herself to be the usher to something greater than herself. It is very strange, I think, to see how very apt any strong sense of duty is to become religious. I turned over not long ago the pages of the *Harvard Biographies*, which many of you know, the lives of the graduates of Harvard who died in the war; and I could not but be struck by seeing how many of them, as their life grew deeper and more intense, became more and more religious, honored God as their Lord, trusted Him as their Father, and made His Son their friend. It was not fear of pain or death. They were not that kind of men. It was that, stung to higher duty than they had known before, all their best needs and powers had come out and, realizing the fulness of the nature God had given them, they had found indeed that "nor man nor nature satisfy whom only God created."

Suppose a moral man in Palestine, in Christ's days, in one of those remote and dingy villages, a man who, with small light, with Pharisees wearying him with their minute and meaningless ceremonial, and with a Sadducee or two singing scepticism into his ears, had still been trying to do right. He had struggled against temptation. He had been sober, honest, kind, and pure. A hard life and a noble one. But now suppose that Christ comes through that village, and, " as His custom was," the Saviour goes into the little synagogue or stops under the shadow of a house and talks with those who come. As He tells about His Father's house, about the grace that brings men back to God, about the inextinguishable love in the Divine Heart, about Himself as the Saviour, and repeats perhaps the parable of the prodigal son; especially as He stands there by His very presence offering Himself as the fountain out of which whosoever thirsts may drink,—who is the first who feels His power and answers to His call? Will any one come before that anxious man who has learned his needs by trying to do his duty? We can almost see his face settle into the repose of peace, and the lines of his anxious questioning fade out of it. Here is the solution of his problems, the satisfaction of his wants. He looks back and sees how all his struggles have been preparing for the day when he should meet this Saviour. The Law, his schoolmaster, has brought him to Christ. He looks back and is thankful for the holiness of duty.

I think that this is just the truth which many people need. You say: " I am not—I cannot be—

religious. There is nothing spiritual in me. I can do nothing holy." Oh, you are wrong! God has not made any soul destitute of that deepest and best prerogative of humanity,—the power to live by the unseen, to worship and love Him. But be you wrong or right your immediate course is clear. However you may think that holiness is closed to you, duty is open. You can do, to-day and to-morrow, what you know you ought to do. And O, my friend, remember that as long as you do not go in through that first and outmost vestibule, you have no right to complain that you do not reach the inmost chamber. As long as you are leaving plain duty undone, you have no right to say that you cannot be religious.

There is great beauty in the dignity with which this truth clothes the ordinary things of life. Duty is busied with small things. But to the things which Duty works with she imparts her own holiness. When her work is perfect and she has brought her souls to the completeness of Christ, they must look back and see a sacredness in everything over which they once conquered a temptation and made themselves do what they did not want to, but knew they ought to. And as any promise of that consummation opens to them now, they must already see some beginning of that sacredness in the material on which their daily task is done.

"The Law is holy." Count your law holy. See what your duty is, and count that duty sacred. Let no hardness or sordidness upon the face of it blind you to the great and blessed things which it can do for your soul,—and will, if you will only let it. First give yourself to it completely. Do it with all your strength. And then let it lead you beyond yourself. Or let it introduce you to your deeper self, to the needs and powers which require and can appropriate Christ. Let it bring you to the help of the Mercy Seat and the pardon of the Cross.

Duty shall never pass away. The hardness will be all gone out of it in heaven. But still there we shall do the right because we know we ought to do it; and thereby we shall be made more and more capable of the knowledge and the love of God to all eternity.

XIII.

PEACE WHICH PASSETH UNDERSTANDING.

"The peace of God, which passeth all understanding."—PHILIPPIANS iv. 7.

WHEN a man of disorderly and loose ways of thinking becomes excited, he will deal in mere exaggeration; but an orderly and clear thinker, the more earnest he becomes, will make all the clearer discriminations and use words with all the more definite meanings. St. Paul was very much in earnest when he said these words. He was invoking a rich blessing on his best-beloved disciples. And it seems to us perhaps, at first, as if it was merely a glowing and beautiful hyperbole when he desired for them "the peace which passeth all understanding." The words charm us with their cadence; and the idea as we vaguely discern it seems very rich,—a peace so deep, so high, so still, that no one can know how deep and high and still it is,— a surpassing, a transcendent peace,—this is what he seems to be asking for his friends. But that is not like Paul. He meant always something accurate. He loved preciseness of thought, and it was one sign of his greatness of mind that he could keep his thought clear and sharp even when it was glowing with feeling. It was not blurred by its warmth and fire. He meant, then, by the "peace which passeth all understanding" not merely a certain degree, but a certain kind, a certain quality of peace. I want to study his expression with you and see if we can know what he is talking of. If we can, we shall do well; for this "peace which passeth all understanding" is really the whole Christian life seen from one of its richest and completest sides.

Peace is the under-desire of all work and life. No matter what struggle men are involved in, and no matter how much men enjoy their struggle, there always is below their labor a wish for peace, a sense that peace is the final and ideal condition of all things. No man who has crossed the border of barbarism or who has any idea of life above that of a bandit and a robber, will ever dare openly to proclaim that tumult and confusion and war are the true and permanent conditions for humanity to live in. The soldier delights in war and chafes at the very thought of stagnant, peaceful days, but still he dares propound no theory except that war is a temporary thing, the purifier of corruption, the settler of old quarrels, and so the true builder of a higher peace. The reformer shakes the foundations of old institutions, but his plea must always be that he seeks to dig deeper and lay stronger the great stones on which he may construct the new. The sceptic touches with his withering finger the fairness of a soul's belief and brings confusion where there used to be the placidness of an accepted creed, but hardly any thinker has ventured to praise scepticism as the true resting-place (or floating-place) of a human spirit. The disturbance of faith always claims to be in order to a readjustment of faith. So everywhere peace and not war is the desire,—nay, peace is the under-desire out of which war springs. War is the means, peace is the end. There may be always tumult about us here; but, whether men's dispositions make them look back or forward, they always discern peace in the distance —a Golden Age behind or a Millennium before.

And this universal desire of peace is the reason why men have pictured it so differently to themselves. What all men wish and no man completely has, each man will image to himself after his own character. It is the universal ideals of the race— Freedom, Strength, Peace—which have been most variously conceived, and so most often misconceived. This is the reason why the sources and the character of peace are so differently pictured by different men, and by different men at different stages of their lives. Now, as we think of St. Paul's life, we can see that there must have been two different ideas of peace—that is, of repose and entire satisfaction— in his mind at different periods of his career; and a comparison of these two will give us at once the fundamental idea of what he said to his Philippians. Paul appears to us first, you remember, as a Jewish student. In the Gamaliel period of his life his object was to learn. Truth, as it could be brought to the understanding, was the object of his appetite; and when he looked forward and thought of the ideal of life, it was of a mind which, having studied abstract truth and human nature and the Word of God, had adjusted all their relations, settled every question, and understood the whole. By and by there happened a great change in his life and he became the servant of Jesus Christ. A new ambition opened to him, a new appetite was stirred. The heart and the spiritual nature asserted their supremacy; and now the peace which loomed in sight and gradually closed around and filled his life with its promise, was the rest of the nature upon that new Master in dependence and in loyalty.

These were the two: Paul the young student was trying to understand the world so that he might harmoniously adjust himself to it, compel its powers to answer his demands, force it to satisfy his ambitions,—it was the mastery of his *mind* making the world his servant; Paul the Apostle was trying to get nearer to Christ by more perfect obedience and love,—it was the *heart* fastening itself upon a perfectness which it loved and whom it trusted. Here are two different conceptions of peace,— one of mastery, the other of dependence. One is conquered by the mind; the other is bestowed upon the heart. One is within the range of the understanding which analyzes and investigates its grounds; the other goes beyond or passes the understanding and relies upon a Being who, in unknown ways and out of infinite resources, provides and supports the entirely reliant life.

As soon as we contrast in any way those resources and helps which come to men through the intelligence and through the heart, as soon as we claim for the heart a power to lay hold on truth which the understanding cannot grasp, we invite of course the ready criticism of sentimentalism and feebleness. But it is needful to assert the true dignity of the human heart, to claim that, rightly conceived, it is neither the jealous antagonist nor the feeble ally of the human intelligence. Rightly conceived, the heart is the completeness of the man, outgoing but embracing the intelligence and reason. The heart cannot be truly given to any work unless the judgment approves; but the giving of the heart is something far larger, richer, fuller, than the approval of the judgment. You can not truly love a man unless your intelligence endorses him; and yet the endorsement of the intelligence is only the beginning. Then comes in the love, and through its warm atmosphere your friend gives to you and you give to him what never could have passed back and forth through the cold medium of the intelligence. No; the heart is larger than the understanding, and through it may come messages and gifts which the understanding has no power to bring.

Have we not, then, already seen something of what the distinction is? There is a peace within the understanding, and there is a peace that goes beyond the understanding and finds its warrant in personal trust and love. The peace within the understanding is the result of a clearly perceived proportion between need and supply, between danger and precaution: "I have seen what peril is likely to occur, and I have guarded against it; I have found out all the weak points in my house where the fire or the hurricane might smite it, and I have strengthened and secured them; therefore I may dismiss my anxieties and sit down at rest."

The peace which goes beyond the understanding says: "I have done all this as well as I knew how, but there are regions of danger which I cannot explore, there are perilous forces which I cannot measure. The universe is large, and out of any distant corner of it there may come a sudden blow striking right at my life. Beyond what I can provide for, then, I find out Him who is in all the universe, and, loving Him, I trust myself upon His love. It is not knowledge, now, of what will come or how it can be met; it is only the sympathetic apprehension of His love and care who is all-strong, all-wise. This is what I rest upon. This is **the** confidence in which I sleep by night and work by day."

It is a peace which passeth understanding and fulfils itself in love.

It is easy to comprehend, because the difference is everywhere. You are on a great ocean steamer, and you go through its wilderness of machinery and see how part is fitted into part and every danger is provided for. Perhaps you know enough about it all to understand how thoroughly the work is done, and to be sure that mechanical art can make no better. Then you go and lie down in your berth and feel safe. But can your safety come from what you have seen and understood? Must it not come finally from something which you cannot see and cannot understand? The final confidence must be personal confidence. It must be on the skill and faithfulness of the captain who uses and commands all this machinery that you ultimately rely. Only on character finally can peace be built, and while we use our understandings to discover characters, our deepest knowledge of them still must come by intuitions that surpass the reason.

The peace that lies within the understanding is what men are seeking everywhere in some of its many forms. Think what two or three of them are. In the first place there is the peace of a sufficient fortune. A man says: "If I can be rich I shall be secure." He counts up the dangers one by one: "Hunger, thirst, cold, heat, fatigue, exposure — yes, I can avoid them all if I am rich. Money can build the house and spread the table and hire the servants. These needs and money meet each other." And so the struggle begins, and the competent fortune by and by is earned. And what then? All that his understanding has anticipated is fulfilled. He *is* warm and dry, and has the food that he desires. The machine is fed with its due nutriment and runs its course perfectly. Only this comes, —that when a need arrives which the mere understanding has not anticipated, when the heart which lies out of the region of the understanding lifts up its voice and demands its satisfaction, or when the conscience grows restless and exacting—then this adjustment which has been arranged between money and the animal wants fails and falls short. Here is a further need, and somewhere there must come forth a further supply. And so the town is full of rich men who are not finding in their riches the satisfaction which they ought to find. They can reason it all out; they ought to feel safe and rest secure, but they are all restlessness. They have earned peace, but it does not come to them. From regions out beyond comes a disturbance and unrest for which they have made no provision.

This same is true of all the self-sufficiencies of life, of all the peace that builds itself only on prosperity. A man is thoroughly well and strong, and every relationship with all his fellow-men is bright and happy. He lives with them in that happy condition in which he never seems to need their help, and yet they are always ready to lavish their help upon him. No care nor sickness seems to break in on his lot. He has plenty of work to do, yet not a work to wear him out. In bodily condition and in well-adjusted relationships he seems to be fit for and equal to his task of life. No doubt such a man is at peace up to a certain line. His quiet home, his calm, smooth-flowing days, proclaim it. He matches his dangers against his power and seems to see how he can meet them all. It is the peace of self-sufficiency. It is a peace within his understanding.

But on what does the permanence of that peace depend? Upon the preservation of that balance between the powers and the dangers. Every glimpse of dangers which these powers cannot match, every suggestion of the decay or loss of these powers of health and independence destroys the balance instantly. That is what disturbs the complacency of a prosperous man of the world when some great demand—the need of spiritual conversion or the necessity of death — looms in his sight. *There* is something which is not provided for in all the armory of his self-sufficiency. *There* is a demand for which his well-stocked life can furnish no supply. *There* is a need which goes beyond his understanding, and only by a reliance which goes beyond the understanding, too, only by reliance on an Infinite Person can these infinite necessities be met.

All this is plainest, I suppose, with reference to the peace of the intellect, the peace which a man has in the truth which he holds. There, more than anywhere else, we can discern the difference between the peace which lies within the understanding and the higher peace which passeth understanding. Here is the universe all full of questions, the problems about truth starting on every side. Suppose that a man thought that he had found the answers to them, that in some creed or system which he had embraced all difficulties were dissolved. He could tell why evil is permitted, and how men shall be judged, and what this continual difference of the fortunes of mankind means. He and his system had fathomed all the depths, unravelled all the contradictions.

There must be a strong satisfaction in a feeling such as that. No wonder that men seek it. No wonder that with one oracle or another men are always trying to think that they have got completely rid of doubt, and answered all the questions, and banished mystery out of the world. That is the peace of the understanding, the pure self-satisfaction of the intellect which seems to be quite sufficient for its task. Perhaps some time some of us have had a dream like that. Perhaps we lived in such a dream some time, and then what happened? What became of it? Simply some question came that defied us to answer it. Some one of the old questions that we thought were answered woke at some provocation of our own experience and pressed home on us with its sharp spear pointed with fire. Our peace was shattered. The settled was not settled. The trim, snug answers burst and broke with the swelling problems. Ah, how continual such terrible surprises are! Who does not know such experiences?

> Just when we are safest, there's a sunset-touch,
> A fancy from a flower bell, some one's death,
> A chorus-ending from Euripides,
> And that's enough for fifty hopes and fears,
> As old and new at once as Nature's self,
> To rap and knock and enter in our soul,
> Take hands and dance there, a fantastic ring,
> Round the old Idol, on his base again,—
> The grand Perhaps!

Thus was the peace made and built up within an understanding broken and lost by the reasserted mystery of life—the little creed overcome by the great world. And what then? Unless *out of that mystery itself* could come a peace, there was no hope. Unless it all—vague, infinite as it was—

could be possessed and filled with a Being whom we knew, and who from His home far beyond our understanding called to us and took us to Himself, we were all lost. God grant that that *has* come, that out beyond the creeds and systems we believe in we have come to believe in God, taking our satisfaction and content that all is well, not from our mind's discernment of the goodness of each detail, but from our soul's assurance of His love and power. If that has come, then a new peace has opened on us, a peace in Him, a peace of soul and not of mind, a peace of love and not of reason, a peace not hedged and bounded by our own intelligence, a peace that passeth understanding, and is sure of all things because it is sure of Him.

How can I possess my soul in peace when so much everywhere is in disturbance? I do not, cannot, dare not, say that I can see the right in every wrong, the light in every darkness, but when I know that God is, and that He sees what I cannot see, only then comes the higher peace,—

> Well roars the storm to those who hear
> A deeper voice across the storm.

Is it not clear, then? Within the world which our understandings can embrace there is a peace which we can estimate. Its assurance lies in a comparison of clearly seen dangers with clearly seen supplies. I see such and such expenses, and lo, here is the money to meet them with. I know of this or that strain coming, but, behold! I am well and strong and prosperous, and I can bear it. Here are hard questions, but here in the other hand are their sufficient answers.

If life stopped there, all would be well. But life will not stop there. Never can we say: "Now I have provided for the last danger and answered the last question—'Soul, thou hast much goods laid up for many years.'" Before the words are out of our lips another danger, a new question, comes down upon us out of the infiniteness of life behind us. There is where the peace of self-sufficiency breaks down. We men here on the shore of human life, with just a little of its very border appropriated, seem to be like Crusoe on the beach of his unknown island. We guard against a few immediate dangers, we build our hut and our stockade, we plant our plot of corn, we light our fire, and we load our gun, and then we sit down and try to call *that* peace and safety. And as we sit there we feel how little way our peace extends. How little of the island we have comprehended! Our peace stops at the line of trees which backs our little beach with its dark shadow. Beyond that all is mystery and danger. What foe may come out from it upon us at any moment we cannot tell.

I appeal to your own knowledge of your own lives to testify to what I say. Is there not, with the most safely guarded of us, a haunting sense of something that money or health or prosperity or study cannot do? We know they all exhaust themselves. We know there is a region of human need which they are powerless to enter. What is there that can help us there? what peace beyond our understanding and our planning? More than we know, that question lies heavily upon many of our souls which seem easy and careless.

And to that question the soul gives its answer in one great word—"God." Beyond our understanding and our planning, inhabiting and filling with Himself that unexplored region, the Source and Governor of all that issues from it, there is God, " the high and lofty One that inhabiteth eternity." It is by apprehending Him that the infinity in which He dwells becomes peaceful and secure for us. And He is apprehended not by the understanding, but by the heart. The understanding tells us that He is, but it is the heart that goes forth after Him and finds Him, and fastens itself upon Him, and in Him makes the infinity in which He dwells its own.

Once more recur a moment to the figure which we used. Still we may think of the man living upon the strip of beach which is all that he has apprehended, where he has built his house and set up his defences; only now the great wilderness behind him, though unexplored by him, is known to and governed by one whom he knows, in whom he trusts and who in many ways has shown his goodness to him. So, when a man loves God, back from the little fragment of life which he knows, stretches the great immensity of life which he cannot know, which passes his understanding, but which God understands, and so which, while it never loses its mystery, loses all its fear for the servant of God who is in communion with his Lord through love.

Is not this what St. Paul means? "The peace of God which passeth all understanding," he says. It is first a peace which God possesses. No fear, no trouble in the universe can touch His perfect mind. He knows, He governs all. With Him the peace is self-contained. It is absolute self-sufficiency.

What thought can be more rich or solemn than this of God so utterly filling the universe with Himself that out of no unexplored corner of it can start any anxiety to surprise Him? His pure peace in Himself—how it throws out in contrast the frightened, anxious, nervous lives we live! This is the "peace of God," the peace which God has that passes our understanding; but, then, that peace is communicable to us—not through the understanding, for that does not reach far enough to take it, but through love. It is something which He may give to us, something on which we may enter as we enter into Him; and then for us, too, there is safety in those realms of life where, save as we go in Him by love, we cannot go at all.

Ah, you watch some poor, ignorant, faithful soul taking up a duty that you see is endless, giving himself to a sacrifice that reaches to the very sundering of soul and body! He does it with a calm, bright face, and you think that he is ignorant, he does not know what he is doing. "My poor friend," you say to him, "have you weighed the cost? Do you know where that task will carry you? Do you know that you can meet the labor and the suffering that it will bring?" "No," he replies, "I know nothing. I know only God, and He is in the task which He has given; and let it carry me where it will, it cannot carry me beyond Him." That is the peace of God which passeth understanding. A little child is putting a fearless foot down into the river beyond which lies eternity. "Poor child," you say, "do you know the eternity which you are going to? Do you know what you will do, what you will *be*, in that mysterious land? Do you understand immortality?" "No," he replies, "I understand nothing. But I love God. I am going to Him. And eternity is not so vast that, in all of it, I can go beyond Him." That is "the peace of God which passeth all understanding."

And this makes very plain to us the work of Christ. What does He do for us? What was He doing in the struggle of His life? What was He doing on His cross? What is He doing forever at His Father's throne? *He is giving us the peace of God.* And how? By making God real to us, and bringing us to God. All is for that. He reconciles us to God. He takes a poor rebellious, restless life; He touches it with His power; He wakens its capacity for gratitude; He makes it penitent and then forgives it; He breaks away the obstacles that lie between it and its Father: He casts His own love into the deep gulf and fills it. And then over that filled gulf the love of the changed soul can go unhindered to God and lay hold upon Him. And there, in Him, it finds the peace it never knew before—a peace that covers every region which God's life covers, a peace which goes where the understanding cannot go, and faces the spectres of the spirit and the conscience, and subdues them in the strength of God.

"There is no peace, saith my God, to the wicked." How could there be? The essence of wickedness is that it is separation from God. And so it cannot have the peace of God. All fear belongs to it. But Christ takes the soul out of its wickedness and brings it to God, and there its peace begins. Once more to turn back to our figure: Christ is the Son and Other Self of Him to whom belongs the infinite land upon whose beach we live. And He comes down to where we are encamped, and, at all sacrifice of Himself, tells us of the love of Him who owns it all and wins our love for Him. This is the peace He brings, His peace which he "leaves" among us.

I am afraid—nay, I am sure—that much which I have said to you to-day seems to a good many of you very mystical. What do we mean by mystical? Beyond our understanding! But it is not to the weakest of us, it is often to the very strongest of us that, many and many a time in life, the narrowness of the understanding grows oppressive and we long to look beyond it. Often, as we sail so steadily on, *from* what and *into* what we know so little, we long to forget the clank of the machinery by which we sail, and to stand on the rolling deck and look out into the mystery of the ocean on which we sail. That mystery of life is God. Shall I guard and watch my engines and never question the ocean and the sky? Shall I watch and guard my business, and never, by prayer, by obedience, by communion, draw near to and ask the deepest things of Him? The soul that loves God has entered into that mystery of His Being. To it come intimations of His Will which it cannot analyze or justify, but which it follows as the laws, the secrets, of its life. To it comes knowledge which men may call foolishness, but which it knows is deeper truth. On it rests a peace which passes understanding, but is full to the outmost borders with living love.

Oh, do not be afraid to let your love carry you beyond your understanding. Our danger is not mysticism. Let the higher life sound to you as mystical and cloudy as it will, nevertheless, enter into the cloud without a fear. Follow Christ, by earnest faith, by obedience, by loving imitation, trying everywhere to keep near to Him by being like Him, and He will lead you certainly to God and to "the peace of God which passeth all understanding."

XIV.

THE RELATIVE AND THE ABSOLUTE.

"And there was also a strife among them, which of them should be accounted the greatest."—LUKE xxii. 24.

THE strife was among the disciples of Jesus, and it took place at the very table where He sat with them on the night before His crucifixion. We say "How strange it was!" and it was very strange, indeed. That the personal presence of their Master should not have taken those men up above all question of precedence or superiority, and made each rejoice to hope and believe that the other was a greater man and a better disciple than himself,—this certainly was strange. But, after all, there is something to be gained out of the story, in the reminder which it gives us that these men were still men, that even with Christ visibly among them, the occupation of their natures by His power had to be gradual and slow, and so that we must not be too ready to despair either of ourselves or of each other. It ought to make us see how the new power of Christ does not destroy, but purifies and uses the faculties and dispositions which it finds in man. This last will be the special lesson from the story on which I shall dwell to-day.

Think, then, of that old picture. Artists have tried to put it upon canvas, and not one of them has satisfied that imagination of it which has been bright in Christian souls that saw in it the essence of their faith. Jesus, the Master, sits at the table, and all around Him are His twelve disciples. He is the Life, and so His presence sheds vitality on every side. It is like the sun shining on a fertile field; all kinds of dispositions and emotions spring up freely. Love, regret, indignation, resolution, expectation—these and a host of others are all there. And among all the rest, out of these fruitful hearts quickened by the warm sunshine of Christ's nature present with them, springs up emulation. The disciples begin to look suspiciously on one another. The clear air becomes thick with comparisons. They are not content to be asking simply how great and good each of them can be, but there grows up in each soul a desire to be greater and better than the others. There is a strife among them which of them shall be accounted the greatest.

We want, first of all, to recognize how perfectly natural this is. There are two ways in which a man may estimate his progress and the position which he holds at any moment. There is the absolute method, and there is the comparative method. Take your profession. You are engaged in some one of the great recognized departments of human action. You have been engaged in it for a long time. You have been working as a mechanic, a lawyer, a merchant, or a physician for many years. You ask yourself some morning, "How do I stand to-day?"

I am sure there is no better test of what sort of man you are than the way in which you go about to get your answer. More significant than the answer which you get is the way in which you go about to get it. On the one hand, you may look round and see how other men are doing. You may take men whose life in your profession is recognized as a success, and ask yourself whether you are as successful as they. "Am I as honest, as prosperous, as well esteemed as this man or as that man who, upon the whole, is accepted as a fair specimen of what a man in this profession ought to be?" You try to find your true place in a long scale marked and graduated by the greater or less attainment of your brethren. That is the comparative method of self-estimate.

On the other hand, instead of looking about upon your brethren you may sit down and try to realize absolutely what your profession and the man working in it ought to be. You try to summon back that vision of it which you saw burning before your imagination when you first set out upon it. You summon its essential principles and pure ideas. You ask yourself how far you have satisfied the final purposes for which your occupation has its being in the world. That is the absolute method of self-estimate.

The difference is clear. And if we let ourselves think, not of two men calmly judging of their lives in these two ways, but of two men living their lives under the impulses which these two ways of judgment will create,—then the difference is more striking still. One man is anxious to outstrip as many of his brethren as possible; the other is anxious to get as near as possible to the true standard of his occupation. One is all keenly alive with rivalry; the other is earnestly set upon attainment.

When we state it thus, I think we see at once how the absolute method and impulse are finer and higher than the comparative, and at the same time we realize how largely the comparative method and impulse rule the lives of men. Look at the boy at school; is it always pure love of learning that makes him struggle so to learn his lesson? Surely not! It is the passion to outstrip the other boys and win the head of the class or the medal that shall show he has surpassed them. Look at the busy citizen, eager in all public affairs, restless, observant, impatient, putting a useful hand to necessary tasks of every kind. Is it a simple public spirit that inspires him? Surely not! A desire to be first among the citizens, to be more valued by his fellow-citizens than any other—that certainly is a large part of what we see kindling in his eye and moving in his tireless hands and feet. It is a race, not merely to do the distance and to do it in a certain time, but to do it in shorter time than other men,—that is what makes it fascination. To see our fellow-runner, who is far in front of us at first, grow nearer as we gain upon him, and by and by to feel ourselves close at his side; and then to hear his footfalls die away behind us as we shoot far ahead,—that is a large part of the fascination of the running. To take out competition, to bid each man do his work from the pure impulse of the work itself, to bid each man run round the race-course of his life alone, do we not know what listless runners that would make?

When we talk thus of rivalry or emulation, we see immediately its dangers and how great they are. We see how rivalry must oftentimes be tempted to detract from the good name of others, and to hold those back whom it is hard to keep up with or surpass. That is one danger. And there also is the danger of too easy self-content, the danger which comes to all of us when we have found no competitors in any particular race whom we could not outstrip, and yet are far from having put forth all the power that is in us, or from reaching the goal which is the only really worthy satisfaction.

Among the men whose struggles are comparative, not absolute, the ugly, envious faces and the complacent, satisfied faces are too common. If they are strugglers hard-pushed by their competitors, they grow jealous; if they have won their victory and are no longer likely to be outrun, they grow self-satisfied. To be eager and earnest, and yet not to want to hinder any other man from doing his best; to be calm and serene, and yet to be full of energy and hope of higher things,—this comes to him whose life aims at the absolute, who strives, not to be stronger than his brethren, but to be ever stronger than himself, ever nearer to the fullest strength which it is in him to obtain.

Rivalry and emulation, then, if they have their places at all in a well-ordered human life, as impulses of action, must be satisfied to be wholly subordinate and accidental. Two regiments start side by side to storm the works of the enemy. On their fierce rush across the plain each may well be stimulated by the desire to beat the other and come first to where the hand-to-hand battle must be fought; but the real inspiration must be in the frowning guns of the foe and the determination that they must be taken.

One would like to speak urgently and earnestly to the young people here, and remind them of how much of the solidity and independent strength of life depends upon their learning very early to depend upon absolute and personal relations to the objects which they desire. Insist on feeling the intrinsic power of the things you seek. So, and so only, can you be sure that even if every other seeker should become discouraged and drop away, your search would still go on. You start upon a course of reading or of study with congenial companions. A generous rivalry begins at once. Who will be quickest and most faithful? Who will pierce most deeply and directly to the author's meaning? That is very good, of course. But if that be all, or be the principal thing, the whole enterprise is weak. The book itself, the author's valuable thought, the truth he has to tell,—in these must be the real attraction. If you are really set on these, then you may gladly accept the stimulus and pleasant excitement which comes from matching mind with mind among your fellow-students; just as a ship bound for the North Pole may easily indulge, some sunny day, in a friendly race with another ship, bound for the same mysterious goal, which it has met on some great, free expanse among the icy seas; but the true purpose of the voyage, the thing which keeps the ship stern and determined, and makes it safe not to be misled by the fascinations of the race, is the unseen purpose of its voyage, the mysterious pole whose deeper fascination has drawn it out of its home-harbor and keeps it steadfast on its way until it finds its prize, or turns back before a hopeless obstacle, or goes down in the midst of storms it cannot weather.

It is not only the persistence of life, it is also the purity of life, which is secured by service of the absolute. The eagerness which comes by rivalry not merely is unreliable and ready to give way, but while it lasts it is of poorer quality than the eagerness which comes from a real desire for the essential natures of the things we see. The essential nature of things has its true and constant relations to the soul of man. The two are made to answer healthily to one another. Learning shines upon its hill-top, and the desire to know in the soul of man leaps up to greet it. Strength calls from the distance with its rugged voice, and the desire to be strong which is in man hears and answers to the call. The struggle and search which follow until the purpose is attained are legitimate and pure. There is no base admixture of low motive. But rivalry, the desire to outstrip our brethren, is always trembling on the brink of jealousy and spite. It is so easy to pull down the reputation which is a little too high for us to match; it is so hard to be glad of the good thing which another man does, when it makes the less good thing which we are doing seem poor and insignificant. And even when the temptation to spite and jealousy is resisted, and the rivalry is absolutely generous and fair, and the victory is honorably ours, the whole side issue of comparison is an alloy and distraction to that pure desire for a noble thing which, quite apart from the attainment of the thing, is one of the noblest educations of a human life.

There is yet another danger that comes from giving rivalry too large a place among our impulses. It lies in the temptation to limit our lives to those companionships in which we can easily be first, and so losing the broader fields of action in which we should get the greatest exercise and growth, even though we were constantly outstripped. "Better be first man in this small village than second man in Rome," we cry; and so we shut ourselves up in the village where we can be first, and all the great inspirations and delights and cultures of Rome are lost. How many men are doing this! What multitudes of souls are spending their lives in playing children's games, because they know the petty cards and can easily beat in them, and letting the brave man's work which they ought to be doing, but in which they fear to be outstripped by other men, lie undone. How one wants to cry to them: "For shame! Go and meet men worthy of your manhood. Go and match yourself with the best men you can find. Go and be beaten. It is better to be beaten in wrestling with the strongest than to win a thousand battles over adversaries just a little weaker than yourself. By such defeats you grow strong. By such victories you grow ever feebler as you become more proud!"

All that is good to say. It is good to bid men run races with feet swifter than their own. But is it not better still to beg them to make as little as possible of the race-running motive altogether? Do not think about outstripping each other; think of getting to the goal! Let your whole soul be set on God, on getting to Him. Entering into Him, filling your life with His, *then* look round with joy at every progress which other souls are making towards that only satisfaction of a human life. Cultivate everywhere the habit of dealing directly with the absolute, and the merely relative and comparative ways of estimating life will come to be profoundly uninteresting to you. You will not care for much which now seems to you of vast importance. "He is the best athlete, the best lawyer, the best merchant, the best Christian in the town,"— that will sound very tame and uninteresting to you. You will not care whether it is true or not when you have really seen the perfection of those attainments shine before you, and your soul is set on being the best athlete, the best lawyer, the best merchant, the best Christian that it is possible for you to be. Only in pursuit of the absolute comes freedom from the slavery of the relative, with its rivalries and comparisons, with its close atmospheres and small satisfactions, and restlessness and jealousy and spite!

I want to turn now to Jesus, and see how in the story which we have before us He dealt with this disposition of rivalry of which I have been speaking at such length, and which he found breaking out in His disciples. I cannot doubt that in general His way of dealing with it was that which I have been trying to describe. The whole great spirit of His Gospel was forever trying to draw men away from the slavery of the relative into the freedom of the absolute. He never encourages men to compare themselves with one another. He is always bidding them be perfect like their Father. He hardly ever says, "Outstrip one another." He almost always says, " Come to me."

And yet it would not be hard to quote passages in which Jesus recognized the power of comparison, and stimulated His disciples by bidding them see how their lives stood beside the lives of others of God's servants. He told them of John the Baptist that no man born of woman had surpassed him in true greatness. He warned the cities of the Lake of Gennesaret that the men of Nineveh had been more ready to hear the word of God than they.

Jesus, then, does not ignore the power of comparison. He does not ignore any of the powers which have their essence in the very constitution of humanity. That is His glory. He takes two powers and says of one: "This is the noblest. Do your work with this by all means, if you can." But He does not forbid the using of the lower power if only it be pure, and be kept in its true degree, and be used rightly. "This ought ye to have done, and not to leave the other undone."

But there is another thing which He does often,

and which it seems to me that He does here. He takes the lower power and makes it higher than it is often made, and rescues it from many of its dangers, by suggesting a higher method of its use.

For powers are not invariable in their character. They vary with their uses. They grow finer when they are used on finer things. The power of thought grows subtle as it deals with subtle problems. The power of imagination becomes more radiant when it is picturing the possibilities of the celestial life than when it paints some base indulgence of the earthly nature.

This is the principle which Christ applies to the power of rivalry. He sees His disciples in danger of using it for low purposes, and so of making it a low thing. They wanted to compete for tawdry reputation and position,—"which of them should be accounted the greatest?" Such a use of it would make the power itself tawdry. Jesus says: "No! If you must use the power use it for a fine, unselfish thing, and so make it fine and unselfish." And then he tells them what that use shall be. "He that is greatest among you, let him be as the younger; and he that is chief as he that doth serve."

How deep and wise and fine that is! Jesus says: "Must you then compete with one another? Must one be greater and the other less? Must you then use this power of competition? It might be better if you did not use it at all; but, if you must use it, make it as noble as you can by using it on noble things. Use it for human good. See not who shall be splendidest, but who shall be most useful.

Let your rivalry be a rivalry in self-sacrifice and in laborious doing of good. Compete with one another in humility. See which can be the truest servant."

As if one took a stream which had been running waste in low and muddy places, and with a strong hand collected it and shut it up into its channel and turned it to the fields which needed and could welcome its fertility, so was it when Christ took this wasted, dissipated power of rivalry and said to it: "Come here. Here is your true work. Do this noble work nobly, and it shall ennoble you!" We can almost hear the stream laugh in its delight as it recognizes its true task. We can almost see the power lift itself to mightier proportions as it beholds the worthy work which it is called to do.

Imagine the difference to the disciples when they once really grasped the new teaching of their Master. They might very likely have looked for a rebuke. They might have expected that their Master would have forbidden them to use this power of rivalry at all; but this is different. He says: "Use it,—but use it for higher and holier purposes. Use it not to surpass one another in honor and esteem, but use it to increase the amount of usefulness and brother-help." How the sword which they were just grasping, of which they were ashamed, which they expected to see snatched out of their hands, must have flashed into a new and surprising splendor when they saw in the light of Christ's words to what noble uses it might be put!

If they did what Christ bade them do, as in some

good degree they did, they must have been the subjects of a continually increasing surprise. The old power, transfigured by its new use, must have amazed them with its possibilities. Behold! there could be rivalry without hate or grudge. Behold! they could struggle to beat and yet rejoice to be beaten; for if they were beaten when they made their most earnest efforts to be useful, it merely meant that their brethren had more power of usefulness than they, and so the thing for which they strove became more perfectly accomplished.

I ask myself what would be the result if the same teaching of Jesus should be spoken to and should be accepted by all of this great world of competing men. Here are these eager hearts all eager to outstrip each other. Rivalry sparkles in every eye, and is the restless, almost frantic power which keeps all this life alive. Suppose some mighty power could take it all and make a change. Rivalry is not abolished, but the object of rivalry is altered. Not now, who shall be richest, or who shall be most powerful, or even who shall be most learned?—but who shall be most useful, who shall be most absolutely devoted to the good of fellow-man?—that is the question. The eagerness is kept just as intense. The city glistens and palpitates with the same active life. Each man upon the street watches his neighbor with the same keen vigilance. Only the purpose of it all is altered. It is a competition of beneficence. It is a rivalry of self-sacrificing service. All these men want to surpass each other by doing a little more good, by taking a little more of the burden of life upon their shoulders, by relieving a little more of misery, by lifting a few more of the fallen out of the mire!

You say it is impossible. You say it is a dream. I answer that I know nothing about that, and I do not think you know much more than I do. I think that more impossibilities are possible and more dreams are coming true than we have any idea of. But what I want you to observe is this,—that if such a great rivalry of unselfish service ever should come to pass, it would probably free itself almost entirely from those evils of which, as we have seen, our present rivalries stand in such danger. Tell me, can you imagine him whose only competition with his brother is, which shall drag the most men out of drunkenness—not which shall get the *credit* of saving the most men, but which shall really save them—the whole impulse which creates the competition being the pity for the men's perdition,—can you imagine *that* man hindering his brother-worker from doing some act of salvation for fear that his brother-worker's list of rescued should exceed his own? Tell me, can you imagine the man, capable of entering into such a rivalry, deliberately drawing in his life and consorting only with the least useful people, so that he may not feel himself outstripped?

Such questions answer themselves. This nobler use to which the power has been put has in large degree robbed the power of its danger. It has preserved its best and cast out its worst tendencies. It has kept all its energy and cast out all its narrowness. It has made man able to struggle with his brother and to work all the harder because his brother is working by his side; and yet to rejoice in his brother's victory as if it were his own. Such transfiguration and purification come to a power when it is put to its highest use!

All this applies not merely to individuals but to those larger persons which, though they are made up of many beings, have still a personal existence of their own. It applies to the Christian Churches and their rivalries with one another. "Which of them should be accounted the greatest?"—how Christendom has rung, how our Christian country rings to-day with the old question! There is not a village in the land where religion is not defamed and almost dying with the competition of rival churches. The country as a whole is distracted with the denominationalism which is simply at heart the wrestling of denomination with denomination, which of them shall be accounted the greatest. What hope is there of any peace? Good people dream of a Christian unity which shall swallow up denominational differences altogether. They picture a day when some great triumphal assertion of some form or principle, perhaps, shall have merged all these contentions and competitions in one millennial agreement on that principle or form. It is a case in which the wish is father to the thought. There is no sign which promises such a consummation. It is not in the killing out of denominationalism that the solution lies. The solution, at least the primary and immediate solution, lies in the turning of denominational rivalry to the most sacred uses. Let the churches of the land stop trying to outstrip each other in the number of their adherents, in the abundance of their wealth, in the magnificence of their sanctuaries, in the stateliness of their service, and let each of them be honestly set to do all that it can—to do, if it can, more than its brethren for the attainment of truth, for the service of the poor, for the salvation of the bodies and the souls of men; and then what a change would come! Still there would be emulation, but it would be a holy emulation. It would be a strange, unworldly emulation, in which each party struggling to surpass the others would still lift up its voice in thankful joy when any of those others had surpassed its best efforts by supreme devotion or capacity. It would be an emulation in which each victor would honestly lament that those whom it had conquered *could* be conquered by such a feeble servant of the Master as it had felt itself to be!

One almost sure result of such a noble rivalry would be that every church, devoted to the profoundest purposes for which any church exists, would speedily develop its own especial aptitude to meet those purposes. And so the several churches—all of which are partial, none of which is final or complete—would speedily find themselves working in different but parallel lines towards one great, broad result, which should freely take all their several successes into itself. In that way they would best come to know their real unity; to understand that neither of them is The Church of Christ, that The Church of Christ is the great aggregate of all of them together — and vastly more!

But let us leave the churches, and come back to sum up in a few words all that we have said to-day about the principle of rivalry as it affects the lives of individuals. Does it not all come to these two exhortations which I press on you as I close? The first is this: As far as you can, get rid of emulation altogether. Live in the absolute, not in the relative. Measure yourself not by the unstable standard of your brother's life, but by the great, eternal, unchanging patterns of life which are kept in the treasury of God. And the second is this: So far as you must still keep rivalry among your impulses, let it be always rivalry for the deepest and truest things. Refuse to enter into the race except for a prize so great that it shall rob the race of all its evil power. Most of all, make the great object of your emulation helpfulness to all who need the help of fellow-man.

He who is Christ's servant, and whom Christ has really brought into the presence and the love of God, must find both of these exhortations gradually fulfilling themselves in him. May Christ become so truly our Master that they may both be more and more fulfilled in us!

XV.

THE STRENGTH OF CONSECRATION.

"And Samson said, Let me die with the Philistines. And he bowed himself with all his might; and the house fell upon the lords, and upon all the people that were therein. So the dead which he slew at his death were more than they which he slew in his life."—JUDGES xvi. 30.

It is in many senses that the Bible is justly called the "Book of Life." No doubt that name belongs to it peculiarly because of the great revelation of the higher spiritual life, the life with God, the life in Christ, which fills its pages; but it would also describe the wonderful profusion and variety of vitality of every sort with which the sacred book abounds. Think over the Bible from beginning to end, and ask what other book so overruns with character? What other book so shows the endless diversity of human action? What kind of man is there that is not here? What human strength and weakness is assembled in this company! Where is there such another Book of Life?

For instance, think of two men, one from the Old Testament and one from the New, one the hero of the verse which I have read you for our text, the other the gentle disciple of the Lord—Samson and

St. John, the savage hero of Dan and the spiritual youth of Gallilee. How large must be the system of truth which can conceive of the relations which both of these men hold to God, which can see God using both of them for His purposes! How broad must be the stage on which these men have both their parts to play! One of them is the world's picture of saintliness and love; the other is the perfection of physical vitality. "As holy as St. John," we say, and "As strong as Samson"; and the same Bible holds them both. The same God uses them both, and so shows, in the long history where they both have part, the completeness of humanity. It is no partial picture. The man who walks the Bible pages is the full man, body and soul together, and so the Bible is the Book of Life.

I am led to speak this morning of the great champion of Israel whose name has become through all times the proverb and synonym of physical strength. I should like to reach with you some of the meanings of his singular life. And first let me recall to you his history. It was a time of depression for Israel. The Philistines had conquered the Israelites, and they were subject to their savage neighbors. In the country of Dan, which bordered on the Philistine country, one day an angel came to a childless woman in a field and told her that she should have a son whom God would use for the deliverance of His people from their enemies. The next day the visit and the promise were repeated, and then the woman's husband, whose name was Manoah, saw and heard the angel. He who gave the promise made the conditions. This child was to be made a Nazarite, set apart, that is, and consecrated to the Lord. The symbols of his consecration were to be two: he was to taste no wine nor strong drink, and no razor was ever to touch his hair or beard.

By and by the child was born, and he grew up to manhood, and he was very strong. It would seem as if there were periods of excessive strength which he recognized as given to him by God for a peculiar purpose. "The spirit of the Lord began to move him at times"—that is the description which is given of the strange phenomenon. Soon he began his attacks on the Philistines, and they all had a wild, grotesque, almost ludicrous character. He played with his enemies as a lion plays with its prey. His full, frolicsome life breaks out in all he does. He is a great, good-natured boy, passionate and excitable, but susceptible and impulsive, and apparently keeping no strong hatred even for the people whom it was the mission of his life to punish. He marries a Philistine woman, and at the wedding feast he provokes a quarrel with the guests about a foolish riddle, which led to his killing thirty of the men of Ashkelon and leaving his wife and her people in disgust. He comes back to find·his wife given to another, and he revenges himself by the fantastic malice of turning three hundred foxes with firebrands tied to their tails among the standing corn of the Philistines. He falls into their hands and as soon as they have bound him, "the spirit of the Lord came mightily upon him and the cords that were upon his arms became as flax that was burnt with fire, and his bands loosed from off his hands. And he found a new jaw-bone of an ass, and put forth his hand and took it, and slew a thousand men therewith. And Samson said, ' With the jaw-bone of an ass, heaps upon heaps, with the jaw of an ass have I slain a thousand men.'" It is the cry, the laugh, of an almost boyish triumph over the havoc he has made.

And so the stream of his life flows on like a mountain-stream, falling from one cascade into another, until at last it sweeps into dark shadow. The catastrophe approaches. Once more he comes among the Philistines. In the city of Gaza he falls in love with a woman named Delilah, and after many times playfully deceiving her, he gives her at last the secret of his strength. He bids her cut the flowing locks which represented his consecration to Jehovah. When those were gone his strength was gone. The Philistines bound him and made him captive and blinded him. As his strength slowly returned they used him for their purposes. They bound him to a mill, and made him labor there like a beast. At last came the day of his revenge and his death together. He was brought out by his tormentors to show his strength at a great festival for their amusement. And there, when he had amused them for a time, he found his opportunity to seize the pillars of the house where the flower of Philistia were gathered for the pageant. "And Samson said, Let me die with the Philistines. And he bowed himself with all his might, and the house fell upon the lords and upon all the people that were therein, so the dead which he slew at his death were more than they which he slew in his life."

Such is the story. It is a story which at once we feel belongs to the youth of any people. Long before David and Isaiah comes this champion of physical power, revelling in the strength of his right arm, doing all kinds of wild, fantastic things in the exuberant consciousness of being so strong. It has been often pointed out how like this story of the Hebrew Samson is to the Greek myths of Hercules and all his mighty labors: There is the same vast strength and the same weakness, the same yielding to the power of woman, the same captivity, the same open, free, fearless, passionate character. Perhaps the stories may have some connection with one another, or perhaps, what is more likely, they only indicate how back of all conceptions of power always lies this first, crudest, but most manifest and indisputable sort of power, physical strength. It is the first thought of God which man receives. "The heavens declare the glory of God, and the firmament showeth His handiwork." "How strong He is!" is the thought that starts the fear or wonder of the soul which is just getting sight of God, and makes the beginning of its religion; and whatever deeper things it learns concerning Him, whatever tidings of His love and wisdom may be brought to it, it never must lose the first thought of God's power. Any religion which loses that loses its masculineness, grows weak and feeble. The "fear of God" comes to mean something very much higher and finer than the mere sense of His power. It comes to mean a deep and awestruck perception of all His perfect qualities, but it can never leave out its first meaning; it can never cease to mean the sense that He is strong, that He can do with our lives and the earth on which they swim through space whatever He shall choose to do. All other truths of what He *will* choose, of the wisdom and the love with which He will select, must be clustered and twined around this first truth of His power, that He can do what He will.

And much the same is true of man. There, too, all higher culture makes us see that there are qualities higher than physical strength in man. In a certain sense civilization is always making physical strength of less and less importance. But no culture, no civilization, can ever wholly do away with its significance. There is still an instinctive admiration for the strong man in our human nature. All young men will begin by holding it in honor, even though old men's philosophy proves that it is of little worth. It is the crudest sort of force, but it is the most manifest and the most immediately effective. Men are always coming back to it, and out of the most artificial standards of what is honorable are always returning to the simplest of all tests and applauding the man who can strike the hardest blow, or lift the heaviest load, or march the longest journey. And if we told the truth, down at the bottom of all our hearts lies an envy and admiration, which perhaps we should be slow to own, but which no higher standards ever totally obliterate, for the man who is very strong. There come times which hear no music in the harp of David and are unstirred by all the aspirations of Isaiah, but Samson is never without his honor.

As we think, then, of Samson's life, let us remember it in its periods; first in its strength, then in its fall, then in its disgrace, then in its second chance.

1. Of Samson in his strength what I want you to notice is how God used him, with all his imperfections, and his crudities, just as long as he was true to the consecration of his life. A wild, irregular, unaccountable creature, full of passion, running into sin, he still kept through it all the broad birth-consecration of his life to God. Before he was born he was named a Nazarite. His unshorn locks were the witness of his consecration; wherever he went and men saw them floating wildly like a banner, men knew that there went a man who, recklessly as he sometimes lived, terribly as he sometimes sinned, still knew and owned that he belonged to God, counted his strength a trust of God—not his, but God's,—and knew that he ought to use it not for himself but for the purposes of Him to whom it belonged. Such a man God could use. A wilful, wayward weapon he would often be in the Divine Hand, but wilful and wayward as he was, far as he was from being a perfect servant, still the confession of servantship was in his heart, the consecration to the Lord was always the under-fact of his existence to himself, and so God used him.

And that is a perpetual truth. One man may be

more wayward than another, the sort of force that men possess may differ vastly, may be in one man crude and coarse and in another fine; but, after all, the use which God is able to make of two men in this world depends on the amount of the consecration-consciousness that is in their lives and souls. One man is fine, clear, orderly, cultivated, finished, but it has never entered into his thought that he lives for any one beside himself. Another man is like Samson, wild and disorderly, passionate and boyish and frolicsome and wanton, but all the time, wrought into the very muscle of his strength, there is a tough, persistent consciousness that he belongs to God. Which does the work? Samson may go blundering through it, doing it in bad taste, dishonoring it very often, breaking as much glass as he saves, never seeming to realize how great the work is that he is doing, frolicking over it and never appearing to get hold of its best motives or meanings, but after all he does it. The Philistines fall before him. He believes that God sent him. But the other man, who has no dream of any consecration, works out his fine conception, criticises and refines, and says what ought to be done, and does nothing. More and more clear it grows, I think, that it is the sense of consecration, however crude and rough be the characters in which it works, that God uses to change and save the world.

2. And this makes clear the next point. If this was Samson's strength, then we can see where Samson's fall came from. *He lost his consecration.* It seemed a little thing. In a weak moment he let a

THE STRENGTH OF CONSECRATION 261

wanton woman cut his seven-twisted locks of hair. But Samson was just the man to whom a symbol was everything. Those locks were so bound up with the vow that had been made before his birth, that they not merely stood for, they *were* his consecration. When he revealed the secret that his strength lay in them, and really bade her cut them off, he knew that he was casting away that tie between his life and God's which had given him all his power.

Ah, men will talk of little things and great things as if they knew what things were little and what things were great. Men read this story and they say: "What a droll, fanciful old legend! As if the cutting of the hair could have had anything to do with the man's strength!" And so they read the third chapter of Genesis and shake their heads and say: "What! could the eating of an apple be the ruin of the world?" As if their own experiences had not been scattered through with events which ought to have explained to them how powerful and influential may be an act which seems insignificant. Have they never come up to a time when one single act, that seemed nothing to the men who watched it, meant for them either the acceptance or the rejection of the mastery of God over their souls, and so had in it all the power of the endless blessing or the endless curse?

Why, we are always taking or refusing to take the apple, sacrificing or saving the locks of our consecration. There was one oath in your life that threw away your reverence, one lie that decided you would not be true, one cheat that petulantly cast off the restraining hand of God, one act of lust that gave your soul up to impurity, one drink that broke the consecration of your temperance. You cannot think of any act so little—the saying "Yes" instead of "No," the going up the street instead of down—that it may not be, when you do it, such a focal act as to assume most tragical importance. It may be the casting aside of the whole purpose of your life, the saying, "I will not have this man to rule over me," the giving up of God, the taking up of self, just what the act of Samson was when he told the secret of his locks. And if any act of ours be thus the sacrifice of the purpose and consecration of our lives, then for us as for Samson there comes weakness. Strength goes when purpose goes; and our unconsecrated powers may be bound with any cords that men may choose to bring.

Is not this what the story of Samson's fall really means for us,—that if we sacrifice our consecration and our purpose all our strength is turned to feebleness? It is true even of our physique, I think. The very strength of the arm is weaker when the man has no faith in his cause and no passionate desire for its triumph. The soul's devotion passes into the muscles and prevails to conquer the foe or break open the dungeon door. "If ye have faith ye shall remove mountains"—those words of Jesus have almost a literal and physical truth. But it is truer of the other forms of strength, perhaps, than of the strength of the body,—at least one wants to dwell on it most concerning them. Of intellectual strength it is supremely true that it gives up its vigor when it loses its moral purpose. How many witnesses there are of that! How many ages full of ability and wit, but with no earnestness! How many men, living to-day, or dead and buried long ago in graves from which no inspiration rises, who had strength of mind, clear brains, vivid imaginations, scholarship, taste, and yet were very weak. They laid no hand upon their time, they exercised no influence on men. What was the reason? There can be only one. They had no moral purpose. They cared nothing for the good of man or the glory of God. They had given up their consecration.

In days when every other element of strength is glorified, and that which completes them all and makes them really strong is so continually forgotten or despised, surely the story of Samson is good for us. It is not, I think, for the labor of science, which, however it may sometimes lose sight of the best truth, is laboring earnestly for the human good,—it is not for this that we ought to regret and fear to-day. It is for the vast amount of wholly purposeless literature,—the way in which so much of the best intellectual ability of this time is working solely for self-satisfaction,—it is in the prevalent selfishness of culture that its greatest weakness lies; for there is no real strength in anything that is devoid of moral purpose. The book that is written, the state that is built, the life that is lived, without a consecration is weak, however brilliant it may be. It is Samson without the locks of his Nazarite dedication.

O my dear friends, let us know—oh, that all the world might know, indeed—that everything, every triumphant work of genius, every assertion of dogma, every construction of system, ecclesiastical or social, is weak, weak and not strong, that is shorn of the crowning glory of moral purpose, that is not bent and bound and dedicated to the achievement of goodness.

3. This, then, was Samson's fall. Think of him next in his disgrace and misery. It is a terrible sight. "The Philistines took him, and put out his eyes, and brought him down to Gaza, and bound him with fetters of brass, and he did grind in the prison house." That last clause has the sting of the story in it. Milton in his wonderful poem has drawn for us the same picture:

> Ask for this great deliverer now, and find him
> Eyeless in Gaza at the mill with slaves,

and when his father Manoah comes to him, he asks

> Wilt thou then serve the Philistines with that strength
> Which was expressly given thee to annoy them?

That is the true depth of his wretchedness. Not merely he has fallen out of his loyalty to God; he has fallen into the slavery of these brutal savages. Look at him where he toils!—the mighty chest, the brawny arms, the limbs like columns, the muscles of twisted power all through the frame, the great form bent down upon the heavy mill-crank which he almost gnaws in his rage as he slowly heaves it around; and all about him, mocking him, goading him, these miserable Philistines who are his masters Oh, if he could have left his strength behind him when he fell! oh, that, if he could not slay them, at least he might not serve them and give them the advantage of his God-given power!

And if the bad man always could leave his strength behind him when he crossed the line into sin, if in proportion as he grows more wicked he grew more weak, his wickedness would not seem so terrible. That was David's ejaculation: "If I forget thee, O Jerusalem, the City of Holiness, let my right hand forget its cunning!" It is the skill, the thought, the subtlety, the work that is laid out for wickedness, the cheat and burglar lavishing an ingenuity that was made to enrich the world, the deceiver arguing with a power, glowing with an enthuasiastic genius that belong to truth;—these are our Samsons, at their mills with slaves. Many a bad man in his better moments curses his skill in badness as Samson must have cursed his strength when the Philistines had it all. "Samson" means "the Sunny." The name belongs to the open, bright, breezy freshness of his better days; see him now as he grinds away, moody, blind, desperate, with his hands clutching the mill as if they would tear it. Yet that is something—something that he should hate himself and hate them as he toiled for them—something that he should grudge them the strength that belonged to God. It were a lower fall still, if he had come to consent to his slavery, to do the will of God's enemies and be happy, without a self-reproach.

4. And so we come to what I called Samson's second chance. While he was toiling at the mill his hair was growing again, his consecration to God was renewed, and his strength became once more complete. Then came the Philistines' festival, the bringing out of the prisoner, his feats of strength, and at last he seizes the columns of the palace and drags it and the Philistines and himself down into death together. There is where the story ends. The champion is himself again, and once more he does the same service for God and God's people; he is the same ruin to God's enemies as at the beginning. "The dead which he slew at his death were more than they which he slew in his life." The consecration has come back into the strength, and once more he wins the fame and works the deliverance.

> Samson hath quit himself like Samson, and heroicly hath finished
> A life heroic, on his enemies
> Fully revenged, hath left them years of mourning.

But see the difference. In this second chance he can conquer only at the price of his own destruction. Look at the youthful hero, rushing with a shout after his foes, clad in a strength which "made arms ridiculous," and then at this gray, rugged, silent man, bent down between the columns of the palace roof and tugging at their weight to drag them on himself as well as on his foes. No longer is there the radiant, sunny, easy, joyous, almost frolicsome, air of his first victories. That is all gone forever.

Now, nothing but the heavy, desperate endeavor to die at work.

Yes, God does give men a second chance; but the first chance never comes back to them. A wicked man turns from his wickedness. An old thief struggles back to honesty. The long accumulations of a godless life are cast aside. The wanderer comes home. The consecration is renewed. There is work. There is patience. There is even hope. But there is not, there cannot be, the exhilaration, the first swing of life which was there before the purity was stained, before the vow was broken. It is worth while—oh, how well worth while!—for the oldest and vilest to take the new chance that God gives him. It may be that even he in his chastened and subdued old age may not merely save himself but do good service for his Master; but let us not, in our glad thankfulness for the willingness with which God takes the wanderer back and gives him another chance,—let us not get to think that the wandering and the fall were anything else but bad. Let us not extenuate it or excuse. There are men now serving God in their old age, serving him nobly in their second chance, but still the first chance was the brightest, bright with a brightness that never comes again,—the daylight before they fell, before those blank, dark years of sin. Most shameful and most terrible, as one sees more of men, becomes that wretched proverb about the "wild oats" which fathers and mothers quote so lightly, which expects men to be bad before they can be good, which robs men of the bright and joyous first chance, and only hopes for them the dogged and desperate second chance of Samson. Let us hate it with all our hearts!

How shall I speak to this congregation, made up as it is of young and old? Here are young Samsons in the freshness of their purity and strength. Here are old Samsons toiling at the mill of sin. Oh, that I could preach to you the double truth—the first and second chance—and let neither weaken the other! If you are still believing—pure true, consecrated to the Lord and to His high works, and therefore *strong*, oh, keep that consecration! Let no promise that some day He will bring you back to Him tempt you to wander into wickedness. If you have already wandered, now come back! It never is too late! If only that you may die in His service, give up your sins, renew your consecration, and do what yet you can for Him before you die!

This, then, was Samson's strength, and fall, and misery, and restoration. Out of the whole survey of him there comes one clear impression which the vividness of his personality is well adapted to convey. It is of the personal responsibility of the man. That is so evident all through! This healthy human creature illustrates splendidly the human mastery over circumstances and events. There is not a particle of feeble and unmanly whimpering about his fate. Philistines conquer him only when he yields and puts himself into their power. Once more to turn to Milton's poem. There is a passage there in which the Philistine harlot meets the hero whom she has ruined, and reproaches him that he should lay all the blame on her. It is a reproach which we can put into the mouth of the world, and fancy it rebuking the man who charges it with having through its allurements and temptations led him into sin. Delilah says:

> Was it not weakness also to make known,
> For importunity, that is for naught,
> Wherein consisted all thy strength and safety?
> To what I did thou show'd'st me first the way,
> . . . . .
> Ere I to thee, thou to thyself wast cruel.

These words tell the whole story of the world's leading men into sin. We say: "If I had not met this companion I never should have been so frivolous or mean." "This sceptic made me sceptical." "This failure made me bitter." "These many distractions drove my deeper thoughts away." "This badness made me bad." And every one of them, all these bad things, and the world which altogether is made up of them, lifts up its voice and flings back our pusillanimous reproach: "'Ere I to thee, thou to thyself wast cruel.' You betrayed yourself, or I never could have betrayed you." It will be the bursting forth of that voice from all the things, animate and inanimate, which we have turned into excuses of our sin, that will make up the Judgment Day. It anticipates the Judgment Day in time, when a man hears that voice now, and stops saying, "These things have ruined me," and begins to say frankly, "I have sinned."

And now, let us come back a moment to where we

began. I spoke at the beginning of this sermon about two strangely contrasted characters—Samson and St. John. They seemed to stand very far apart; can we see anything which they have to do with one another? In other words, what has the Christian faith to do with Samson, the man of primitive human nature, strong in the first strength of man, and making that strength powerful as he used it in dedication to God?

We answer, that Christianity, if it took this Old Testament giant in hand, certainly would not try to destroy or to restrain the fresh and breezy freedom of his life. Its joyousness and spirit she would try to keep. Its simplicity and humor she would love. Its childishness she would undertake to educate, but its *childlikeness* she would treasure and exalt.

To make Samson a Christian! In our modern ears, with our modern associations, that sounds ridiculous. It makes us laugh to think of taking this boisterous young savage, and teaching him our doctrines, and bringing him to our meetings, and making him talk our religious talk; for that is what we often understand by being a Christian nowadays. But Christ could have made a Christian out of him, and it is easy to see how. Keeping his strength, that strength which, as we saw, depended wholly on his consecration to God, Christ could have made his consecration to God perfect. First, He could have shown him God as that poor bewildered boy of Dan never saw Him. Instead of that dim Jehovah after whom his dull imagination reached, He could have set before him the love and richness and perfection of Divinity in His own perfect life. And then, having shown him God, He could have bound him to God by personal love for Himself. Imagine this brave young soul in all its freshness, perfectly seeing God and perfectly bound to Him by love, seeing Him and devoted to Him in Jesus. How strong his consecration then! What tempter could have overcome it? How brave his onset! What foe could have withstood it? Where shall we find the picture of what it would have brought him to, except in that Christ Himself, who, stronger than Samson, had in Himself perfectly what Samson had so imperfectly? Jesus is the Samson of the divine life—strength filled with consecration. His strength was perfect because His consecration was perfect. "Verily, verily, I say unto you," He said, "the Son can do nothing of Himself, but what He seeth the Father do." That which He was, He would have more and more made His servant; not robbing him of one glorious flower of his strength and freedom, but making all his strength pure and permanent by filling it with God through the channel of consecration to Himself.

The Christian Samson, then, is simply the man in whom Christ does this work to-day. Fighting and conquering the enemies of God, joyful and radiant with present pleasure and perpetual hope; springing up with a sleepless fountain of vitality; so free that nobody can bind him from doing what he knows is right and thinking what he thinks is true; so strong that no wickedness can stand before him or in him; happy and busy, and making happiness and work about him as the sun makes light;—but all this only because he is perpetually and completely consecrated to God in love and service of Jesus Christ. To him there can come no blindness. No man can make him a slave, or chain him down to any work of sin. He is strong in the Lord and in the power of His might; and he goes from strength to strength until at length in Zion he stands in perfect love and consecration, and so in perfect power for his eternal work, before God.

XVI.

THE DANGER OF SUCCESS.

"Verily I say unto you, They have their reward."—MATTHEW vi. 2.

THE soul of Jesus was stirred within Him as He went about the streets of Jerusalem and saw the multitude of hypocrites who passed there for pious men. He saw the Pharisees standing in the synagogues and in the streets, distributing their charity. They came in with a crowd and a noise. They stood upon the highest platform. They were surrounded by their fawning sycophants. They insulted every poor man with their arrogance before they helped him. They made every coin sound as they dropped it and tinkle the praises of their generosity, so that all the synagogue or all the street could hear. There are such public and ostentatious almsgivers in the East to-day doing the same thing in almost precisely the same way. And here, where we live, in the West, where this particular way of doing it would be ridiculous, there are plenty of people doing the same thing after an Occidental instead of an Oriental manner, "doing their alms before men, to be seen of them." These are the men that Jesus looked upon, and the comment that He made upon them is well worth our study. He saw them doing a certain act with a certain object. The act and the object for which they did it were exactly suited to one another. The act was unspiritual and selfish, and the object was unspiritual and selfish, too. The charity they gave was cold and formal and unfeeling, and the praise that they expected for their charity was the cold, formal adulation of men whom they had convinced of their importance. In their charity there was no deep yearning after God and the children of God; and in the applause that they expected they found a perfect satisfaction. They never dreamed of creeping by their charity a little nearer to God, and entering by sympathetic action a little deeper into His heart and mind, which is what the really devout soul is always longing for.

And so Jesus, looking at the meagre nature of their charity and seeing how it just matched the superficial applause which it excited, said: "Yes, verily, I say unto you they have their reward." They get what they are after. They get no more. They *have* their reward. There is no more to come, no great, unrealized future fruitage of their action into which they shall enter one of these days. It is all there. Those clapping hands, those praising voices are all. They have their reward, and it is over. But yet they do certainly have it. Such as it is, they do not miss it. In their own little region their actions are certainly successful. Nay—for, as Jesus speaks, we feel as if His words were certainly telling the story of condemnation,—they are successful, and it is that very success that ruins them.

They are certainly deep words—these words of Christ. They are not such words as many of us would speak, for He did not see with eyes like ours. His words touch and start a distinction which is always appearing in the different treatments of the low and selfish lives of low and selfish men. You see a man doing a selfish thing, or living a selfish life. He is working for a low and little purpose; what shall you say to him to turn him? You may tell him that he will fail in what he seeks; that, struggle as he will, he never will be rich; that, seek to be prominent as he will, he never will make men look at him; that, desire and work for peace and comfortableness as he will, very few men attain what he is working for, and it is not likely that he will attain it. You try to scare him off with the prophecy of failure. That does not do much good. Your friend knows that while his success is not absolutely certain, still he is in the direction of succeeding. Corrupt men do get rich and powerful, he knows, and hypocrites do pass for saints, and men who aspire for popularity do get it by their arts. He will not ignore facts. A few exceptions here and there will not make him believe that on the whole men do not get what they are struggling for, and so he plunges on all the more eagerly for your warning.

But now, suppose you take just the other tone. Suppose you say to him, not "You will fail," but "Probably you will succeed." That was what Jesus said: "Verily, they have their reward." The low ambition gets what it desires. The cheat does get the fortune. The demagogue gets the popularity. The hypocrite gets the name of piety, and the flippant sneerer gets the name of wit. You say to your friend: "If you go on, you will succeed. You will get the reward that properly belongs to the life you have chosen. But look at that reward and see what it is worth. See whether, painting it at its very brightest as you will, it is indeed worthy of your seeking. See whether such a success is not really a dreadful thing for a man to come to and be satisfied with, when there are in him powers of such a different sort that might bring him to such a different issue. Is it not in the rewards to which they come that the real hollowness and wretchedness of the things that you are doing show themselves out most manifestly?"

Now surely this is the truest ground to take. It looks the facts most truly in the face. I do not believe that you will ever make the drunkard leave off drink by telling him that drink does not exhilarate, nor even by pointing him to the headaches that follow when the exhilaration is all over; but only by showing him what a poor, low thing that kind of exhilaration is,—of how much better a man like him is capable. Point him to the crowd of rollicking inebriates, happy up to the very height of their desires, in the complete enjoyment of that for which they have given up clearness of brain, and tenderness of heart, and the joys of pure friendship, and the respect of men; point him to them in the full glory of their success and say: " 'Verily, they have their reward,'—what do you think of it?" I do not believe you will ever rescue a man from the unreasonable slavery of business by telling him of the chances of his not succeeding, but rather by taking him and showing him what success amounts to. Show him the man who, by the mere business standard, has perfectly succeeded. Show him a life all given up to trade, and now travelling down towards the grave with hands burdened with a fortune that it cannot use. Show him the stunted nature; show him the table spread with food that the sick man cannot taste, the library crowded with books that the uncultured man cannot use, the free admission won at last into a society that the mere business machine cannot enjoy. Show him success. Show him the rich man, whose life has been given up to getting his riches, at last in full possession of all he has been struggling for; and then, with the gorgeous picture glowing full before his eyes, ask him: "Is that, then, what you want? Does that then, satisfy you? Verily, he has his reward,—is that the reward you want?" And many a time, he who would have braved defiantly every threat of failure, will feel the scales fall from his eyes and turn away disgusted as he looks at the poor, drudging mortal cursed by his complete success.

I should like to speak to-day about the danger of success. We hear a great deal about the danger of failure, and yet there are many things in which it is much more dangerous to succeed than it would be to fail. So many men have been ruined by succeeding in what they undertook, who might have been saved by failing. Let us look at it, and see what are some of the most prominent of the dangers of success.

And perhaps I can show it by certain illustrations, by citing certain common cases. Take a man who goes into public life. His object is to win public applause and so to win power. He has looked no higher than that. He has never aspired to true servantship of the people, nor to a real incorporation of the great principles of government into the life of the people he is set to rule. There is nothing either of the philanthropist or of the philosopher about his politics. Well, by-and-by, he succeeds. The people begin to praise him. He comes up to higher and higher office, and he wins little by little the power that he wants. To keep that power and to use it then becomes the business of his life. He looks no higher. He values no other sort of attainment. He has done his best, and has succeeded. What shall we say about him? If he were a friend of yours and if you had been watching him and really desiring his best good, and if you really saw how poor that prize was which, if he should reach it, would almost certainly have cut off all chance of spiritual growth and progress into higher ambitions from him forever, would you not rather have seen him fail than succeed? Would not failure, perhaps, have cast him back and, even if from mere disgust at first, still have compelled him to cast aside the unsuccess of policy and perhaps to have taken up with principle? Certainly, there have been public men enough who have seemed to learn what princi ple was for the first time only when all their plans of self-advancement had come to woeful failure. And there have been plenty of public men who seemed to say good-by to principle and pure ambitions the moment that their public life, after long disaster, graduated from failure into success.

Or take the success of many a merchant. In a mercantile community like ours this must be what oftenest forces itself upon our notice. In every occupation there are certain special faculties employed. To seem to have those faculties supremely is the pride of him who is ambitious in that special occupation. To seem to be supremely shrewd and practical, to seem to be sharp, smart, quick at the turn of a bargain, able to make money and able to keep it,—this is the whole ambition of many a business man. This is what multitudes of clerks are striving for in emulation of their principals. When they have reached this, they will seem to themselves to have reached the purpose of their life. But when we see what such a success makes out of many men, how it hardens them with selfishness and narrows them with pride; when we see how many young men who started full of various generous desires, aspiring after self-culture, dreaming of knowledge, craving usefulness, sensitive to religion, gentle with reverence, are swept by their mere business success into the close and confined career of the man who has no desire but for money,—as a wide river that lay open to the sunlight and lavished its fruitfulness on broad banks and on the shores of happy islands, is by-and-by all crowded and cramped in between narrow granite walls, where it foams and frets and rages and is hurried on like a whipped slave,—when we see this (and it is what our great business cities are full of) are we not ready to cry of many a man: "Oh, if he had only failed and not succeeded!" Are we not ready to pray for a friend, whose best good we desire, that he may not succeed too much? Do we not feel the danger of success?

But I want to apply the same idea in a higher field —in the field of religion. What I have just been saying all will agree to; what I would say about religion is no less true, though perhaps not so clear. Can there be a danger of too much success in religion? Is it possible that there can be peril to a man from being too easily prosperous in the religious life?

Let us remember what religion is, what its great purpose is. The purpose of religion is to bring the human soul to God. The soul religiously successful is the soul that really *has* come to God, and laid itself on Him in perfect love and absolute obedience. Of that success there cannot be too much. To all eternity the soul of man redeemed shall always be coming nearer to, deeper and deeper into the soul of God. But that final and complete attainment is reached through other attainments; and one of these subordinate attainments is the clear and certain holding of doctrinal truth. It is a subordinate attainment; not to know truth but to come to God is the ultimate glory of religious life. And now, if it is sometimes the case that the easy and comfortable acceptance of truth, the ready belief of these great verities of Christianity, hinders instead of helps the soul in its approach to God; then, even here, there is an instance of the danger of success that is most striking and that we ought to understand. It is not easy to state. I think—at least I hope—that I have made it clear to you often enough that I have no sympathy with nor tolerance for the disbelief that disbelieves for the mere pride of disbelieving. God forbid that I should ever lead any soul to think that the simplicity and directness of its faith was a sign that its faith was superficial or insincere. Let me never seem to teach that doubt in itself is better than belief as such. But while I say this strongly, none the less I am sure that there is a certain doubt that is better than a certain belief. There is a belief that is traditional, easy because it never asks a question, placid because it is so shallow, and that, calm as it looks, is not so good as the tumult of eagerness, which, making religion a thing of life or death, will not be satisfied till it has had an answer to a hundred questions, to know the answers to some of which a man must verily be God Himself.

And now, if a man makes it the object of his Christianity not to come near to God, but merely to establish himself in a certain set of doctrines; and if in time he reaches his desire and stands with his creed all compact and formulated, each part fitted into its neighbor part so that, whatever happens, no shock ever comes to the structure of his well-jointed faith,—what shall we say of him? What can we say but just what Jesus said? "Verily, he has his reward." He has built up his faith, and he keeps it so abstract, so apart from these terrible live problems that are rampant in the world, that it never feels their disturbing influence. While other men are shaking with bewilderment, while David is perplexed and troubled at the dreadful mysteries of Providence, while Paul is wondering at God's treatment of him, this man's faith stands apart and unshaken. He looks with pity or contempt on every doubter. He lives a more comfortable mental life than they do, but he does not accomplish so completely the real purpose of all religion—he does not come so near to God. He has his reward in careless days and peaceful nights. But it is not good for him. Some time or other God blesses him if He lets a great sorrow or a great bewilderment plow down through his easy faith, and turn it up in great furrows to the very core.

And what is true about faith is true also about peacefulness. That, too, is dangerous if it is not pure and thorough and profound. A man accepts some superficial and mechanical notion of Christianity. He learns to think that his soul is in danger; by which he does not mean that his best powers are in danger of degradation and that his spiritual vitality—his love and truth—is dying away from him. He means that he has been wicked, and God is going to punish him with suffering. To get rid of that suffering is his one desire. And by and by he convinces himself that, by some one thing that he has done, that suffering is got rid of, that God has let him go out of His revengeful hands and he is free. The moment of his freedom he may describe differently. It may be the moment when he felt a certain inside emotion; it may be the moment when he submitted to a certain outside sacrament; but the peculiarity of all such thoughts of Christianity is this, —that they put the whole work at one special moment and, that once past, the soul released from the threatened penalty, thenceforth the whole is done, the man is among the elect, among the saved, the chosen, and he has nothing to do but be at peace and rejoice in his already perfected salvation. The soul convinced of this settles into the consciousness of its own happiness and easily grows pharisaical as it looks at the poor, troubled spirits which have not reached the rest it has attained.

What is there that shall disturb it? Salvation, for it, means the escape from everlasting punishment; and the warrant of that escape it holds firmly, written in the red blood of Christ. What shall it seek for more? For it, no daily struggle to grow near to Christ, no daily sense of how far off from Christ the soul is living, keeps the whole nature in disturbance. No fight with sin, no dissatisfaction with itself, no half-despairing sense of its own feebleness ever coming up into sight, no impatience after the Christ who as the soul approaches Him seems to loom up all the more forbidding as He is the more tempting in His purity,—none of all this ever disturbs with a ripple nor darkens with a cloud the perfect peacefulness of the soul which, with its purely mechanical conception of religion, thinks itself safe, and with its cushions and its comforts travels along to its assured and entirely unawful heaven. God forbid that I should depreciate or deny the

Christian's peace in Christ, but this is something wholly different from that. *That* is a peace consistent with eagerness, anxiety, and toil. "Woe unto them that are at ease in Zion!" The man who gives up seeking to be like God, and makes his religious satisfaction to consist in the assurance that he is not going to be punished in the other world, gets what he seeks. He attains a comfortable peacefulness. He has his reward; but it would be better for him if he never had it, for that very peacefulness and satisfaction keep him away from God.

And the same thing is true of Christian influence. We all know that we ought to do good to one another, that what the Lord has given us was not given us for ourselves alone, but for our brethren too. And there are powerful and effective ministries which, as we look about, we all know that we can render to some one or some number of people by our side. But the best ministry, the real ministry of one soul to another is always of a laborious and quiet sort. It requires studious sympathy. It must draw near to the nature that it wants to help, in patient, silent ways. Very often it must sacrifice the favor of its object, and even provoke his enmity, that it may deal frankly with him and do him good. All this is laborious and makes no noise, and so it is no wonder that a more prominent and easier type of work for fellow-men, an external and unsympathetic lecturing of men's sins, takes the place of this unseen, painful work which goes on so toilsomely, so silently, between soul and soul.

Oh, it does almost anger one sometimes, when

one is in his weakest moods, most capable of being angered, to see who are the most recognized laborers for fellow-men, the helpers of their brethren whom all men praise. The cheap satirist of social vices, who never goes down to their bottom to cure the social discontents out of which they spring; the professional philanthropist, the preacher or the lecturer who only abuses his fellow-men and never tries to understand them; the busy-body giver of advice who flutters here and there like a stupid gardener through his garden, pulling up all the flowers that will not grow just his way;—all these are the men whom people praise and say, "See how much good they do!"

But where is the good really doing? Not where men see it or praise it at all. There is a great upward movement of humanity, the better part lifting the worse part always, but it is as silent a process as when the hidden leaven creeps through the heavy loaf, or when the subtle springtime pervades the sluggish earth. Wherever any soul, without the slightest pharisaism, is just infusing its noblest power by sympathy into some brother soul—father helping child and, quite as often, child helping father; teacher entering into the life of scholar, employer touching his clerks' temptations with the strength of his maturer life; and friendship everywhere creating the atmosphere of life which makes unconsciously the moral strength of one to be the moral strength of many;—in all such cases the real help of man by man, the real influence of man over man, is at work. While more and more suspicious, certainly, seem the loud professions of those who claim to be the helpers of their fellow-men, more and more beautiful and precious seem to me the unconscious ministries by which earnest and loving souls win other souls, and never know the blessed work they do. The first win their brethren's applause; the others win their brethren's souls, and that is better. The first win applause, and they have their reward; but if success is dangerous anywhere, it is never so dangerous as when men succeed in making other men believe that they are self-sacrificing and devoted, because the risk is so great that they will rest in their fellow-men's fond gratitude, and never do the hard, unnoticed work by which alone men do really come close to and give real aid to one another.

So we might go on with many illustrations. The fact which all of them illustrate seems only too plain. Is it not this? I beg you to notice it, remember it, see if it is not true—that every work which it is right for man to do has its legitimate and true result, hard to attain, and more manifest to God than to men when it is attained; and that these perfect results of things have always certain copies or imitations or counterfeits which look like them, which are easy to reach and which attract men's attention; that the counterfeit result is always trying to slip itself into the place of the real result, and, furthermore, that a success in the attainment of the counterfeit is dangerously apt to delude men and distract them, and turn them off from the reality they ought to be pursuing.

I do not know the occupation to which this will not apply, in which the true ambition is not always haunted by a false ambition that is always trying to slip into its place. The merchant's service to the community and his own self-interest—the politician's public spirit and his ambition—the school teacher's desire to teach his scholars and his desire to make them shine—the minister's wish to save souls and his wish to be popular—the lawyer's love for justice and his love for technicalities—the church-member's love for men's souls and his pride in the growth of his denomination—the Christian's longing for truth and God and his satisfaction in a creed and in safety,—everywhere the sham besets the reality, the counterfeit lurks close beside the genuine and tries to make men accept it in her place. If men do take it they get their reward, but the temporary peace or pleasure that they gain is paid for by the loss of fuller culture and the final joy which only the real and perfect things can give. Oh, for more thoroughness, no matter what it costs! for more determination to be satisfied with nothing but the highest and the best!

It would seem as if this subject of ours was closely bound up with the most fundamental things—with the largeness of life, and the limitation and sin of man which make it impossible for him to comprehend it all. In a perfect world, inhabited by perfect and sufficient men, every good act would have four facts manifestly and necessarily belonging to it. In the first place, it would *be good*,—there would be its own inherent and essential righteousness. In the second place, it would *do good* to a world all ready to receive it,—there would be its immediate usefulness. In the third place, it would give pleasure to the pure nature out of which it sprang,—there would be a spontaneous and genuine pleasure. And, fourthly, it would win applause from all men, since all would instinctively recognize it,—there would be its easy and ungrudged popularity. Righteousness, usefulness, pleasure, popularity,—all these belong to the perfect action done in the perfect world; all these shall come to it in the world that shall be perfect. In heaven every good act shall have not merely its own essential excellence, but it shall leap at once into some blessed influence, it shall fill with unmixed joy the soul of him who does it, and all the multitudes of the New Jerusalem shall see its beauty instantly and praise it with hearts incapable of envy or detraction.

But *now*, in this imperfect world, with these imperfect men, how is it? Where is the act that wins all these deserts of goodness? Where is the act that is righteous and useful and delightful and popular all at once? Once in a lifetime there may come such a golden act, but how few they are! The experience of any noble life seems to be very largely occupied in cutting off and giving up the inferior and more accidental characteristics of goodness in order that its more precious and essential ones may be maintained. We begin at the bottom of our list. My righteous act ought to win men's praise, but let me surrender their praise without a murmur if only my own soul finds joy in doing what is right. But even that may have to go. I ought to enjoy doing righteousness, but if there is a righteous thing that will help my brother at my side, let me do it, though I get no pleasure from it, though I dread and hate it. And even that usefulness may have to go. Not even to help my fellow-man, dear and sacred as that duty is, not even to help him must I do anything that is not righteous in itself.

My dear friends, may we not describe the difference in men's lives simply by saying that it depends on whether they begin at the top or bottom of that scale in their choice of actions? One man begins at the top and runs down: Righteousness, if it is convenient; usefulness, if it comes in my way; pleasure, if I can arrange it; but popularity anyhow! Another man begins at the bottom and runs up: Applause, if men choose to give it to me; pleasure, if God bestows that privilege; usefulness, if I may have so great and sweet a boon; but righteousness certainly, though everything else must go with one sweep to attain it.

Which class do we belong to? As we look at the life of lives, the life of Jesus, there can be no doubt about Him. He trod popularity under his feet. He let pleasure go, and lived a life of pain. He would not, even to help men, go out of the way of righteousness. Nothing could weigh with Him against the necessity that He should do His Father's Will. Do you think He did not care for all the others? Was not the praise of brother-man sweet to His intense and genuine humanity? Did not that perfect nature delight in the pleasures that humanity was made to feel? Let us never picture to ourselves the Lord as an unsensitive, hard man, to whom it cost nothing to give up the things that other men yield to and that occupy their lives. He felt every surrender as we do not know how to feel it, but He turned away to do that Will which He had come to do, that Will which was to Him the one precious, absolute thing in the universe; and as He looked back on His brethren seeking their pleasure, winning one another's praise, it was with a keen appreciation of the lower success which He had sacrificed to reach the higher, with a clear sense of its value, though without a shade of regret at its loss, that He said, "Yes, verily, they have their reward." It was as if the man who had climbed a snowy peak stood cold and tired in the midst of all the glory on the very top, and looked down into the valley and thought how warm and comfortable were the peasants by their firesides, and was never so thankful as just then that he had not been content to tarry by the fireside, but had struggled through every difficulty to the top.

How the very thought of Jesus gives us the true spirit in which everything that duty calls us to surrender ought to be given up! It is not good for any man to give up any success for the sake of a higher success, and yet to go about grudging that success which he has surrendered to the men who are still satisfied with it. You give up riches in order to be honest and do good; thenceforth the joy of doing good ought to be so great to you that no shadow of envy should sweep over your face as the carriages of the rich men spatter you upon the street. You choose the happiness of sobriety; thenceforth it is not worthy of you to feel vexed at the temporary exhilaration which the carousing drunkards get out of their dissipation. You deliberately make your religion a serious and thoughtful thing; you determine not to be satisfied with the mere surface of it; you open its deep, puzzling questions and you let in upon your soul many a puzzling and bewildering doubt:—it may be you are doing well, but at any rate do not complain of the price you pay for the more intelligent faith that you are seeking. Do not complain that you have not the smooth and careless life of the traditional, undoubting believer who never asks a question and so has none to answer. It is a beautiful satisfaction in the highest success which can look the brilliancy of the lower successes in the face, and say, without a shade of grudge or bitterness, "Yes, they have their reward,"—say it without conceited superiority and without feeble envy.

This seems to me important. I think I see so many Christians, men who have chosen Christ, who are not deeply, thoroughly satisfied with the Christ whom they have chosen. They have really chosen Him. They know there is a happiness in Him that wickedness cannot give, but this happiness lies so deep! They know that it is there, but they have not uncovered it yet—not all of it. They see some fragments of it, and they know that the rest is there. But here lies the happiness of wickedness—all plain and open. It sparkles in the sunshine. Its laughter rings out on the air. I think that there are a great many good people who wish that wicked people did not seem so happy. It puzzles them. They know that they are happier, but somehow their happiness is not so palpable. It lies far off. It lies deep down. The eating and drinking and merriment bewilder and amaze the patient toiler after righteousness, who has given up everything else that he may win Christ. He is not able all at once to measure their success and see its value, and say ungrudgingly and pityingly: "Yes, that is the joy that belongs to that kind of life—the joy that I put behind me once for all when I chose Christ. They have their reward. Let me press forward, and every day a little more and more have mine."

What shall such a half-discontented Christian do? He does not dream of turning back and giving up his Master. He is only bewildered. All he must do is to stand firm. In ever new obedience let him give his Master ever new opportunity to show him the deeper and deeper richness of His love. As he goes on, as he learns more of Christ, as he sees more of what it is to serve Him, he will leave all these half-regrets behind him. It will no more trouble him that lower ambitions find their lower rewards, than it seems an injustice to the strong man, toiling in the delight of health and self-dependence for his daily bread, that his little dog frisks by his side, or sleeps in the sunshine and does no work. It is the satisfaction of the soul in Christ that makes the injustices of this world seem all right and clear. **We** shall have **it** perfectly when **we get** to heaven, and we might have far more of it than we do have now.

The danger of every success except the highest! Let us be afraid of every prosperity and rest that our souls find, except that which they find in righteousness and Christ. And when they come there, and are found in Him, then let them be satisfied; for all things are theirs when once they are wholly Christ's.

XVII.

THE SPIRITUAL MAN.

"But he that is spiritual judgeth all things, yet he himself is judged of no man."—I CORINTHIANS ii. 15.

ST. PAUL is always aware of two kinds of men: one of them he calls the natural man and the other the spiritual man. He sees them living together in every group, in every family, in every church; and the general aspect of the world becomes to him most interesting because these two kinds of men are always mingled in it.

Indeed, the mingling of the natural and spiritual men in the world seems quite as universal and fundamental a fact as the mingling of the higher and lower elements in nature. The two in some degree correspond and illustrate each other. In nature there is a constant penetration of the grosser and coarser by the subtler and finer parts. The grosser portion presents itself immediately to our sight; the subtler part eludes us, and only gradually do we find out that in it the real depth and richness of power lies. The black, dead clod is found to be all teeming with the powers of growth. The heavy cloud is packed with electricity. Heat lies latent everywhere, and the atoms of the most solid things are in perpetual change. Everywhere behind the surfaces of living things lurks the great mystery of life.

Perhaps the most delightful feeling which the great discoveries of modern times have brought with them is that which comes with this ever-increasing knowledge of how a higher spirit works in everything. Dead matter is *not* dead, because it is capable of such a marvellously intimate reception of life. There is a natural and there is a spiritual; and the natural is fed and fired by the spiritual always. Each owes the other a debt. The natural would be heavy and base without the spiritual to inspire it. The spiritual would be weak and wasted without the natural for it to manifest itself through. The two together make complete nature.

It is the same thing in the great world of man. The natural and spiritual are there. The grosser part (do we not know it?) is in the men whose lives and thoughts are occupied with material affairs. The men who deal with the outsides of things, the men who carry on business, the men who administer the details of government, the men who manage social life, the men who study the material world and write the chronicles of history,—such men as these are what St. Paul means when he talks about the natural man. They are not wicked. God forbid! They are to the whole world of human nature what the black earth and the brown rocks are to the whole substance of the globe. But, just as through the rocks and earth run subtle forces which redeem them, so in among the masses of the natural men are scattered men of fire, men of imagination, men of unselfish charity, men of enthusiasm, men of religion, men who know and love the purposes and spiritual ends of business and government and society and science. These men are what Jesus told his disciples that they were: "The light of the world"; "The salt of the earth." Think what a dreary place the world would be without them. Think how flat history would lie if there were not always these buoyant and aspiring elements in it, lifting it, making manifest its principles, showing how it belongs to God. Think what your own little circle would be if there were not among its natural men some spiritual manhood. It may be a child, it may be a strong woman, it may be a brave, unpractical, protesting man, it may be a quiet dreamer; whoever it is, it is a being with a poet's soul, for this is the poets's office always—to live in and to make powerfully manifest the heart of things, their inner principles and diviner purposes.

If in these words I have made clear the difference between the natural and spiritual man, then our next step must be to see how they both co-exist in every full human creature. Just as the entire earth comprises both the earthy clod and the living principle which pervades it, so every true man has both the natural and spiritual manhood in himself. What I was saying just now may have sounded like invidious discrimination; I may have seemed to be declaring some doctrine of a spiritual aristocracy, a lofty and superior caste, made out of finer clay than the ordinary men about them. Such doctrines have been preached. Such claims have been made. But always they have proved how wrong and false they were by the way in which the self-styled aristocracy grew foolish and lost its insight; while out of the mass of men whom it dared to call base and sordid came by and by some prophet's voice, full of spiritual meaning and revelation. The real connective of such thoughts lies in the deep but simple truth that every full man carries in himself both the natural and spiritual manhood. We all have our coarser and our finer parts. There can be no mischief in the claim that the little kingdom of every man's life should be an aristocracy, and that the best part of us and not the worst part of us should rule.

And if in every man, so in every action: there are both the natural and the spiritual elements when it is perfectly performed. Not merely in the highest as we call them, not merely in worshipping and teaching and healing,—not merely in the singing of poems and the building of cities, but also in the making of bargains, and the travelling of journeys, and the clasping of hands, and the playing of games —if each of these is done as completely as it may be done—there are a natural action and a spiritual action present together. The natural action is the formal deed; the spiritual action is the motive out of which it springs and the affection which is its soul.

How life starts into new vitality when the spiritual act completes the natural action! Often, as St. Paul wrote to the Corinthians, that is not first which is spiritual, but that which is natural, and afterward that which is spiritual. Material development goes far in advance of education, of philanthropy, or of religion. It builds a splendid structure which the higher activities of man are afterward to occupy and to inspire. Is not this really the condition of the world to-day? The eager enterprise which has possessed the earth for all these centuries has created this noble, this wonderful civilization. Commerce, war, government, art, learning, social refinement, and luxury—they have all contributed, and here it stands. How wonderful it is, with its great columns driven deep in the unchanging rock, with its flashing pinnacles reaching to the sky, with the exquisiteness of beauty filling all its courts! What is it that it needs? What is it that our civilization needs? for surely it needs something. Surely it almost begins to weary of its own splendor and completeness, as if, without something else which they have not they were incomplete and unsatisfying, almost ugly and tawdry things. What is it that our civilization needs to-day? Is it not a spiritual man? Is it not a worthy occupant of this worldwide palace, a man who shall value and seek after character above everything, who shall honor and rank men by the standards of character and by no other?

Think what our civilization would be with such a manhood occupying it. Think what our business streets would be if they were all alive, as this or that office in them is now alive, with the enthusiasm of charity,—our railroads laden with men and women bound on benevolent and lofty errands, our telegraphs flashing finer and more sacred messages, our systems of government purged of selfishness, our beautiful houses filled with beautiful lives! "A dream! a dream!" we say; but, if it could be more than a dream, is it not the thing we want, is it not the thing which we must have before the world with its vast civilization can really be a sight to satisfy the eye of God or of a truly godly man?

May we not say again that the same is true of the condition of every man which is true of the condition of the world? You and I also have our natural side in advance of our spiritual side. What we need is that our natural part should be overtaken and occupied and inspired by a completer spiritual life. When that shall come, all our faculties, all our dexterities, all our leanings, will be filled with and used by the most sacred purposes. Our powers will be radiant with unselfishness. The powers themselves will be more perfect under the power of such occupation,—we shall see farther and run faster and learn more richly; but the great difference will be that the powers, great or small, will all be obedient to the spiritual purposes within them, and transparent with their light. Humility, purity, devoutness, simplicity, unselfishness,—these will be the characteristic qualities of the powerful man. Are they the characteristic qualities of the powerful man to-day? Are not rather their very opposites?

I wish that I could make you feel that I am thinking not of a few choice men for whom these lofty spiritual things are possible; I am thinking of all men,—absolutely and literally of all men. It is as true of the lounger at the street corner, of the wretched tippler in the grog-shop, of the fashionable idler in society, as it is of the earnest reformer or the high-souled saint, that there is in him somewhere a true spiritual man which, if it could awaken, must occupy and rule his life.

What can awaken it? We must not go on longer thinking about spirituality, talking about it as we have been talking, as if it were a subtle something, a sort of substance or element or quality, like heat or electricity, which exists in a greater or less degree in connection with other elements or qualities in human nature. Spirituality is God. To be spiritual is to be in communion, in communication, with God, who is the Source and Father of all spirits. When we say that every man has in him a true spiritual element, what we really mean is that every man is a child of God. The awakening of the spiritual element in any man is just his coming to know, and acting on the knowledge, that he is the child of God. And who shall teach him that?

Ah, there we come home immediately to Christ. He is the Revelation. Therefore, it is through Him that God enters into the soul. And how through Him? Under the most simple and universal of all laws: it is through obedience to Him. This law runs everywhere. To get the good out of any being you must obey that being; you must do his will. If you obey Christ, then, He will reveal God to you. The spiritual side of your life will awaken, and you will be the spiritual man.

Is that a theory or is it a fact? It is a fact, my friends! Plenty of men I have known who have *studied* Christ and yet remained unspiritual. They have turned His words this way and that; they have dissected the history of His religion; they have been wise theologians sometimes; but it has all been as if they studied physics or astronomy. But never has a man tried to *obey* Christ and not been lifted into spirituality. It cannot be otherwise. You cannot step abroad into the sunlight and yet breathe the damp air of the prison or the mine. When Christ is always bidding those who would obey Him to love God, to love their fellow-men, to live for eternity, it is impossible for any man to obey Him and yet be earthly, selfish, and short-sighted.

It would make one impatient, if it did not make one sad, to see how unreasonable men can be about this thing. One of you young men sees a comrade whom he honestly admires. That comrade lives a higher life than his. Where he is coarse that other man is fine; where he is weak that other man is strong. You would expect—what? Why, certainly, that, honoring that other man's life, he would begin to live that life himself. Instead of that you see him going on in his own life unchanged. He lives basely and he praises goodness both at once. And when you ask him for some sort of explanation, he declares: "Oh, this man has a religious nature! I have not." A religious nature! It is as if the jewel lying dark in the shadow looked out upon its brother jewel blazing in the sun, and said: "Oh, he has a brilliant nature. He is made to blaze and burn." Go forth, O darkened jewel; go forth into the sunlight. Give the sun a chance to find the power of brilliancy which is in you. Do not dare to say you cannot shine until first you have put yourself where shining is a possibility! And so one wants to say to the young man who thinks he was not made to be religious: "Try to do what Jesus Christ wants you to do; try to do His will and see what happens." Very slowly it may be, breaking out with great difficulty through the crust that lies above it, still the spiritual sense must stir, the spiritual man must come out to the light and know himself. That is the new birth which Jesus promised, whose unexpected richness has taken by surprise so many souls.

You know how Christ is always saying to people in the Gospels, "Follow me!" What does He mean? It is not that He wants a mighty company for the glory to Himself that it would bring; it is simply that He sees that if men follow Him, then He can give them God. He knows a power of receiving God which He longs to bring forth in them. So He calls to men one after another through the Gospels, "Follow me."

And so He calls to us. It is the sum of His religion. If we can follow Him, we shall grow spiritual. Then how strong and safe we are! Age and trouble and death cannot touch us any more than the spear can wound the air. He who lives in the spirit never grows old. The outward man perishes, but the inward man has a perpetual youth; and sorrow only touches the spiritual life with a more mellow happiness, and death only opens wide the door through which it passes into perfect union with God.

But it is time to pass on from this attempt to describe what is the spiritual man, and see what is meant by St. Paul's statement of the functions which belong to him. "He that is spiritual judgeth all things, yet he himself is judged of no man." Judgment and independence—those are the rights of spiritual manhood.

Think first of judgment. The impulse to form judgments is almost irresistible, and yet Jesus says, "Judge not, and ye shall not be judged," accompanying His injunction with almost a threat. And we ourselves are always hesitating between our duty of judging and our other hardly less imperative duty of not judging. We ought to discriminate between our fellow-men, and yet who are we that we should pronounce upon our brethren? May not the solution of the seeming contradiction lie in St. Paul's words? It is not that we must not judge, but we must judge with the right faculty; the right part of us must judge. Here is some man who stands before the world,—what shall I think of him? But before that comes the other question: "*With* what shall I think of him? What faculty shall I bring to bear upon him? Shall I judge him merely with my eyes and my æsthetic sense, and see whether he is beautiful? Shall I judge him with my social instinct, and see whether he is pleasant company? Shall I judge him with my commercial skill, and see whether he is growing rich? Shall I judge him by my sensibility to other men's judgments, and test whether he is popular? Shall I test him by my knowledge, and see whether he is learned? All of these are judgments *about* the man. If I take them for judgments of the man, deciding what he really is (as men are always taking them), I am all wrong. Nothing but the part of me which is spiritual can judge that,—can judge him. That part of me fixes its eye upon character, discerns motives. That is the only true judge.

Certainly, it is the only judge that any action which is worth the doing, any action which has loftiness or meaning in it, has much thought of or regard for. You do some little trivial thing, some one of the small actions of society, and you are anxious to know what the lower and smaller parts of your brethren will think about it. Will it please or offend their taste? Will it help or hurt their liking for you? But when you do some moral act, some act which has a true character in it and is really *you*, these little questions fade away. If men praise your action for its beauty, you resent it! If men say it will make you rich or honored, you turn aside from them and will not listen. Only when some man who evidently values goodness for its goodness calmly says: "The deed is good. Whether it brings wealth or poverty, whether it brings repute or scorn, the deed is good," then you are satisfied. Here is a judge who has a right to judge men, a judge whom no man can resent.

It is none the less true if the judgment is a condemnation,—if the man who is spiritual says, "The deed is bad," and not, "The deed is good." Have you never seen a group of boys submitting to the judgment of one comrade who, quietly living in the midst of them, was purer, braver, and loftier in his standards than the rest of them? They may have wished he was away,—very often people do not like the judges whom they most respect. They may have resented something which seemed arrogant about his goodness, but it was his arrogance and not his goodness that they resented. And all the time he judged them. He unmasked them to themselves, and with a wonderful meekness they acknowledged his judgment, and owned themselves for what they really were before the standards which his life made clear.

And many a group of men is just the same. "Do ye not know that the saints shall judge the world?" wrote Paul to the Corinthians and the saints,—by which is meant just exactly this: the men who are spiritual, the men who believe in things unseen, the men who care for character, do judge the world to-day. Let a bad man stand up in the community, and however he is praised and imitated and promoted by all sorts of men, he is aware and all the community is aware that he is being judged by a quiet, patient, earnest body of men, who, going their way through the familiar tasks of life, are all the while filling the air with loftier standards. The bad man may not see them, but he knows that they are there. His very bravado and bluster often mean how perfectly he is aware of them. He knows how helpless his ordinary acts are in their presence. And, wrap the adulation of his own friends and sycophants about him as closely as he will, he never can shut out this judgment of the spiritual man.

And here comes in again the truth of which I have

already spoken, that every man has the power of the spiritual manhood in himself, as well as close around him. The felt judgment of the men of higher standards wakens the higher standard in the man's own heart. Oh, self-reproach is far more common than we think! Many a man whom, in our easy confidence that we know each other, we call reckless or hardened, is really being judged all the while by his own spiritual self, is standing and trembling before the judgment-seat of his own better nature.

Put these two things together, and have you not got the Judgment Day? Already through the thick cloud of daily incidents we can see the Great White Throne. Already in the remonstrances of a man's own conscience, stirred to life by the protesting witness of the goodness in whose presence he lives, there is heard the thunder of the eternal verdict.

And then go higher still. Instead of the weak spirituality of the best men the world can show, let us see God, the Father of all spiritual life, God the Holy Spirit; and instead of the feeble appeal which the best man's goodness can make to his brother's conscience, let us hear the arraignment of the child by the Father, let us think of the terrible awakening of the child's reproachful better nature when he stands in the full presence of his Father's grieved and wounded righteousness and love,—think all that, and have you not the Judgment Day? No man can tell us its geography,—where in the universe that mysterious valley of Jehosaphat may be, that valley of decision where the "multitudes, multitudes" shall be gathered,—but it will be wherever God in His perfect spirituality draws back the veil and looks full in the face of His assembled world. I believe there shall be something corresponding to the scenic picture which the Scriptures draw, but the essence of it must be in the eternal right and power which spirituality has to judge unspirituality. The essence of it is already wherever the spiritual is judging the unspiritual in any little judgment-seat on earth.

Sometimes we hear good men complaining that goodness is so powerless; the effort to do right and to keep a pure soul and to live by highest standards is dishonored and despised, we hear. All such complaints are utterly unworthy of the good man. There is nothing more refreshing and magnificent in the whole world than the satisfied good man, the man who lives to do right, who is entirely above such weak complaints and never dreams of making them. In the first place he is too busy, too perpetually occupied with the enthusiastic struggle of his life, to think whether he is powerful or not. He is a being in himself, and if he can so bear this life of his that God shall see it and approve it, and be able to fill it with Himself, he must be satisfied. But then, if he does lift up his eyes and look about, he cannot count himself powerless. Rather he is overwhelmed and oppressed by the power that he carries. For is he not the judge of all things? O my dear friends, it must be that a truly spiritual man has nothing to complain of in the world! It is not that he must struggle on in misery and contempt until he gets to heaven, and only there be happy and content, but now, here, all that is best in life is his. Let him not degrade the high dignity of his lot, nor make it less tempting to other men by talking of its sacrifices or disgraces. He that is spiritual is already the king of the world.

One other declaration the apostle makes about the spiritual man, which we must not entirely neglect to speak of. "He that is spiritual judgeth all things, yet he himself is judged of no man." The spiritual man, while he stands judging by the highest standards whether men and things and institutions are good or bad, is all the while himself based on a foundation of his own which does not move with the perpetual changes of the things about him. I feel a truth in those words the moment they are spoken. Think of the man whom I have tried to picture, who stands in the centre of a group or a community and makes the men and things about him know whether they are good or bad. Where do his standards come from? Does he get them out of the community which he is afterward to judge by them? That would be very insignificant. Not many days would his fellow-men consent to be judged by him, if that were so. Such judges there are, men who pretend to do nothing more than just to reflect back on their brethren the standards of life which have first been caught from them. But the true spiritual judge of men, whom men acknowledge,—we immediately feel something quite different concerning him, —he stands on a footing of his own. He tests the currents of his race or of his time, because, while he stands in the midst of his race or of his time, he is not drifting with it. His foundations are his own;

and while the waves that pass by him take their bearings and measure their speed by him, they never dream of moving him at their will. He may move with them, he may even use them in his movement, as the steamship uses the waves on which it floats, but they do not give it its direction or its speed. He judgeth all men; yet himself is judged of no man!

Such men there always are,—alas for the world if they should ever fail! The greatest of such men was Jesus. "The Father hath committed all judgment unto the Son," He said. Wherever men touched His life they were judged instantly. It was as if an object of indistinguishable color floated out into the sunlight, and at once knew itself and showed to all who looked on what its color was. John, Peter, Nicodemus, Herod, Judas, Andrew, the nameless centurion, the nameless young nobleman,—how we see instantly what they are when they touch Jesus! He judges them all, and yet what one of them judges Him? He goes apart from them all when the day is done, and climbs up the hill and lays His soul upon the soul of His Father, and so, alone, is judged.

Oh, there is a real consciousness in all of us that no man is really strong unless this which is true of Jesus is also true of him. In our imperfectness it may be true of part of us, and not true of the whole. There may be one side of my being in which I do accept and depend upon the judgments of my fellow-men; while, at the same time, on another side, I insist on coming to absolute righteousness and absolute truth and being judged by them alone. On this second side only am I strong. On this second side only will my brethren really feel that I am strong, and make me their judge. There only am I really spiritual, and so there only can it be possible for me to judge all things.

What will be the temper of the man who thus stands on his own convictions and judges his fellow-men? Will he be arrogant and intolerant? Not if he is really spiritual; for, as I said before, all spirituality is God. He who is really spiritual makes himself but the channel through which God can declare Himself. The judgment, when it comes, is not his, but God's. He must be humble, for he has laid himself low that God may flow over his life into these other lives. And he must be full of sympathy, because where any part of God can flow, the whole of God will flow, and "God is Love." Humility and sympathy must fill the strong judgments of the man who judges all things because he is spiritual.

And so it all comes to this,—that if you and I can really give ourselves to God and be made His men in Jesus Christ, then we shall attain to that which we dream of, which we desire, but which so often seems very far away. We shall be able to understand and help our fellow-men without being their slaves. In very virtue of our freedom, we shall be able to understand them, and reveal them to themselves, and help them. And there is nothing better, nothing happier in the world than that. May we be made fit for it by being made God's men in Christ!

XVIII.

DELIGHT IN THE LAW OF GOD.

"I delight in the law of God."—ROMANS vii. 23.

IF we know what a man delights in, we know what sort of a man he is. "Where do you find your greatest pleasure?" is certainly one of the most searching test-questions by which men may try their own or their friends' lives. Our circumstances tie us down to the things we have to do; but when our circumstances let us up and we are free, what do we fly to with delight? One to the pleasures of the senses,—the appetites and the lusts; another to the social joys; another to the charm of books; another to the glory of nature; another into the struggle for influence and fame. How they scatter as soon as they are free! It is as if you opened the doors of a great menagerie, and all the beasts that had lived monotonously there together felt their primal instincts once more, and the lion sprang with a glad roar toward the forest, and the eagle swept upward toward the sun, and the snake shot out of sight into the grass of the thicket. In all the confusion that pervades this world and perplexes us about the characters of the men that we know the best, would there not be a clearing-off of every doubt and mystery if every man for one appointed hour should do the thing in which he most delighted? It would be an hour of strange revelations, but when it was over it would be like the morning after the Judgment Day. We should know ourselves and one another.

St. Paul gives us his statement here. He tells us what he delights in, and it is so remarkable, it is so different from what delights most men, that we may well give it our study. It is the story of the new life which he was always talking of, the beginning of which was his most precious memory, and to grow in which was his supreme desire.

"I delight in the Law of God," he said. What is the Law of God? As we live in the world we look around us and see a multitude of operations going on. How manifold they are! How confused and intricate they seem to us at first! The stars, the plants, the waves, the men, the nations—all moving back and forth on one another; everything restless, nothing still. Now, to a low order of intelligence there is sufficient pleasure in the mere confused movement of this mass of life. A low, dull-minded man is satisfied with the mere variety and vitality of the moving universe, as a child will look out of a window for hours and be amused enough with the change and liveliness of the scene before him, and never ask whither the procession that he sees is moving. But as a man improves, this mere unreasoning sight is not enough. He must look deeper. The confused variety, the ever-shuffling movement, cease to give him pleasure, and only tantalize and provoke him unless his eye can fasten on some law or principle which, if it does not tell him by what force, at least can tell him by what method, the perpetual movement is maintained. He must find a uniformity in the circling of the stars and the growing of the plants, and the coming and going of the tides; and when he has found it, when, through the clash and murmur of mere noise, beats out at last, first indistinctly and then clearer and more clear, the rhythm of harmonious order,—then he has come to a new kind of pleasure: he delights in a law.

Much harder in some respects, and yet much easier in others, is the effort to which the man is driven to discover a law in human action. The simplest instincts suggest it, and yet the most acute analysis cannot wholly trace it. But in human action man can least rest without a law. His own heart will not let him believe that, however it may be with the trees and stars, the actions of mankind are things of chance, capable of being submitted to and governed by no principle; and so he does discover various laws under which men act, and at last down deep under them all he discovers the fundamental law of conscience, the law of right and wrong, and sees that, however other influences have come and gone, have crossed it and recrossed it and mixed themselves up with it, still, always recognizable, there has always been, underneath everything, the principle of righteousness—something which proclaimed that certain deeds were right and must be done, and that certain other deeds were wrong and men must not do them.

Now, when a man discovers this, and begins to test the world by it, he has entered into a new capacity for pleasure. Deeds which before gave him delight only because they stirred his blood and touched his taste, now fall with quiet and profound satisfaction upon his sense of righteousness. "It is *right*," he says of some event of which the world is talking; and above any half-sensuous joy that comes from its picturesqueness or its bravery, that righteousness of it, that harmony with the sense of rightness that is lying in his soul, gives him a profound and peaceful satisfaction. He delights in the law of righteousness.

We pause here for a moment just to say how pitiable the man's life has been who has never known what this satisfaction is. As indescribable as the color of a rose to a blind man or the sound of a trumpet to the deaf, is the joy of righteousness to a man with no moral sense. "The thing is right,"—to say that unqualifiedly of anything, to feel the deed you see fit itself into the conception of goodness that is in your soul, so that the two claim one another like the embrace of mother and daughter, like the mutual recognition of seed and ground,—that is a joy, pure, deep, and indescribable to any one who has not felt it. I hardly dare believe that there is any man who *never* felt it; but just as to some men the sight of the stars is a rare luxury while other men study them night after night, just as some of us go once in our life and look at the great pictures while other men almost live in their sacred presence, so this delight in the law of righteousness, which is a sensation once or twice in a lifetime to many, is a continual passion to some men. They could not live without it.

But how cold it is—how abstract—this simple adoration of a law! By-and-by the man's soul must have something else! Who made this law? Whence comes this beautiful, imperious standard of righteousness? And then (we need not try now to tell how), by various revelations comes out into sight as the background and source of everything, the dear, vast personality of God. How solemn and sublime it is! "*He made us*,"—man has never done more than floated on the surface of that thought. "He made us! And all that we are, all that is in us, came out from Him. And if there is a principle of righteousness in us that makes us test and judge things morally and say that they are right or wrong, He put it there. And if He put it there, it was *Himself* He put there. This law of right and wrong is but the projection of His nature, the inspiration of His being. When I say that a thing is right, I mean that it meets and finds and harmonizes with Him. I, the child, have this of my Father in me— His standard and pattern of righteousness. And when my brother here by my side resists a temptation, when he flings back a bribe, when he drags a wrecked life to the shore and saves it, I know at once that between that deed and the purity and love of God there is a bright, true harmony; it is an act that God would smile on,—nay, it is an act that God might *do*,

And now, this God, who is He? My Maker! My Father! My everything! This beautiful world, He made it! This deliciousness of life, He gave it! I put out my hands and they come back to me loaded with His ever-falling mercies! I walk my daily path and my feet are set upon His thick-sown benefits. Ever since I was born He has been showing me how He loves me, and tempting back my love to Him. And now, if I find that this law of righteousness is His law; if, instead of tracing everywhere the beautiful persistency of an abstract principle, I see everywhere Him, my Friend and Father, working on men's natures with an influence which I have felt impressing itself on me, what then? There is nothing cold or abstract any longer. Every triumph of righteousness is an assertion of my Father's nature. Every sign of the law's working is a signal of His presence. It is not "it" any longer. It is "He." I delight not merely in the law of righteousness, but I delight in the Law of God.

I do not know whether there is anything here that seems to you strange or obscure. It has seemed strange to some men. But surely it is very simple. If I live in and love the Fatherhood of God, then every desire of mine that righteousness should be done is warmed and fired with all the intensity of my filial love to Him. It is just such a feeling as might be in the mind of a loving son of a great prince or governor. He would see the absolute righteousness of the commandments that his father gave, and for their own sakes he would desire that they should be obeyed. Having his father's nature, he would see just as his father saw when he made the law—that it was good and just in itself; but this would not conflict with a profound enthusiasm for it because it was his father's. All his filial love would fire his devotion to it. If he went out to fight in order to sustain it, there would be no separation of the motives that moved his arm as he struck one single blow for the abstract right and for his father's honor. It is his perception of the law's justice, made warm and tender with his love for his father, that fills his heart as he delights in his father's law.

Now, with all our unfilialness, let us lift up our hearts and imagine ourselves for a moment the perfectly filial children of our Heavenly Father. Let us forget the sins of yesterday, the ingratitudes and forgetfulnesses which to-day have stained our love. Let us imagine ourselves all that God's children might be, and then let there come to us, as we stand with quick, attentive ears, the story of how all over the world there is a Law of God at work. It rustles right by my feet at first. Some child I know is tempted to steal or cheat, and does not do it because God has forbidden it. Some man, burning with lust, is held back from his sin because he knows that it is wrong. And then more faintly I hear the same tidings come from a great distance. Some hero in China has laid his life down in self-sacrifice. Some good deed in the Sandwich Islands bears witness that there are souls there struggling for the right. And then sounds come out of the past. Some martyr in the sixteenth century went to the stake rather than deny his Lord. Some old-time Greek would not betray his friend, and so he gladly died. What is the sum of all these tales of goodness, these testimonies of righteousness from all the ages and from all the world? Children of God, what do they bring to us? At once a joy in righteousness and a joy in our Father. A delight in the Law of God. There is no conflict, no jealousy. God is the Law, the Law is God. And added to the deep, pure sense of satisfaction that I spoke of, that rises cool and sweet from the perfect fitting of the action to our sense of right, all mingled with it and setting it into a glow, there is a happiness in the new exhibition and the extended sway of Him whose glory and power are our light and life—our Father, God.

In its broadest way this is, I think, the soul's delighting in the Law of God. It is a noble life. This, I think, is what Paul meant. But now we must turn for a moment and remember that, while Paul meant this, he meant this in a more special form than that in which I have stated it. Paul taught a theology; we must not forget that. We dishonor and misunderstand him if we make his theology, as it has been so often made, so special and narrow that it does not coincide with and explain the problems and questions of ordinary, universal life. But while we must always shrink from turning him into a mere local Jewish teacher, we must get at his full meaning always by putting ourselves as far as possible into his place and time and way of thinking. Now, when Paul speaks of the Law of God, he is thinking especially of the Law of the Old Testament, by which his people had been trained for the coming of

Christ. He is thinking of the Bible history of the moral experiment of humanity. He is thinking of the Bible as the Book of this universal law of which we have been speaking. That is the Law of God which he delights in. And so we may apply what we have been saying not merely to the universal law of God which is written everywhere and made known to us in many ways, but to that special revelation of the Divine Will which is given to us in the Bible. Surely, if there is in us such a soul as longs everywhere to discover the intentions and purposes of God in this perplexed world where we live, the very idea of a written Law of God—a Book which shall so utter Him that any man studying it shall know what. He desires, and find His commandments written plain and clear—must be the most welcome blessing that it can dream of. And that is just what the Bible is—a Law of God, an utterance of a regulative word. That is the side on which it approaches us. That is the claim with which it comes to us. It is not a mere satisfactory account of the universe, appealing to our intelligence; it is not a poem of beautiful life, appealing to our imagination; but it is a law appealing to our conscience, and just in proportion as men read the Bible with their consciences does it satisfy them and send them away saying, "I delight in the Law of God."

I am glad to say this because it seems to me that very often nowadays men and women (we here, perhaps) are not getting the comfort and pleasure which we ought to out of our Bibles, because we do not go to them with the right idea. We miss, it may be, in ourselves that eagerness and joy with which we know that other Christians have turned to the Bible constantly and lingered over its pages. We read it, and it interests us; but it may well be that there are some of the young people whom I speak to, who have often reproached themselves that they could not feel that intimate and dear affection for the Bible, as the friend of their souls, the treasure of their lives, which they have heard older people tell about. It is not good that it should be so. It is a sad loss to the life not to love the Bible. Of course there may be other reasons, but may not one reason be that, in the midst of all the discussions and discoveries about the Bible in our time, the primary purpose of the Bible has been too much dimmed, too often lost? The histories of the Bible have been analyzed. Its poetry has been magnified. It has come to be treated in many circles as a literary work, and so we do not easily regard it as our fathers did, as a Book purely for regulation. It has been so much a Book for criticism that we do not easily make it the Book of Life. What many of us want, I am sure, is to get back to the very simplest thought of the Bible. It has all one plain, direct intent. There is nothing told us in it to satisfy our curiosity or to gratify our taste; nothing that has not the one great purpose—to regulate our lives. God is shown to us in it, not in His absoluteness as the Lord of Heaven, but in His relations to us, as our Maker, Master, Father. It is a *Law* of God, and will open its heart and beauty only to those who come to it as a law, with hearts asking for commandment and promising obedience. Certainly if we could go to our Bible thus, if to-night when we open its pages it could be with hearts feeling their failures in governing themselves and longing to have God govern them, anxiously asking Him, "Lord, what wilt thou have me to do?" the Bible would speak to us as it does not speak now; and, entering into its new mastery, finding it really the lord and ruler of our life, we should learn to love it as we learned to depend upon it, and it would no longer seem strange or extravagant for us to say: "I love my Bible"; "I delight in the Law of God."

I think, then, that, both with reference to the universal law of righteousness and also with reference to the special revelation of the Bible, we have seen that a delight in the Law of God means simply this —a love for God and a profound and peaceful satisfaction that One whom we love and trust entirely is ruling us and everything about us. It is as simple as that. Look at the life of Jesus—was there ever a Being who so delighted in the Law of God as He did? It was His meat and drink to do His Father's Will; and that calm face, unmoved among the tumult and the roar, kept its perfect calmness because in, under, through it all, He knew that God was fulfilling His purposes, manifesting Himself. That satisfied Him entirely. "Ye could do nothing against me unless it were given you from above," He said to His persecutors, and so He let His persecutors do their worst. "Even so, Father, for so it seemed good in thy sight"—that was the end of everything for Him. He knew what God's Law was. A portion of the Deity Himself, He had felt it control the throbbing pulses of the universe, and had seen the bright, endless ranks of Cherubim and Seraphim bow before it, and uncounted hosts of angels fly to do its bidding. And now, a man, weary and dusty and bewildered, it seemed glorious and sweet that His life as He toiled back and forth between Jerusalem and Galilee, up the steep hill at Nazareth, and at last out of the gate to Calvary, was all held and sustained and regulated by that eternal, supreme Law. It rested Him and strengthened Him. He delighted in the Law of God.

Sometimes it seems to me as if we, with our imperfect obedience to and realization of God, getting so little of what He wants to give us every day, wrenching ourselves by our wilfulness out of His care,—as if we, living thus and looking from our disordered lives at the calm, obedient life of Jesus, were like a wrecked and broken ship lying dismasted on the ocean, feeling the winds that it could not obey, tossed by the waves on which it could not steer,—as if that ship should see bearing down upon it a ship like itself, only perfect,—every sail set, every breeze caught, ruling the waves that carried it, borne on in all its stateliness by the very ocean that seemed ready to open its black mouth and swallow the poor, helpless wreck that floated like a foreign and unwelcome thing upon its bosom. So Jesus, perfectly obedient to His Father, delights in the same Law of which we are so apt to be afraid. We love to look at His life. And most of all the stately ship is beautiful to us if she bears down to us that she may help us. The perfect obedience of Jesus, beautiful in itself, is a thousand fold more beautiful if it gives itself to the rescue of us from our disobedience.

If we understand, then, what it is to delight in the Law of God, I think we can see easily enough what must be the blessed consequences of such a noble condition in the life of the happy man who has attained it. It will sweep out of his life the two great hindrances that most impede and vex the life of every man — selfishness and restlessness. O my dear people, look into your lives and tell me, what is it that keeps you unhappy and ineffective? Is it not these—these which came in across the pure happiness of Eden and ever since have held men in their power. I open the old palace of the Cæsars and I open the squalid hut of some Fiji barbarian, and in both there is just what makes miserable your house and heart, the old, undying tempters and tormentors of the human soul—selfishness and restlessness. What is there that can cast them out and bring in their bright opposites, devotion and peace? What but just this, a delight in the Law of God; such a new state of being that the soul shall be happy in knowing that God reigns, and in obediently helping His government to its complete results. Is there any selfishness left there? What room is there for it when the one wish is that God's Will may be done? Is there any restlessness left there? Where can there be any flaw for it in the entire peace of a soul trusted away from itself into the hands of a

Lord of perfect wisdom and entire love? O my dear people, all the while that you are selfish and restless there is a region of unselfishness and peace right by your side in which you might be walking. If you would only make one effort, leap one fence, you would be in it, and your life would be changed. That leap is taken, that change comes, when you begin to delight in the Law of God.

Am I painting what is only a mockery? Am I telling of something which is very bright and tempting, but which is utterly out of your power or mine to attain? God forbid! It is not an easy, matter-of-course thing, I know. I have talked, perhaps, as if it were very easy for St. Paul. It is time for me to read you his other verse and show you how hard he found it, what a perpetual struggle it was to him. He says there were two men in him, one of which was capable of this supreme delight, while the other lived in lusts and low desires. "I delight in the Law of God after the inner man," he says. "But I see another law in my members warring against the law of my mind, and bringing me into captivity to the law of sin, which is in my members. Oh, wretched man that I am! who shall deliver me from the body of this death!" He saw the beauty and peace of living in the delight of the Law of God. Part of the time he lived up there in that high employment; but then his lower passions were always dragging him down. Just your life and mine exactly; and certainly it may help us when we see that the great Paul—that Saint of God—had not escaped from this harassing and fluctuating life in which we are living.

He has escaped it now. In God's very presence, there in heaven where he stands through his Redeemer, he has left selfishness and restlessness behind forever and has entered into entire devotion and perfect peace. But when he wrote these words he was just where we are—trying to delight in God and yet dragged back always by pride and selfishness to his own restless self.

If Paul could speak to us to-day he would tell us how he finally escaped, by what divine and loving ways God led him out of the power of his lusts and into the glory of that pure delight in God in which he is now laboring. "Be patient," he would say,—"be patient, my brethren, and never be discouraged. Your God is able to deliver you, and will deliver you at last."

Shall we venture to put words into the mouth of the glorified Apostle and think what he would say to us if he should speak to his brethren who are wandering and struggling in the darkness which he must so well remember? We run no risk, for we know well enough what he would say to us.

First of all would he not say: "Never forget that you have the power, the capacity of delighting in the Law of God. Let no tendency to grovel and to love low things blot out of your soul the certainty that there is in you a capacity for a higher happiness. Do not think it impossible, even down where you are in the depths of degraded passion, do not think it impossible that you should sit in heavenly places with Christ Jesus and delight in the Law of God. Cling to the possibility of the highest life, however low you sink." Would he not urge us with some such words as these?

And then again he would say: "Obey the Law of God even if you have no love for it, and so you will learn to love it. Even if obedience be only a task, even if righteousness be a burden and a cross to you, even if you have to force yourself to your duty—still, *do* it. The Law of God is delightful; force yourself up to it and you shall know its delight. Do your duty, even if duty be wearisome and hard, for then you are in the place where it can become joyous and easy to you." That he would say with all the emphasis of his own brave duty-doing life.

But then (and we can almost hear his voice rise and see his face glow as he advances), then he would go on to what he would most love to say. "I escaped," he would declare, "purely and solely by the help of Christ. He took me, and, drawing me into His love, made me delight in God's Law by my delight in Him. He took me and showed me the Beauty of Holiness by offering me Himself as the Master to serve, the Law to obey. Look at Him! —He is the Law of God. To be conformed to Him is to obey God perfectly. Can you love Him? Can you *not* love Him? He lived for us, for me and you," the old Apostle would say, putting himself right by our side. "He lived for us, He died for us, He lives for us forever,—can you not, must you not love Him? Must not your soul delight in Him?" And then, turning back to the life and work of heaven, we should hear him say as his voice ceased from our ears: "To delight in Him, that is to delight in the Law of God. Christ is the end of the Law for righteousness."

We can at least do this which he tells us,—we can believe that there is in us the power of loving God's Law. We can obey God's Law even before we love it, doing our duty however hard it be. And we can pray to Him who came to show God to all men, that He will show God to us, and make us delight in His Law.

Oh, let us claim our souls for their highest joys, for it is sad and terrible that men and women who have the power of loving and obeying God should be loving and obeying the tyrants of this world—houses and fortunes and the poor standards of Society. May God set us free and lift us up to Himself!

XIX.

THE ARK OF THE COVENANT.

"And the ark of the covenant of the Lord went before them."—
NUMBERS x. 33.

WHENEVER a Jew read these words they must have presented to him a very vivid picture in his people's history. They present the same picture only less vividly to us. The host of Israel is leaving Sinai on its long journey across the desert. Their caravan in its vast numbers has trailed its slow length out of the camp at the foot of the mountain where it has tarried so long and is stretched out toward the Promised Land. It goes slowly crawling, like a vast serpent, along the dreary stretches of sand. And there are other caravans in sight. Just as to-day, the Arab from the South, the Egyptian from the West, the mixed nomadic tribes who live on the bright spots of the desert itself, are moving hither and thither, breaking the monotonous horizon and giving some variety and interest to the desolate sameness of the scene. But among all the caravans this one of his forefathers is marked and separated to the Hebrew's eye. Not merely by its size, not merely because it is a moving nation, not merely because it is his forefathers, but mainly because of something which is always carried at the head of the procession, which gives a tone and character to it and all its movements. It is a certain box or chest; not very large, some five feet long and three feet high and broad, covered with cloths and hidden from their sight. This is the Ark of the Covenant. No other caravan in all the desert has anything like this mysterious and sacred chest. Wherever it moves the eyes of all the host are on it. Whenever they encamp the tents of the host are pitched around it, as if that they might protect it, and it might bless them. Whenever it started upon the march the voice of Moses is heard, crying aloud: "Rise up, Lord, and let thine enemies be scattered; and let them that hate thee flee before thee." Whenever it rests and stands still the same voice cries: "Return, O Lord, unto the many thousands of Israel." This is what marks the moving army of the Israelites, that wherever they go, the Ark of the Covenant of the Lord goes before them.

At first it looks like superstition and some foolish dream of magic. But it is not that at all. The following of the ark has a reasonable meaning. Really, that golden chest, wrapped in its curtains, represents a truth, and that truth it really is which is moving on before them and on which their eyes are always fastened for direction and for inspiration. The truth is that centre-truth of Judaism, that they are God's chosen people. That truth, not any mere box of wood and gold, it is which is leading them and keeping up their courage. It is inside the ark, this truth of their national belonging to God, in the shape of three sacred and venerable relics,—two stone tables, on which God had written their fundamental law, a pot of manna which God had sent from heaven to satisfy their hunger, and a rod with buds upon it which had been the symbol of God's life and inspiration imparted to their national High Priest, Aaron. God's law, God's care, God's communication,—these three facts grouped together in the ark represented the one truth,—that God was their God, that He had taken them for His, that He and they belonged to one another. It was that truth which they set at the head of their army; around that truth the silver trumpets blew, and behind it the whole multitude of the people marched. They followed after it all the day-time, and they clustered close around it all the night. No wonder that the ark in which the symbols of that truth were enshrined came to seem almost as if it were God present in their midst. When it was lifted up, it seemed as if it were indeed God rising to go against His enemies and theirs. When it was set down upon the ground it was almost as if God Himself planted Himself among the many thousands of Israel.

This covenant ark was to the Jews the promise of two things which they needed every day and hour — safety and direction. It was not safe for them where they were, and they did not know which way to go. There were the Midianites and Moabites about them, and there were the pathless sands before them; what could they do without a protector and a guide? And He who helped them must be both of these to them. It was of no use to them that He should protect them if they were still left to wander hopelessly. It was of no use to them that He should guide them if it were only into dangers from which He could not keep them safe. Both wisdom and power they must have to look to. As David sang long afterwards, their Lord God must be a sun and a shield. And both of these they knew were in that symbolic ark which they followed as they marched, and clustered around while they rested. Wisdom and power met in the stone tables and the miraculous manna and in the budded rod.

And now, how far off all this seems! How long ago, how far away this caravan of Jews trampling along through the weary sand between Arabia and Syria, with their strange ark borne along before them three thousand years ago! How far away from us here on this Sunday morning! It startles and delights our sense of picturesqueness to lift our eyes all at once from this modern life and let them rest away off across the ocean and across the centuries upon this foreign picture. But have we nothing more to do with it than that? If we have really got at what the picture means, and if you have really minds and hearts to look not at the forms alone but at the hearts of things, I hope to make you see in that procession following the ark the picture of a possible life of yours—the picture of a life that, reconciled, covenanted, given away and dedicated to God, follows the truth of its dedication, makes that the leading and inspiring truth of everything, and gets safety and guidance out of it every day it lives. The Christian life so often seems to men a weight and a restraint. It seems so often as if it put a man's life into danger and bewilderment, instead of into safety and clearness, to give it to God, that I wish we could see it all differently; I wish that we could really see, among all the purposeless, defenceless nations of the desert, wandering without a plan, unsafe, unguided, this one procession of the Israelites moving safely and surely day after day because they alone had God, because they followed the Ark of the Covenant.

The soul led and protected by its covenant with God—that, then, is our subject. But first of all, I think we often hesitate at that word "covenant." It has an ancient, Jewish sound. It was a word under which Abraham, Isaac, and Jacob conceived their relationship to God. But now it often seems as if the word had a hard kind of contract sound about it.

It appears to picture God as standing and weighing out His love and benefaction, grain by grain, against the scrupulously exacted equivalent which man was called upon to render. It seems to miss the whole idea of freedom and spontaneousness which we rather love to make prominent in the thought of God blessing man. But I am sure that there is danger of a great deal of our modern talk doing injustice to the grand, straightforward religion of the old Jews, partly by attributing to them ways of thinking which they never had, and partly by losing sight of the real eternal value of a great many of their broad and simple truths which modern subtlety has refined away.

For instance, the Jews no doubt had deeply engrained in their religion the notion of the necessary mutualness of every relationship between God and man. They believed, that is, that it was impossible for God to do anything for man, without man's meeting God with a responsive activity of his own. God could not bless a people unless the people were obedient. God could not speak to a soul unless the soul would listen. God could not lead a man unless the man would follow. The necessities were not artificial but essential. Now, that is a great idea. It is an idea which it is dangerous, nay, absolutely fatal, for religion to lose. We look around, and is there one thoughtful man among us who is not often in fear for the religion which we see the most of now-a-days, lest it should grow weak and perish from its losing just this idea of the necessary mutualness of the relation of God and man?—men expecting to be blessed without being obedient, expecting to be enlightened without humble devoutness, expecting to be led to truth and righteousness when they make no attempt to follow. These are the indications of how that old Jewish idea may be lost, and of what is the peril of losing it. Now, this is just the idea that the Jew pictured to himself under the form of a covenant. He was to do something and God was to do something. "Draw near to me, and I will draw nigh to you"; "Do this, and you shall live"; "If you will be my people, *then* I will be your God." The mutualness was essential and necessary, not merely arbitrary. It was pictured in sacrifices minutely described and punctiliously demanded; but at the bottom it was this great, true, everlasting idea,—that for God and man to come together both must do something, that God cannot meet live men as the sunlight strikes a dead rock, merely giving itself to what is helpless, but as the sunlight strikes a live tree which must open to receive its bounty. There is no covenant with the rock. There is a covenant with the tree.

No doubt the Jews dropped away from the lofty simplicity and truth of this idea. With perhaps the same tendency to barter which has characterized the Hebrew in all times, they did degrade this great mutualness of life into a close, hard bargain in which, by doing certain formal things, they might bind God down to certain mercies of which they could not otherwise be sure. The prophets found this state of things, and in strong opposition to it they proclaimed the perfect freeness of God's mercy: "Ho! every one that thirsteth! He that hath no money, come ye, buy and eat, without money and without price."

Jesus found the same state of things,—every mercy of God ticketed in the price-list of Rabbinical scrupulousness,—and He, too, exalted the freedom of God. "Whosoever will, let him come." "If any man thirst, let him come unto me, and drink." No doubt the high idea of covenant did run down into a low idea of contract; but in itself it is a high idea, the high idea of the necessary mutualness in the life and relationship of God and man.

As a Christian man, I believe fully that all the modern discussion of the being and work of God, more or less connected with natural science, which often sounds like atheism, is really tending, under God, to a better knowledge, on our part, of what He is and how He relates Himself to us. And sometimes it seems to me as if, with its strong assertion of the human side, it were just this covenant idea which the modern discussion of God is destined to restore and to confirm,—as if without weakening the absoluteness of God it were bringing forth the way in which He has bound Himself to man and made it seem impossible for Him to send His best mercies until men have risen to their part in the mutual relationship. The modern physical philosopher, solemnly insisting that the price of health is cleanliness and decency, often reminds us strangely of the Hebrew Prophet denouncing pestilence upon the people who refused to hear and obey the word of God. At least this covenant truth of mutualness is in them both.

I have dwelt upon this truth of the covenant because it appears in its perfection in the relation which the Christian holds to God. I hope that after what we have said there is no trouble for our minds in carrying over the word "covenant" to the richer relations between God and man which Christianity makes known, and hearing Jesus called "the Mediator of the new covenant." The Christian has made a covenant with God! It was a phrase more common once than now. But still it is a great and precious truth. What does it mean? Not, surely, that the Christian has bargained his obedience against a certain forgiveness and a certain help, not that he has undergone a certain humiliation and contrition in virtue of which God has bound Himself that he shall not be punished but shall go to heaven: nothing of that sort. But this,—that he has entered into a mutualness of life with God; that he has met God's willingness to help him with a willingness to be helped; that he saw God wanted to forgive him, but could not because he was impenitent, and so he repented and received forgiveness; that he saw God was willing to pour light and strength into him, but could not because he was proud, and so he humbled himself and the light streamed in; that he took God and God took him; that he could not have taken God without God's taking him, and that God could not have taken him without his taking God; but that by mutual love they met, one bringing submission and the other help, and that those two meeting made the soul's salvation-time.

That is a man's covenant consciousness. And when the man becomes aware that out of that covenant is coming the impulse and the safety of his life, that what is guarding him from sin and throwing light on duty, and keeping up his courage and filling him with hope, is the certainty that all this has taken place—that he has given himself to God,—when a man knows that, the power by which he lives all issues from the certainty of the position in which he stands with the great Lord and Master of his life. He is the man—walking on strongly behind and in the light of this sublime transaction between his soul and God—he is the man who is following the Ark of the Covenant.

Years, years ago, perhaps, a young man somewhere, in some church, some shop, some school, who had before lived as if on this green earth, under this blue sky, there were no greater being than himself, came to know God. God came to him! He came to God! Both of these sentences tell the story of what happened. It was not an unwilling God who laid His hand upon the soul and blessed it. It was not an unwilling soul that laid itself upon the bosom of the mercy. The soul and God met in the covenant of life. Well, years have passed away, and now the man is old. How many acts the man has done, how many thoughts, how many words have crowded in since that day of his boyhood, when he and God gave themselves to one another. But ask him, and he will tell you that all his life has just been following out the promise of that day. All that he has done or been of good was wrapped up in that perfect gift of himself to the Eternal Good. All that he has received of blessing really descended on him when the Lord became his God. When he has doubted, he has looked up and seen His promise shining; when he has been tempted that promise has sustained him. He is where he is to-day in character and life because of that meeting of his life with God's, in church, or shop, or school, so many years ago. What shall we say of such a life? *It has followed the Ark of the Covenant.* How it brings out the difference in men! They have traversed the same desert, been parched with the same thirst, drank of the same springs, had the same comforts or discomforts; but one has had peace and purpose, and the other only unrest and discontent. One has walked in the footsteps of an apprehended God; the other has gone in the ways of his own will. One has lived the Israelites' life, and the other the Midianites' life; and so one comes to Canaan, and the other is lost among the sands.

But take one step more. How is it possible that a conscious and remembered relationship to God should constitute a rule of life. "I grant," one says, "that it is good for you who are God's child to know your Father and to come to as true an understanding as you can with Him; but tell me, how does that practically help you? How does it unravel for you this snarl of life? How does it make you know what you ought to do to-morrow morning? How does it teach you how to treat this troublesome, ungrateful friend? The Jews' Ark of the Covenant was different. It was not merely a memory and an idea; it was there in wood and gold. They could see it; when it turned north they saw it; when it turned south they saw it. They had only to keep their eyes on it and they were safe."

But remember the experience to which the Christian soul looks back; its covenant which it remembers was not a mere emotional transaction, begun and ended in itself. Just as in the Jews' covenant, something came in,—the tables and the manna and the rod,—which were mediators, as it were, which brought the authority and mercy on the one side to the need and the submission on the other, so in the Christian's covenant there was a mediator, not a *thing* any longer, but a Living Person who brought the willingness of God and the willingness of man together. The Christian's whole remembrance of his new covenant with God is bound up in association with the Christ in whom it was made. "He brought God to me, and me to God, and we met in Him," the Christian says. "I never should have known how God loved me, and I never should have known how I needed God, if He had not shown me both." And then when the Christian looks up and says, "Where is this covenant of mine to lead me?" when he asks just the question that you asked—"How will it make for me a rule of life?"— behold there, walking before him, a Human Life which lightens up all human living, goes He in whom the covenant is represented—Jesus Christ, its Mediator. What the golden and wooden chest was to the Hebrew, this Saviour in His own flesh and blood is to the Christian. He goes before His people. He is the Ark of our covenant. To follow the Christian Ark of the Covenant is to follow Him.

O my dear friends, I promise you that I will never preach to you any mere vain theological speculations, that cannot touch your life; but I must tell you of what so many Christians here among you know so well, of how the covenant between the soul and God issues into the service of Him in whom the covenant is made, and the life of the Christian becomes the following of Christ. "To follow Christ! —that sounds vague. Christ lived so long ago! If

I had been there, I could have followed Him. I could have kept close to Him and imitated every action. But now the times have altered. Here in our modern homes, now in our youngest century, how can I shape these daily acts upon such different daily acts of One who lived so long ago, so far away?"

But if you ever tried it, you would cease to wonder. For this is the power of that life of Jesus,—a power which you cannot know till you do try it, a power which all who have ever tried it will bear witness to,—that they who enter into living sympathy with Him by gratitude do truly see not merely how to do those certain things He did, but how He would have done, how He would wish to have His servants do, every most different and modern thing which it may come into their lots, so different from His lot, to attempt. The Christian, thoroughly in sympathy with Jesus, knows how his Christ, who never bought or sold, would manage his great business; knows how his Christ, who had no wife or child, would rule a household; knows how his Christ, who lived the patient subject of a despotism, would vote as the free and responsible citizen of a Republic. He finds his Lord a legible and shining Law in every strangest place to which his duty calls him. And, doing everywhere what he knows that there the Christ would do, in and through whom He has been brought near to God, he is living a larger service than any Jew tramping through the sands after his ark, or any disciple following Jesus about the city streets. In a higher and fuller way than either of them, he is following the Ark of the Covenant.

I said of the ark that went before the Israelite in the desert that it gave him two things—safety and guidance. These same two things come to the Christian out of his following of Christ. He has both security and progress. He is at once kept from danger and led on to ever greater things. And it is clear that both these things must meet in any strong and happy life. Merely to be safe, to rest outside of danger, but to make no advance, to conquer no new ground, to grow to nothing greater day by day—that is a most depressing life. And merely to advance when every step is uncertain, when the consciousness of danger is haunting every footstep, when you cannot tell whether you are going right or wrong—that is a most distressing life. And yet almost all our expedients of living seem to aim at one of these ends, not at both of them; either at safety or at progress, not at the two together. Conservatism with all its forces tries to make men safe, radicalism with its forces tries to keep men moving, till safety in thinking and acting comes to sound of deadness and torpidity, and progress to many ears is full of the ideas of reckless peril and destruction. It is the privilege of the true follower of Christ that these two, so often separated, meet for him.

See how it is in thought. A man whose whole life is led by the consciousness that his life belongs not to himself but to his God—led by the Ark of the Covenant—is armed most strongly against the worst dangers of thinking men. Every thought that comes to him is brought into that obedience. He cannot think wilfully merely to please himself. He cannot think servilely merely to please other people. Whim, pride, the love of novelty, the fear of novelty, these, which you all know are the perils of thinking men, are swallowed up in the conviction that he must not think anything lightly or unworthily of Him whom he follows. But at the same time the limitlessness of the Christ who leads him, the certainty that He has infinitely more of truth to show than He has yet made known, makes His true follower impatient after new ideas and broader fields of thought. The Israelite host was at once safer where it stood, and yet surer to move onward to new camping grounds, than the loose tribes of Moabites and Midianites around them. So the Christian thinker ought to be at once surer of what he holds and more eager to move on to new truth than the disciple of any other master. If he loses either his safety or his progress, if he grows either a sceptic or a bigot, he surrenders his privilege. The intellectual man, following the Ark of the Covenant, learns the true harmony of positive convictions with free and enterprising thought.

And it is with life and conduct just as it is with thought. Here, too, there seems to be a struggle. Safety and progress will not blend with one another. One man says: "Let me be safe. Let me be sure of doing nothing wrong." And so he shuts himself up to a little circle of conventionally good things; he cuts off a multitude of innocent pleasures which he chooses to consider doubtful; he never dreams of enterprising and original goodness; and all his life grows meagre. Another man, seeing him, grows afraid of the paralysis of virtue, and goes forth recklessly in the fields of wildest license. He casts all thoughts of safety aside. What good men have most called wrong shall become right for him. He will walk through the midst of impurity and yet be pure. He will go to the bottom of fiendishness and bring up a new kind of saintliness from thence. The movement, the zest of life, is everything. Safety is too low a thing to think of.

And then comes Christ and His follower; what does He do? He binds the follower's heart completely to Himself by love. He makes His life and His disciple's really one. He makes it His servant's one desire to be like Him. This great desire, as a triple wall, He builds about His servant's purity. He makes him safe with the protection of His own character and standards always present there through love. The Christian is assaulted by temptation. He looks up and sees that the sin to which he is tempted is a desertion of his Lord, is a wrong and pain to Jesus, and he will not do it. Is there any safety so complete as that? But then it is no safety of mere laws. It is no limited and bounded negative. It is an infinite and boundless positive. As his loyalty to Christ restrains him, so also it incites him. As he will not do anything in disobedience to Christ's nature, so he will not be satisfied until he has completely matched that nature with his own. It stretches before him into new realms of growth and duties that have seemed impossible. Virtue is no longer paralysis, but inspiration.

What is the result? A fear of sin that does not bind the feet, but loosens them, and gives them wings towards holiness. A longing for holiness that is all the more tenderly conscious of its danger of temptation. The Christian will always surprise men with this mixture of fear and freedom. He will refuse to do things which men see no harm in, saying: "I dare not. It is not safe. I cannot expose my soul." And then he will boldly go forth into some new field of adventurous duty that men think most perilous, doing most unconventional work there, saying, "The Master whose I am and whom I serve is leading me."

I am talking all in vain unless you who are Christians understand me. Do you remember an old life when you alternately stood guard over your character and tried to live a live, real life? Sometimes it was one and sometimes it was the other; sometimes safety and peace, sometimes progress and action. And then came Christ. You gave yourself to Him. The new life opened. You have lived since then with a new consciousness—that you were His—filling everything, sinking down and spreading out through all of you. Tell me the story of that life. Is it not that safety has ceased to be sluggish and action has ceased to be dangerous to you, now that safety is rest in Christ and action is work for Him? He guards you, and that stimulates you. He sets you to work, and that rests you. Righteousness and peace, which used to be at variance in your life, have kissed each other and are reconciled.

Is not this what we want?—to be safe with a security that is not cowardice or palsy, to be alive with a vitality that is not wearing us out—safety and progress? And we can have them both only as we do not dare to try to make these lives our own, but give them up to God, and live them not for ourselves but for Him. The Jew who wants safety only stays ignominiously in Egypt. The Jew who wants freedom only starts out by himself across the desert and is seen no more, but leaves his bones whitening among the sands. The Jew who wants safety and freedom both gives himself to God and follows the Ark of the Covenant.

And so the Christian follows Christ. Now upon this side and now upon that he wanders in his weakness, but he always comes back to the central track in which the Ark has passed. He will carry nothing with him that cannot go through the often straight and narrow places where his Leader walks. He will never let a thought of fear come in so long as he sees that Leader out before him, to show him that he is on the right road. And so at last, just as the ark led the Jews across the Jordan and into the Promised Land, and there they set it down in its new place, and lived the new life of their new home around it; so when Christ has led us safely into Heaven, He who has led us shall take His place in our midst, and, gathered around Him, the new life of the redeemed soul shall begin and go on, by His grace, in perfect safety and unhindered growth forever.

XX.

SONS OF GOD.

"Beloved, now are we the sons of God, and it doth not yet appear what we shall be."—1 JOHN iii. 2.

"WE are the sons of God," St. John says, "and it doth not yet appear what we shall be." He says *we*. He binds his own experience to his disciples.' He does not stand apart, either telling them of something which belongs only to himself or announcing what concerns only them. He does not say "I" or "you," but "we." His present and future are theirs, and theirs are his. And this is almost always St. John's way. It seems to be the necessary character of all the truest and deepest religion when it is experimentally conceived. The profoundest experiences admit of no monopoly. The attempt to limit them strips their whole value out of them. I cannot believe in the highest spiritual privileges for myself, unless I believe in their possibility for you; nor can I really think them possible for you unless I know that I too may have them. So it is by the experimental character of all his religion, the way in which his theology comes out of his life, that St. John is brought into clear understanding of and sympathy with the spiritual life of others, and says, "*We* are the sons of God."

We want to look at this statement of the Christian life, with reference to its present and its future, which John makes for himself and those who believe with him. Servants of Christ together, they lived the same life now, and the same prospects stretched out before them all. They were the sons of God, and that sonship must open into a fuller life which they could not yet grasp or understand. It did not yet appear what they should be. These were the two elements of their life.

And notice, first, how these are really the elements of all the highest and most successful living. All the best life that we see about us, all the truest parts of our own life, have been characterized by a certain combination. They have united a clear, tangible, intelligible present to a vast and indefinite future. Out from some fixed and certain point, where everything was solid and indisputable, they have reached into a distance which stretched beyond their ken and lost itself in visions of unexplored possibilities. The best moments of all our lives, as we look back upon them, seem, I am sure, to be the times when we were clearest about our present position and present duty, and when the possibilities of life seemed most infinite to us. The best scenes in the ever-moving panorama have been those which had in them the elements of the best pictures —a clear, strong foreground, where the foot was planted solidly, and a vast vague outlook, where the imagination might find endless room to range; a steady point to stand on and infinity to look into. Both are essential to the happiest and largest life,— not merely a vast future and not merely a solid present, but the two together.

Just look at one or two of the points of life where these two characteristics supremely meet, and see if they are not the strongest and most beautiful. They meet in childhood most pre-eminently. Nowhere is the present so definite and clear as there. The simple relations that surround his life, the few plain duties that belong to every day, the narrow circle in which his habits move, the comprehensible authority that presses him on every side—all make the child's life tangible with a distinctness that is lost in the complicated relations that come with later years. He is *one* thing—his father's son. That is his everything—his fountain of enjoyment, his law of work, his rest, and his incitement. But at the same time, what wide outlooks from that strong simple standing point! What visions come to that boy, shut in to the limits of his father's care! How vast life looks to him! Just because the foreground is so sharp and real, the distant stretches into a more measureless infinity. Because he understands the limited present so clearly, he dreams of the future so enthusiastically. But is it not the union of these two, of the limited present with the limitless future, that makes the charm and romance of his childhood? He knows what he is now, but it doth not yet appear what he shall be.

There is another moment in which the same union appears, and to which something of the same charm belongs. It is the time when the young man has just chosen his profession and looks out into the possibilities of that work in life whose new tools are thrilling the unfamiliar hands that have just grasped them. I think that there is no more interesting or beautiful time in life. He is a boy no longer. The boyish fixedness in the limitations of his home is over. Those doors have opened years ago, and let him out into the unsettledness that belongs next in life. He has passed through the years of early youth, the years in college, when everything is vague and doubtful, when the boy does not know either what he is to be or what he is. At last his feet have touched the solid ground. "I am *this*," he is able to say once more. "Here is my ground. Now I am a doctor, a merchant, a minister, a lawyer." It is not mere conceit in the new signboard or the new surplice that you see glowing in his face; it is a healthy satisfaction in being something, and knowing what he is. But in that glowing moment does he see what he shall be? Do any limits of his new work stand up in the distance? Is it not just then, when his feet are set firm on the strong ground, that the horizon of his profession sweeps away from him? Never before and never after does the work seem so vast. To be the perfect lawyer, the perfect minister, the perfect merchant, never before and never after seems so unattainable. By and by, among the ridges and the hollows of his professional life, the horizon of its possibilities contracts, and he gets some point in his eye which is the farthest that he can attain; but the glory of this first moment is that the new work allows itself no limits, and the neophyte, strong in a definite task and gazing into an indefinite prospect, can say: "I am this now. What I shall be doth not yet appear."

The same is true of the clear and convinced acceptance of any strong, clear truth. You come to the unhesitating belief in any fundamental principle in philosophy or politics or social life, and are there not two elements in the satisfaction of that strong moment when you fasten yourself upon it? You say: "This is strong; how good it is to be here!" and you say also: "I wonder where this will carry me,—what other thing shall I come to believe because of my believing this?" At that good moment when you thoroughly believe in a new truth, your feet plant themselves firmer and your eyes look out wider. The ground grows solid under you and the distance vast before you.

As one says this, he longs to stop and point out to the young people who listen to him what a lesson and law of life all this involves. Fixity and range, a definite working-place and a vast prospect,—these are the necessary conditions of the best and most effective life. Every man must have these two conditions, or his life grows weak and narrow. What then? One wants to say these two things: First, find yourself a place. Do not be drifting hither and thither, ready to do anything and doing nothing. Be something as early and as wisely as you can find for yourself a place in some profession, in some of the clear, tangible, definite tasks of men.

Do not let the accident of wealth be your curse by standing between you and a work in life. Do not let anything hinder you from the deep satisfaction of knowing something, doing something, being something, having something,— of which you can say to yourself and other people, "I am this." However it may be in other lands, there is no chance here in America for a man to do his best good or live his best life except in some definite and recognized employment of his powers. But be sure your work is large enough to give you prospects, and be sure you see the prospects that it offers. No profession is worthy that does not give a man room to look out into more usefulness and higher character than he can comprehend at once; but any honest task is capable of being so largely conceived that he who enters into it may see stretching before him the promise of things to do and be that will stir his enthusiasm and satisfy his best desires.

So this is the lesson of our truth: Be something definite and special, but let that something be so large, and *be it* in so large a spirit, that you shall not be able to be it all at once, but that it shall tempt you on forever to indefinitely greater things. Two kinds of creatures haunt our city as they have haunted cities ever since Cain, the son of Adam, built the first. We know them both, and we have seen the harm that both can do. One is the visionary and the other is the drudge. The visionary is the man who has no present; the drudge is the man who has no future. The visionary never can say, "Now, I am this." The drudge never lifts up his eyes and says, "It doth not yet appear what I shall be." To the visionary all is future; to the drudge there is nothing but the present. One's life floats off like the smoke from the city's chimneys; the other's runs off like water from the city's streets. To be saved from being either, to be strong and permanent and useful—that can come only by joining a clear, sharp, solid work to large hopes and great ambitions; by seeing visions from some peak of rock.

But now we turn from all this general discussion to find the same principle which we have been describing at work in Christian life. St. John says, "Now are we the sons of God." There is the present for him and his disciples. Ah, my dear friends, we must put ourselves back into a time when the simplest truths of Christianity were all new; we must strip off all the familiarity which Christian thought and love have clustered about the idea of God's Fatherhood before we can understand how strong and clear a fact that was in the experience of those first disciples. "We are the sons of God." Except in some inspired poet here and there, the first sense that all men were God's children had been lost. Men had counted themselves and treated their brethren like brutes. They had drifted alike out of the responsibilities and the joys of sonship to the Almighty. Then Christ had come and made them again, so far as they would accept His blessing, the sons of God. "To as many as received Him, to them gave He power to become the sons of God." What does that mean? Not that He made men something which it had never been in man to be before; He made it possible for man to come where he always had belonged. Not that He established a new relationship between man and his Creator; He declared the beauty and glory of the first relationship from which man had voluntarily departed. It was a redemption. It is nowhere said that Christ made God man's Father. He made man God's child by showing him the unquenched love that was in his Father's heart, and then by the touch of love, made vital and strong by suffering, wakening up the divine consciousness, the power of godliness, the power of living like a child of God, in the human heart.

I said how new and strong a fact that was to those disciples, but how new and strong it is to any man now who really plants his feet upon it! You have been living like a child of the world or a child of the devil. Nothing that you ever do or say would ever indicate—nay, you have yourself forgotten—that there is anything divine about you. None of the restraints and none of the incentives of high parentage are in your life. But Christ comes, comes to you as truly as He came to those peasants fishing on the lake, or to that tax-man sitting at his table. He brings and sets before you a human life. How human it is every act in it bears witness. If any one tells you that He is different from you, of another race, you cry: "No; this is a man indeed, the type, the pattern, the interpreter of this humanity of mine. He is a man like me, and yet behold He surely is a Son of God. Behold the filialness that runs through all His life. He has the divine nature in Him everywhere. He calls God His Father not merely in His words but in His actions. My Brother, and the Son of God! What am I, then?" You think, and the thought grows into a new consciousness that floods your life with peace and solemnity and strength: "Why, then, I too am God's son. Then He was right when He talked about 'His Father' and ' My Father.' He has taught me that God is my Father. He has made me a son of God." That is what it means! You have received Him and He has given you the power to become a son of God. And what then? Standing strong upon that point how clear it is! The old doubts of your life—the doubts about what you are and how you came here and whether it is worth while to be here at all—are all answered in this new certainty that you are God's son. You are no longer bewildered about duty; you have accepted your Father's law. You are not in doubt how to treat these men about you,—they are your Father's children. Everything has grown definite and plain in that. The sand under your feet has turned to rock. You have a strong and sure present standing-place, now that you can say, "I am a son of God."

But yet, with all that new preciseness, has not the other element of strong life come too? Has not the future widened as the present has grown firm beneath you? Is not life more infinite, now that the central point of life is clear? While you did not know what you were, it did not seem very likely that you would ever be anything more. Now that you know you are God's child, you are sure that there are untold, unguessed regions of life and character. This is but the beginning. It doth not yet appear what you shall be. The end is very far—a whole eternity away.

I feel sure that I am touching here one of the commonest consciousnesses of the Christian life. Its vastness is bound up with its first simple certainty. As it assures itself of a present relationship to God new features open before it. The clearer it becomes in realizing what it is, the more vast and vague becomes to it the prospect of what it is to be. I should like to suggest to you how this appears in several different departments of the Christian life.

First, it is true of Christian belief. I think that this forces itself upon us constantly—that it is the shallow and not the profound, the half and not the whole believer who thinks that he has exhausted the capacities of his belief. The more profound a man is in his belief the more he looks forward and expects developments and enlargements of what he now holds to be true. Take two believers in any doctrine—of the Trinity, for instance, or of the Atonement. Let one of them be the ordinary flippant matter-of-course believer, of whose kind our churches are so full. And let the other be a man whose very soul has drunk in the truth that he believes, who lives upon it, who has seized it with the strong eagerness of a hungry heart. The first of these will surely be the man who will expect no opening or richening of the faith he holds, who will expect to believe in the Trinity or the Atonement always just exactly as he believes in it to-day, and who will insist that other men shall hold his truth just after his pattern, and be indignant at every least departure from it. On the other hand, the man who holds the doctrine more profoundly will be the man who says: "This doctrine I shall always hold, but the very preciousnes of it shows me that it is far too rich for me to have comprehended it completely. I have not mastered all its power. I have not fathomed all its mystery. New sides it surely has to turn to me. I shall see it new forever." And so he will look with tolerance upon his brethren who already see this truth in other lights than his. The deepest faith is strongest in hope and charity. He who most profoundly knows that he is the son of God is most ready to leave the future to his Father, most ready to own that it doth not yet appear what he shall be.

And the same thing is true about the Christian affections as about the Christian faith. They, too, as they grow deeper and stronger under the influence of Christ, become aware of their own present limitations and look forward to a vast, as yet unknown, extension. The man who has never learned that he is a son of God is satisfied with the little ordinary exercise of his affectional nature in the common relationship of daily life. To love his children and his country with the ordinary warmth of parentship and patriotism, and so do his duty respectably to both out of this commonplace affection, seems to him enough. He thinks of nothing further. But make that man God's son, deepen his life with

Christ, give to everything about him the sweet solemnity which it gathers from the Father's hands that hold it, and how that man's affections strengthen! With what new vehemence he loves and hates! How the new holiness he sees summons an unguessed power of admiration, and the meanness which he used to disregard stirs him with passionate indignation! How the sight of misery evokes a new kind of pity, and the sight of joy a strangely heightened gratitude and congratulation! But in this deepening of the affections they find out their imperfection. There are some tasks they cannot undertake. Do you not know it? As you grow more sensitive there open to you efforts to which your sensitiveness is not equal. There is a virtue above praise, a pain that outgoes pity, a voice that is too terrible for blame, a joy that we dare not congratulate. All these we pass back beyond ourselves to God who alone is fit to deal with them; but yet they open to us prospects of growth, hints, and suggestions that the affectional life in us has only just begun its work and is some day to attain a power of enjoyment and culture which is yet unimagined.

Everywhere with the strengthening and clarifying of any of our powers, its range and outlook widens. It is so with Christian work as well as with faith and affection. A man whose labor has been desultory, purposeless, unintelligent, begins to work as a son of God. I have often tried to describe what that change is. It is not that the occupations alter. They may go on just the same. In his store or in his study the man still handles the same tools, and all his outside life remains unchanged. The difference is in the spirit which he works with. Once it was for himself, now it is for the Father he has found. Once it was as his own slave, now it is as the willing servant of that Christ who has made him a son of God. What new power will that put into his work? It will make it certainly more precise and conscientious in every least detail. Just as his Lord is more sacred to him than himself, just as the desire to do His will precisely becomes stronger than any old impulse of self-seeking, just so will each minutest part of all his work be faithfully and scrupulously done; but at the same time the greatness of the Christ for whom he works will enter into his labor and spread it out to infinite results. His work will enter into the great fulfilment of the Divine Will which is going on all through the universe, and be inspired by the anticipation of its endless prospects. Still the new son of God works at the forge or the bar, but wherever he works, working for Christ, he is able to meet Christ's command and labor not for the meat which perisheth, but for that which endureth unto everlasting life. Ah, my dear friends, is it not what we need? Something which shall take these daily tasks of ours which are so trivial that we either neglect them or else are slaves to them, and redeem them from their littleness so that we shall do them with a joyful conscientiousness, and at the same time find in them continual suggestions of larger tasks, of the infinite issues of every faithful work in the unknown future? And that can come only by our whole life being taken up and set over on to new ground where we shall do everything for God.

Here, then, are these three—knowledge, affection, work. In each of them do we not see the power of Christianity at once to intensify the present and to expand the future? As we look at the men in history whose lives have been most full of the sense of their own sonship and of the Fatherhood of God, something of the same character seems to shine out in all of their diversity. Think of Moses, the patient, faithful governor, the man of affairs, shaping out for his people a scheme of government full of minute details, alert, vivid, strong, feeling the present always under his feet and yet yearning for the unseen things to which all these seen things pointed, the prophet of the future as well as the toiler in the present, enduring the present "as seeing Him who is invisible." Look at David, with the clearest present experiences of pain and joy, of rapture, sin, and repentance that any man ever had, at least that any man ever told, yet always suggesting larger experiences than his own, so that the Psalms which he wrote about himself have even availed to sing the story of the humiliation and the triumph of the incarnate God. Think of the Prophets, those real seers of the Old Testament, seeing the future because they saw the present so profoundly, coming by insight into foresight. Think of Paul with his clear creed, yet glorying in his ignorance of what was still beyond. "I am this now," each of them in his own way seems to cry, "this now certainly and clearly, but there is more beyond. This is only the beginning. It doth not yet appear what we shall be." There lies the charm and strength of all of them. Nay, why should we stop with them, why should we not dare to speak of Jesus?—fastening Himself into His own present there in Palestine, with a strength that has never been equalled, and yet reaching out and claiming eternity for the fulfilment of His purposes. He was the perfect Son of God, so eager about His Father's business, and yet using those mysterious words, "Of that day knoweth no man, no, not the angels which are in heaven, neither the Son, but the Father"— the vivid present and the unknown future. "Now are we the sons of God, and it doth not yet appear what we shall be."

It is strange how, if we look widely enough, the needs of life, the things that are wanting to make life what it ought to be, are everywhere the same. What do we need in religion? Greater clearness and greater breadth, a sharper faith and a larger expectation, less vagueness and less bigotry. What do we need in politics and public life? More faithfulness and more outlook, a more honest and devoted care for every day's details of public business and a more inspired prospect of the better possibilities of government, less unfaithfulness and less routine. What do we need in education? More concientious hard work and larger thoughts of learning, less superficialness and less pedantry. What do you need in your daily life? Ah! do you not know well enough? Is it not that you should do your duty and hold your truth at once more strictly and more largely? You want to go to your life to-morrow morning and take it up with other hands, to delight in it, to dwell on every detail of it with joy, to do it with a thoroughness that you have lamentably lacked before; and yet not to be crushed by it, not to be reduced to a mere school-teaching or shop-tending or housekeeping machine,—but to see beyond your work into eternity. Everywhere the need is still the same, from the senator at the capital down to the school boy at his desk,—a sharper present and a vaster future; not either gained at the expense of the other, but both together making life shine with the intensity and the broadness of the sun. And can that need, the same everywhere, be ever everywhere supplied? It can, if men can ever really come to be the sons of God, if life can be all over the wide earth the doing of His will in grateful love, —if everywhere men can feel His eye judging their hourly faithfulness and see His hand pointing them on into infinity. When that comes for all the world, then the world's redemption is attained and its new life begins. When that comes for you and me, then we are redeemed and our new life is begun.

We grow profoundly weary of hearing narrow men—wrapped up in the present, given to some little business, shutting their eyes to all the vast outlooks of life—pour their cheap sneers upon any feeble effort that any poor soul near them makes to realize a higher or a little broader life, to live for other people, to live for their own souls, to live for God. There is hardly any such attempt, however clumsy, that is not more respectable than the miserable cynicism with which men, who know nothing of the impulse out of which it springs, stand round and try to sneer it down. But still the weakness of very many of such attempts is evident enough. Men try after the vague and distant who have not first fastened themselves in the tangible and near. To be a maundering philanthropist, and weep over the woes of men half-round the globe while your brother begs in vain at your door; to long for the conversion of China while the heathenism here in Boston does not kindle you or shame you; to dwell with rapture on the service you will do for God all through eternity in heaven, and yet let the task that He has given you to do to-day lie unattacked; these have been the subjects of cheap satire till it is commonplace enough. But it is not always, by any means, the contemptible hypocrisy that men suppose. It is a foolish, helpless reaching out after the future, with no strong foothold in the present. Still it does show an aspiration, however ignorant, a longing, however shallow. But it must deepen itself with present duty. It must strongly fasten itself in the near. So only can it reach out to the future and the distant worthily and strongly. The philanthropist whose care for the poor child who has fallen in the street here is intensified by the cry of suffering that reaches him from a suffering world, the Christian who is first in evangelizing the home heathen and the heathen of China too, the saint who, dreaming of heaven, makes earth heavenly with the daily doing of duty and service of the Lord,—there are no sneers for them; or the few poor creatures who venture to pour their feeble contempt on lives like these have it blown back in their own faces, and find themselves despised.

I dare to hope that what I have said to you to-day—if it meets any of your experiences and falls in with any of your desires—will give you help. It may be that there is some one here who has found just the dissatisfaction with life that I have aimed at. Such an one says: "I would not be what I have been. I vacillate between two wrong conditions. When I try to do my duty faithfully I grow a slave to its details, and every lofty expectation and spiritual wish is lost. When I fling my soul out into the future and expect eternity and reach after heaven, my present work, the life that I ought to be living now, grows weak and lies neglected." Ah, if it were only as easy to help you to the remedy as it is to tell you what you need. You must be a son of God! That is your only salvation. And if you ask me, "How can I be God's son?" the answer is: "You are God's son already, if you only knew it." And if you say, "How can I know it?" then you give me a chance to tell you once more what it is always such a joy to tell: "Jesus, God's Son, your Brother, came to show it to you. He must show it to you. You must go to Him,—nay, you must let Him come and speak to you. You must see His filialness. You must hear His message. You must feel the power of His Cross telling you how your Father loved you. 'He that hath seen me hath seen the Father,' He declared. You must see Him with your soul, and so you shall see God."

When that is done, then the new consciousness of sonship shall fill you. Everything you do and think and say shall be deep and strong and happy with your Father's presence. You shall go on your way singing, "Now I am a son of God." And what then? The infinite future shall open around the clear and beautiful present. "What is this new life to come to? I cannot tell. It doth not yet appear what I shall be." Suspicions and faint glimpses of it shall come to you as you work; the thought of those who once were with you and have gone on before you, to learn more of the mystery of love, shall strengthen and encourage you; but yet you shall not be impatient. Enough that now you are God's son, and that all which that sonship contains is waiting for you. Enough that you are on the sea, with your ship's prow set towards the perfect shore. What does it matter whether the storms make your voyage a day more or less? The distance before you you cannot read, but in it is the same God who is with you. You live *by* Him, and so you live deeper and deeper *into* Him. Your life is full, through Him, of those two powers by which a human life is saved,—faithfulness and hope,—faithfulness made enthusiastic by hope, and hope made clear by faithfulness. That is eternal life—to know God by Christ.

XXI.

THE FEAST OF TABERNACLES.

A NEW YEAR'S SERMON.

"And I that am the Lord thy God from the land of Egypt, will yet make thee to dwell in tabernacles, as in the days of the solemn feast."—HOSEA xii. 9.

THE Jewish Feast of Tabernacles must have been most picturesque and striking. Every year, as the seventh month came round, the city of Jerusalem bloomed into a forest. The houses were deserted and all the people took up their abodes in booths or tents built temporarily and slightly wherever any room for them could be found. They were set up upon the flat tops of the dwellings, and along the crowded streets, and in the broad court-yard of the temple, and in the public squares. The staid, respectable inhabitants of the houses came out and lived in primitive fashion under the extemporaneous shelter of leaves, alongside of the homeless wanderers who knew what such outdoor lodging was by the whole habit of their lives. The palace and the hovel alike turned their inhabitants into the streets. Every morning while the feast lasted it must have seemed as if the entire population were ready to forsake the beds where they had spent the night and move on like an army on the march, or a host of pilgrims ready for the next stage of their journey, and leave the old city of David empty on its hills.

And what was the meaning of the feast of tents?

"That your generations may know that I made the children of Israel to dwell in booths when I brought them out of the land of Egypt. I am the Lord your God." This is the explanation of its purpose which Jehovah gives in Leviticus. It was a perpetual memorial of the life in the wilderness. God wanted to be to them always "the Lord their God which brought them up out of the land of Egypt, out of the house of bondage." He never wanted them to forget those forty years. And so the Feast of Tabernacles restored it every year.

And the value of such reminiscence lay in three things. First, it reminded the people of God's mercy which had led them through all their dangers. Then, it made them feel the comfort and security of the settled life into which they had arrived. And yet again, it suggested to them the deeper sense in which they will still and must always be wanderers; the way in which, though the wanderings of their feet in the wilderness were over, the higher part of them, their spiritual part, must always be a wanderer in a world which has no final satisfaction for the human soul. Every year the great acted parable proclaimed this truth. As the multitude left their solid houses to live in travellers' tents, could be heard the heart of the people saying to itself: "We

THE FEAST OF TABERNACLES 367

have here no continuing city, but we seek one. We are strangers and pilgrims on the earth."

In this last meaning of it, is not to-day a Feast of Tabernacles? On the first day of a new year, with the sense of transition strong within us and the atmosphere of change everywhere about us, is it not exactly as if our souls went out of their solid houses and lived in booths? We leave for the moment some, at least, of our well-built certainties and dwell for awhile amid the realized doubtfulness of life. Our well-built certainties are not pulled down. They stand there still like the Jews' houses in Jerusalem. We shall go back to them after our Feast of Tabernacles is over. But for the time the narrow walls are forsaken and we live in larger air. The possibilities of life seem greater. The skies and stars and waving branches of the booths are over our heads.

And here comes in the verse out of the prophet Hosea, which I have made my text. "I will yet make thee to dwell in tabernacles," says God to His people, "as in the days of the solemn feast." May not the words mean for us something as large as this?—that the dispensation of tabernacles is perpetual; that always in the midst of man's most settled life there shall come times when he shall be compelled to remember his unsettledness; and then, what seems to be suggested in the last words of the verse, that these times of realized unsettledness, shall be and ought to be feast-times,—in other words that, truly understood, it is a joy and privilege and exaltation to the soul of the true man when he is made to realize that his most fixed condition is not really fixed, but sure of disturbance, exposed to all the winds of change. This is a great truth—worthy of being set forth in picturesque and elaborate symbol. For not the things which happen to us, but the meanings which the things which happen have for us, are the real facts of our existence. Not that we dwell in tabernacles, but whether our dwelling in tabernacles is a fast or a feast is the really important thing.

To many men it is a fast. They crawl out of their solid houses and take up their abode in their tents of uncertainty because they cannot help themselves. They dwell there with groans and tears. They chant the litanies of sorrow. They eat black bread and bitter herbs. They are all gladness when the *Fast* of Tabernacles is over, and they can go singing back to their dear solidity again, to forget that things are not to be forever as they are to-day. To other men the whole experience is a festival. The anticipation of it makes the long year bright and saves it from monotony. To be reminded that the most settled routines are after all but temporary habits, that the most permanent abodes are only halting-places on a journey, that change and not continuance is the true condition of the deepest life; —all this is full of exhilaration and delight. The soul's booth under the waving branches is glad and bright with song; and by and by when the soul returns into its well-built routine again, it carries with it the newly felt certainty of change, to burn like a candle in the house until the next time to leave the house for the wide-open sky shall come.

What makes the difference in these two sorts of men? "It is a difference of temperament," we say —covering our puzzling question with a large-sized word, as one puts the cover on a boiling pot in hopes that the confusion within will boil itself out of itself to some result. "It is a difference of temperament," we say, as if temperaments were absolute, eternal things, with no beginning and no end, which came from nowhere and which issued in nothing. Temperaments are but the habits of the soul, which have become unconscious of their causes, as habits do, but which have their causes nevertheless. What really makes the difference in the two sorts of men is their willingness or unwillingness to think of the infiniteness of life.

Does that seem a great name to give to the reason why men like or dislike to face the changefulness of the world? But remember that the deepest differences of human natures must of necessity declare themselves in superficial varieties of act and feeling. The heart of the earth is convulsed and a small crack on the earth's surface tells the story first. And so when one of God's Feasts of Tabernacles comes, and all mankind together are driven out into the thought of instability and changefulness, one man goes reluctantly and bitterly because the summons disturbs that which he had dared to think of as final, and another man right by his side goes triumphant and joyous because the whole event satisfies his deepest expectation and his fundamental thought of life. "I knew this could not be the end," he says; "I knew that there can be no end until the infinite perfection has been reached. The tent-life is the true life until the building of God, the house not made with hands, is reached. Therefore welcome this signal and token and reminder of it, breaking in upon the hardening security to which my life was settling." Is it not clear how to the first man the Feast of Tabernacles is a fast while it is a true feast to the other?

All this is true of every department of life. It is true about men's thoughts. A man learns all he can learn, and is satisfied. His creed is fixed and settled. He and the men about him think alike. There is no dream of growth or of enlargement. To change an item of this faith is of necessity to wander into error. Another man no less sincerely holds his faith. It is his light and law. He lives by it and works by it; but all the time he knows that the entire truth is more than any creed can state, is vaster and more mysterious than any human soul can comprehend. He not merely holds this as a conviction; it fills him through and through and colors all his thought. He never slips out of the certainty that what he holds, true as it is, is only a small part and fraction of the truth.

Now to these two men, standing side by side, comes one of God's Feasts of Tabernacles. Do you not see now what that means? There comes one of those times in which God makes the whole world feel how large is truth and how far all men are from having found its end. These two men have to go out together and live in their booths side by side. The law of the Feast is universal: Neither can stay behind in his house, however much he wishes. But how differently they go! To one the feast is no feast, but a mournful fast. To the other it is full of solemn joy.

I think all this is most familiar to us now. This day of ours is one of God's Feasts of Tabernacles. In things of faith and creed what hosts of the people of God are living in tents, seekers not finders, sure that they have not yet reached the "continuing city" of final and established truth. To some men it is a perpetual misery. To other men it is a perpetual delight. For them to think that they had reached the fullest truth which they were capable of knowing—that would be misery to them. For it would mean, "We are not then capable or worthy of dealing with and seeking the infinite. Here in this little limit we must rest"; and so man's noblest conception of himself and noblest ambition for his future perishes.

There comes some great disturbance on a land—a war or a commercial crisis. There are the two sorts of greeting for it in men's souls. One kind of man goes into it as if he went to the funeral of everything. Another man goes to it as to a feast—"a solemn feast," as Hosea calls it,—not a time of frivolity or lightness, but a time when the world grows large and the souls of men shake themselves free of the fixed littleness of life. Such days as these are Feasts of Tabernacles. You walk the streets and see men's faces anxious and perplexed. The quiet complacency is gone. These men evidently do not hold to-morrow's bread in their safe hands. They do not know where to-morrow's bread will come from. They listen to each other's prophecies and turn away incredulous. "What does he know about it more than I do? What does either of us know? Is it not all uncertain?"

Yet have you not sometimes, in the midst of such uncertain days, seen here and there an eye that kindled and a face that flushed? Have you not sometimes caught glimpse of a look which made you think of the words of Jesus: "Then look up and lift up your head, for your redemption draweth nigh?" It was a look of liberty. It seemed as if to some men this confusion meant the breaking of cables and the scattering of clouds. In the disappointment of their immediate hopes, the deepest instincts and expectations of their souls sailed forth into satisfaction. "Behold, then," they say, "business is not everything; and business success is not the end of living. A man can live without it. There are higher things, —we have dreamed of them in the visions of the night. Now our eyes see them in the broad light of this tumultuous day."

Men used to think that the constitution of Society was fixed forever. Just how class was to live with class, —who was to command and who was to obey, who was to sleep in luxury and who was to do the work, all this was settled and decided in the nature of things. The axioms were all found out and folded away. They never could be changed. Within these solid walls we were to live forever. There, too, the Feast of Tabernacles has arrived. The trumpet has blown and man after man is seen, under a compulsion which he cannot resist, coming out of his solid house of absolute conviction and taking up his abode in the frail booth of uncertainty. Some men—perhaps most men—hate it and would be thankful to be let alone. To other men the change is full of a mysterious and awful joy. The whole of this mysterious life is a "solemn feast."

To the more personal and private Feasts of Tabernacles I need only to refer, and your own memories will recognize them. Your own hearts and homes are full of them. You said: "My household's way is fixed for many years. There is nothing here that will not last." You limited your thought and wish to what your walls contained. And then, just when you were surest, the solid walls turned to tremulous branches, and you were out among the winds, under the stars, and nothing was fixed. Anything was possible. It may have been a joyous or a melancholy change. It may have been a glad or sad event which broke the spell and brought the difference. That does not matter. The change from certainty to uncertainty, from fixedness to instability, is the great thing. And then, oh, how the real question stood in the midst of your astonished household, and looked you in the face, and asked each one, "Have you then any hold on the infiniteness of life?" And each one answered by the way in which he met the new life of the opened household. A solemn joy or a despondent dread was in the face of each.

This, then, is what I mean when I say that the way in which the Feast of Tabernacles becomes a fast or a feast to any man depends upon whether he has learned to live in the infinity of life. There is a nature to which the thought of the temporariness and transitoriness and changefulness of things is absolutely necessary, and brings the highest inspiration, —not from mere restlessness and the superficial weariness with circumstances which have been but half exhausted and enjoyed, but from the need of some symbol or expression of that sense of incompleteness and aspiration of which the heart is full. The outward change is but a symbol and in some degree a means. If it goes no deeper and does not get at the soul and make it live a new life, and think new thoughts, and be *another soul*, it comes to very little. Indeed, there are very many of the noblest natures who are realizing the instability of life by the continual fluctuation of thought and feeling even while every outward circumstance remains unchanged. There is great beauty in this unseen Feast of Tabernacles which very often is being held in a man's soul, when it seems to all his friends who live about him as if he were dwelling in a house of the most solid unchangeableness. At the very time when his life seems to be most absolutely monotonous, he may be going outside of his most treasured and well-built convictions and recognizing how partial they are, how they cannot be the final home of a soul's faith. And so he may be dwelling for the moment in the open booth, into which come freely suggestions of undiscovered truth and revelations of the distant future.

Whether the changefulness be that of outward

and visible conditions or the subtler one of inward thoughts, there are men to whom it brings inspiration which they could not lose without losing their best strength. Every disturbance and unsettlement opens anew the infinite prospect. Every jolt and jar assures them that the chariot is moving. The fact of present change is a satisfaction for them, because it justifies their hope that they shall not always be the poor thing which they are to-day, but shall attain diviner things.

And then, what follows from this? Must it not be that any power which opens the infinite life to any man must be the interpreter and transfigurer to him of all the petty special changefulness of life? And so, if Christ "brings life and immortality to light," if He truly compels the man who becomes His disciple to look far on and see vast things before him, then He irradiates changefulness and makes it a satisfaction and assurance to the soul.

I feel so strongly that here, and here alone, we are on the highest and the strongest ground! We make most feeble efforts at consolation. Mostly our efforts at consolation, either for ourselves or one another, are merely, in one form or another, the reiteration of the fact of the inevitableness of change. "Why is it that nothing will stay fixed or settled?" And you think that you have answered the querulous and puzzling question when you say: "Oh, they never have! In the days of Julius Cæsar, in the days of Queen Elizabeth, things changed just as they do to-day. They always have. They always will. Go back and take it as it always was and is and will be to the end." There is no consolation there. Suppose not you, but Christ, tries to console the puzzled soul; suppose He begins not here in the detail of the man's present existence, but far off, far on in the great purpose of the man's being, in the far range of his eternal life. "You are eternal," He declares. "You belong to the Eternal Father, and you share His immortality. You are a stranger here, a stranger and a traveller. This is no place for you to live in. You can be at rest only when you have reached the Infinite and have found your home in God." Let Christ teach the man that. Let Him fill the man with that consciousness. Let Him make the man enthusiastically, triumphantly aware that not here and now, but far away, is the completion and rest of his soul; and then let Christ turn back with him suddenly to the present moment of which the man was complaining, and say: "With all this future prospect vast before you, what do you want here and now? Do you want everything to speak of fixity and settlement, as if there never could be any alteration? or do you want the sound and sight of change to be in everything?" Does not the man's soul answer truly: "Let me not root myself too deeply where I do not mean nor wish to stay. Let me have ever round me the promises and prophecies of the great freedom, the great progress to which any soul belongs. O, for the Feast of Tabernacles, in which I shall know myself but a pilgrim! O, for a perpetual Feast of Tabernacles, in which all shall seem a pilgrimage, and the infinite prospect shall shine ever through the scattered dust of these earthly experiences, broken with perpetual change!"

It may be that it seems to be asking too much of man that he should thus desire and demand perpetual disturbance and continual change. Let us be thankful, then, that God does not wait for him to demand it, but sends it to him whether he will or no. He treats us as you treat your children. Not what they wish, but what they need, you give them. It would be cruel to wait for the conscious desire before you, seeing the unconscious need, sent the supply. God does not wait for us to say: "Now it is time for me to be uprooted. Now let my health be shaken. Now let my riches disappear. Now let the solid landscape fade in mist, and the great dispensation of uncertainty arise." That would be cruelty indeed. As well might the surgeon wait till the sufferer himself called for the knife. God, by His own will, knowing Himself that the time has come, beckons, and we follow Him, often reluctantly, often in tears. And it is only as we follow Him that our hearts respond to His heart, and we see the beauty of the new life into the midst of which He leads us, and by and by are surprised at our own voices praising Him for giving us that from which we shrank, that which we never should have had the courage or the strength to ask.

Thus we have sung our Psalm of Changefulness and have felt through it all, I trust, the music of God's purpose. It is not accident. It is not because this man's roof leaked and this man's wall was crumbling that all the world have come out of their houses and are living on the streets of Jerusalem in tents. It is the utterance of a fundamental truth of life. It is the recognition of an unchanging fact. That fact is change; whose perpetual and necessary recurrence is the most changeless thing in all the history of man. But it is not the only fact. It is not the deepest fact. And now it is quite time for us to remind ourselves, and to say, before we close, that unless beneath every change there runs a deeper identity, change becomes demoralizing and corrupt.

See how it was in this historic instance which has made the basis of our study. God says, by the lips of Hosea: "I that am the Lord thy God from the land of Egypt will yet make thee to dwell in tabernacles." "The Lord thy God from the land of Egypt!" All that was hundreds of years ago. Change after change had come, following quick upon each other, from the time of that great change which brought the chosen people out of the house of bondage. The Feast of Tabernacles had been kept every year. And yet all the time there had been, behind and under all, the identity of God and their identity and the unchangeable fact of their relationship to Him. Everything else had changed; but these three things were always there: "The Lord," "*thy* God," and "from the land of Egypt." And now, five hundred years afterwards, when the people are summoned once more out of their dwellings, the great identities are reasserted in the very midst of the renewed demand for change. "I that am the Lord thy God from the land of Egypt, will make thee to dwell in tabernacles."

We must not take half the teaching and not take the whole. God summons us to constant change, but it is *God* that summons us, the God who is unchangeable; and we who pass under His summons from one region of life on into another are the same beings always, and between us and Him there is the unalterable kinship and memory of manifested love. Whatever be the variations of the ever-richening music, that theme runs through it all and keeps it all compact and real and simple.

O my dear friends, do you not know the picture of all this in your earthly life? You go from field to field. The landscape changes constantly. The ground under your feet is now barren and now rich. The sky over your head is now stormy and now clear. Onward you go, and every year is a new field with other foliage and other soil; but, as you go, the same Friend always holds you hand-in-hand. He is the same. You are the same. And the same love and duty bind you to each other. That is the identity which sounds its steady cadence under every change and binds the years together. Personal identity is everything. Could you live in the same house—every least bit of furniture the same—with the dear faces of your family vanished, and make life seem the same? Could you live with your unbroken family about you in the depths of Africa or Hindostan, and make life seem very different? To live a life of changing circumstance, with great lifelong friendships running through it from end to end, that is the lot of highest privilege. It keeps change and identity both, but identity always as the deeper fact,—change woven on identity, as the golden pattern is woven on the golden cloth.

There is no limit to this truth. It stretches out from world to world and fills eternity. You know nothing about the world beyond the grave save that your father or your child is there. You know nothing of what will happen to you as you enter on that world, but you believe that your father and your child will greet you, and that you will know each other—you and they. That makes the unseen world exactly what it is best that it should be to you. That makes it mysterious, yet real,—real, yet mysterious.

Can you not lift all that and feel how through the confusion of change runs the identity of God and of your soul, and of the love and duty which have place between them? Everything is changed since twenty years ago. Only God is the same, and you are the same, and as you were loving Him and obeying Him then, and He was loving and protecting you, so now you love Him and obey Him, and He loves you and protects you still. Everything will be changed ten years hence. Only wherever you are, whatever you are doing then, God will be the same and you will be the same; and you will be loving and obeying Him, and He will be loving and protecting you.

I glory in the vitality and the solidity together which that truth gives to life. I see the practical law of life which will result from such a truth. Be sure of God and of yourself, and of the love between your soul and His, and then shrink from no changefulness, cling to no present; be ready for new skies, new tasks, new truths. This is the voice that comes to us out of the ever-changing world, which has the unchanging God at its heart.

May that voice be heard in our Feast of Tabernacles now! We will not, we cannot, shut our eyes to the certainty of change to-day, but, O Christ, into the midst of our change bring the changelessness of God! Then it shall be indeed a feast that we celebrate, for every change shall only make the changeless more manifest and sure. And at the last the world shall fade away from us only to let Him, in whom the preciousness of the world has always lain, shine out upon us in His perfect glory and unhindered love!

THE END.

A Library of Information in One Volume

THE TEMPLE BIBLE DICTIONARY

Edited by
The Rev. W. EWING, M. A.
The Rev. J. E. H. THOMSON, D. D.

> *Indispensable to:*
> The Student
> The Preacher
> The Class Leader
> The Foreign Missionary
>
> *As well as to*
> Every Christian Household
>
> ---
>
> *A mine of rich instruction and interest*

1100 Pages   500 Illustrations   8 Maps

One Volume 9¼ x 6¾   Handsome Maroon Cloth
Tinted tops and edges   Price $4.00, *net*.

THE EDITORS OF THE DICTIONARY.

THE REV. W. EWING, M. A., the Editor-in-Chief, is a native of the South of Scotland. He graduated from the University of Glasgow with distinction in Logic and Moral Philosophy. After taking a post-graduate theological course at the Free Church College, Glasgow, he studied at Leipzic under Delitzch, and after ordination went to Palestine as a missionary—his work there being centered principally around Tiberias, on the Sea of Galilee.

Here his proficiency in the native tongues and his persistent activity made him an influence throughout the surrounding country, both in the villages of the peasantry and in the encampments of the wandering Arabs.

Returning to England in 1893, Mr. Ewing has occupied important pulpits in Birmingham, Glasgow, Stirling, and Edinburgh.

He has also contributed a great deal to current literature on oriental subjects. He wrote many of the articles dealing with the East in the dictionaries edited by Dr. Hastings, and is the author of the well known book, "Arab and Druze at Home."

For upwards of seven years he has contributed articles on oriental subjects to the American Sunday School Times, thus—so to speak—preparing himself for the very responsible position he now occupies as editor of the TEMPLE BIBLE DICTIONARY.

DR. J. E. H. THOMSON, D. D., the Associate Editor, is also a Glasgow University graduate, but took his post-graduate work at Edinburgh, where he was medallist in Logic and Moral Philosophy.

After graduation he engaged in literary work, and travelled on the Continent of Europe. His first important book, "Books Which Influenced our Lord and His Apostles," appeared in 1891 and at once took rank as a standard work on Apocalyptic literature and gained him admission to the staff of the "Pulpit Commentary."

In 1895, Dr. Thomson went to Palestine as Free Church Missionary to the Jews, and was stationed at Safed, in Napthali, the loftiest city in Palestine. From this point he made frequent journeys throughout Palestine to all the points famous in the Old and New Testaments.

Briefly, the practical experience of both Editors has put them in a position to know what is needful in a Bible Dictionary which is to be used by practical workers and students—and has given them that thorough, first-hand knowledge of Bible Lands and Peoples, which only actual contact can bestow.

THE LIST OF CONTRIBUTORS includes many of the best orientalists and archæologists, the names of such men as Professor Margolioth, M. A., Litt. D., etc., professor of Arabic in the University of Oxford, Professor A. H. Sayce, LL.D., D. C. L., Litt. D., professor of Assyriology in the same University, the Lord Bishop of Ripon, Professors Mackintosh of Edinburgh University, Wenley of the University of Michigan, Dalman of Leipzic, Anderson Scott of Cambridge, James Robertson of Glasgow, being guarantees of accuracy, scholarship, culture and precision.

THE OBJECT OF THE WORK:

The results of the research and criticism have in the last few years been cumulative in their effect. Egypt and the Euphrates Valley, Asia Minor, Syria, and Palestine itself, through the researches of Ramsay, Petrie, Conder and others, have yielded up enough of their secrets for us to be able to lift with practical completeness the veil which has for centuries obscured Bibical lands from the accurate comprehension of Western people.

At the same time the vastly conflicting views of scholars with regard to the date, authorship, mode of composition, trustworthiness, etc. of the various books of the Canon of Scripture have settled down to a stable mean which is not liable to vary very much for many years to come—either in the direction of conservatism or in that of radical departure from accepted values.

Consequently it has seemed to the editors that this is a favorable period at which to put forth a work which shall embody late results in both Biblical Archæology and Critical Inquiry without the prospect of its almost immediately becoming out of date in either department.

Excellent work has been done in some larger Dictionaries of the Bible recently published, but their size and price put them beyond the reach of many who are keenly alive to the necessity for competent and trustworthy guidance in the study of the Scriptures.

The Editors therefore believe that there is room for a Dictionary such as this, which, leaving aside all that is merely theoretical and speculative, presents simply, shortly and clearly the state of ascertained knowledge on the subjects dealt with, at a price which brings the latest results of scholarly investigation within the reach of every earnest student of the Bible, and which for the working clergyman, the local preacher, the class leader, the Sunday School teacher, the travelling missionary, offers an indispensable vade-mecum of scientific and critical knowledge about Biblical lands, peoples and literature.

THE BOOK ITSELF:

The volume is a singularly handsome one of eleven hundred pages, 9 inches by 6½ in size, bound in dark maroon cloth, with gilt back and tinted top and edges. There are over 500 explanatory illustrations—many from entirely new photographs—and eight colored maps.

A sensible series of ingenious contractions, not only of proper names, but of ordinary words also, has made it possible to pack information very much closer in these pages than is usual elsewhere.

The Dictionary to the Apocrypha is in a section by itself, with a special introductory article. There are also special articles on: The Influence of the Bible on English Literature; The New Testament Apocrypha; Apocalyptic Literature; The Targums; Versions of the Scripture; Philo Judæus; Josephus; and The Language of Palestine in the time of Christ; while in the Text of the Dictionary everything possible has been done by the use of thin opaque paper, appropriate sizes of type, and a serviceable system of cross-references to make the book more legible, more intelligible, and more generally comfortable to read than any other book of its kind in existence.

It is the devout hope of the Editors that at last a Bible Dictionary has been produced which will be the standard of its kind for many years to come, both as to fullness and erudition of contents and to mechanical excellence of bookmaking.